Also by Ronald G. Walters

The Antislavery Appeal: American Abolitionism after 1830

Primers for Prudery: Sexual Advice to Victorian America   (editor)

American Reformers
1815 – 1860

American Reformers

1815–1860

RONALD G. WALTERS

CONSULTING EDITOR

Eric Foner

American Century Series

 HILL AND WANG   NEW YORK

A division of Farrar, Straus and Giroux

Library of Congress Cataloging in Publication Data
Walters, Ronald G.
American reformers, 1815–1860.
(American century series)
Bibliography: p.   Includes index.
1. Social reformers—United States—History. I. Title.
HN64.W2136   1978   301.24′2′0973   78–7545
ISBN (clothbound edition) : 0–8090–2557–4
ISBN (paperback edition) : 0–8090–0130–6

Twelfth printing, 1989

For Nathaniel

Acknowledgments

It is a scholarly custom to impose on friends, colleagues, spouses, students, and institutions. I did, and I want to thank those who bore the heaviest burdens—John d'Entremont, Anita and Michael Fellman, William Freehling, Tom Leonard, and Kenneth Lynn. Their comments on portions of the manuscript were generously given and extremely useful. They have no responsibility for the people, events, and nuances I omitted in order to make this a brief, interpretive work.

I also want to give special thanks to Charlotte Walters, who helped much and put up with much, and to the National Endowment for the Humanities for generous aid and for continuing moral support from its staff. Arthur Wang and Eric Foner were extraordinarily helpful and supportive—everything publishers and editors should be, and more. For their sake, I regret that I was everything authors usually are.

Preface

Reminiscing about the 1840s, Thomas Wentworth Higginson recalled "there prevailed then a phrase, 'the Sisterhood of Reforms.'" It referred to "a variety of social and physiological theories of which one was expected to accept all, if any." The phrase was apt. There was an incredible proliferation of reforms in the pre-Civil War years and it was a rare person who engaged in only one of them. Higginson himself was primarily involved with antislavery, yet he also worked for temperance, woman's rights, and health reform. His comment was misleading only in its chronology. The causes he had in mind were at high tide in the 1840s, but the majority were ten or more years old by then. As early as 1815 Americans had begun to generate what would be the most fervent and diverse outburst of reform energy in American history.

It was not, of course, to be the only such outburst. American reform has come in waves, with a decade or more of intense activity followed by periods of relative apathy about social problems. Arising after the War of 1812, antebellum reform crested in the 1830s and 1840s, declined in the 1850s, and seemed almost quaint by the 1870s. It had virtually no influence on Progressivism, the next great collection of reforms. The Progressive era (roughly 1900–16) emerged after a period of corruption in the late nineteenth century and nearly disappeared from view in the moral laxness of the 1920s. It left a bit of a legacy to the 1930s, but surprisingly little. The reformers and radicals of the 1930s, in turn, found themselves denounced or forgotten by the youthful rebels of the 1960s. This lack of continuity marks one of the chief characteristics of American reform: a failure, or inability, to build traditions and institutions capable of surviving across generations.

In most instances war played a major role in destroying reform impulses—the Civil War, World War I, and World War II. (The radicalism of the 1960s was killed by peace, but that is another story.) Wars lead to great social change and even to the fulfillment of some reform objectives: the Civil War ended slavery and World War I helped bring about Prohibition and voting rights for women. But wars have other, and quite stifling, effects on reform. They channel moral energy into service to the nation, either drawing social critics into the war effort or else silencing them and making them appear selfish, unpatriotic, or simply irrelevant. At war's end Americans often fall into moral exhaustion, too shattered or too relieved at being alive to care much about others. Yet even in peacetime and under the most favorable circumstances a reform commitment is difficult to make and to keep. The majority of reformers, as well as many radicals, have come from the middle classes and America offers middle-class men and women more profitable, comfortable, and popular alternatives than spending a life in the service of causes.

Some reforms, naturally, originate as responses to new and disturbing situations. Certainly what reformers and radicals did in the 1930s was largely a reaction to the Depression. In other cases, however, it is hard to find direct connections between periods of reform and the social and economic conditions of the day. For example, the quality of life probably was no worse in the Progressive years, when many men and women tried to improve it, than it had been between 1870 and 1900, when most people had done less about it. Similarly, antebellum reformers attacked evils that had been around for generations. North American slavery was two hundred years old before abolitionists raised the banner of immediate emancipation in 1831. Drunkenness, war, and sexual discrimination were ancient follies by the time the temperance, peace, and woman's rights crusades got under way. Most reform and radical movements, past and present, have addressed themselves to real problems, but it takes something more than the existence of real problems to create reform and radical movements. Finding that something is the historian's job.

There are several ways of going about it. One is to try to explain reform in terms of the moral character of reformers. Sympathetic historians have pictured them as noble idealists who saw wrongdoing and tried to stop it—which begs the question of how people become idealists and why idealists appear, or are effective, only at certain moments in history. Unsympathetic historians have dismissed reformers as irresponsible fanatics or as neurotics and malcontents, a view which ignores the possibility that there might be genuine problems in the world and that it might be reasonable to want to solve them.

A variation on that approach likewise emphasizes motivation while avoiding making obvious judgments on the rightness or wrongness of reform objectives. It consists of searching for sociological or psychological factors which characterize reformers and of which they themselves may have been unaware. At one time the most prominent studies of this type argued that antebellum crusaders tended to come from social groups of declining status. Presumably reform was a mechanism to preserve their social influence and to resolve their "status anxieties." I do not accept that interpretation but I feel this kind of analysis has been useful. It has shown clearly that reformers tended to have been evangelical Protestants from New England families, and that their strength was greatest in New England and its cultural provinces, particularly areas swept by revivalism and economic change. (The prime examples of the latter were the Western Reserve of Ohio and the "burned-over district," a portion of western New York transformed by the Erie Canal.)

Although it has been helpful for historians to examine the family, regional, class, religious, and psychological backgrounds of reformers, it still is a risky business to generalize about what caused people to participate in antebellum crusades. For one thing, we know much more about leaders than about the rank and file. For another, the linkages between a particular kind of background and a moral commitment are not always clear or consistent. There are, indeed, almost as many exceptions as rules—evangelical Protestants, young people, New Englanders, and people of declining status who were not reformers; and non-evangelicals, old people, Southerners, and men on the make who were. Most likely, we will eventually discover that people became reformers out of quite diverse motives and that their commitments satisfied a great range of personal, social, and cultural needs. At the moment, the best we can do is say that reformers tended to be of such-and-such a background and admit that we usually do not know, with absolute certainty, why particular individuals committed themselves to particular causes and crusades.

Fortunately, there is more to reform movements than the psyches, motives, and sociological characteristics of their members. Reform starts when a few men and women declare that something is evil and they know the cure for it. Their statements are worth examining carefully. What do reformers claim is wrong with the thing they attack? Why do they feel it is evil? The answer seldom proves to be as obvious as it might seem. There were, for example, hundreds of objections that could have been made against slavery, but abolitionists made only a handful of them. Why those and not others? The question leads to another approach to reform, which involves exploring the social and cultural conditions that permitted reformers to see reality as they did. That leaves open the issue of what motivated individuals and places emphasis on the relationship between reform rhetoric and the situation producing it. My preference for such an approach is clear and this book owes much to it, even though I firmly believe we should learn more about the sociology of reform and radicalism. But rather than agonize over *who* American reformers were, I have devoted most of my energies to finding out what they said and why it was reasonable and emotionally compelling for them to say it.

It is time to face up to a serious difficulty in terminology. It concerns the words "radical" and "reformer." By radicals I mean those who wish to change the structure of society. By reformers I mean those who wish to improve individuals or existing social, economic, and political arrangements. In theory, there is an important distinction here. Radicals seek to overturn the present order while successful reformers may actually strengthen it by making it work better.

In practice the distinction frequently breaks down. Some people are radical from one perspective but not from others. In the 1950s, for instance, civil rights activists demanded an end to segregation. That was radical in the context of American race relations of the day. Yet most civil rights workers did not ask for a change in the basic American political or economic structure. They just wanted to open it up for black people. Do we judge them as radicals for being integrationists in the 1950s or as reformers because they did not seek a total alteration of American society? My answer is "reformer," but it is a fine and debatable matter.

In their choices of rhetoric and tactics, activists themselves do much to obscure the difference between radicals and reformers. It is common for people to take extreme (or "radical") stands merely to jar institutions or politicians into making concessions that are, in effect, reforms. That is as it should be. Above all, radicals and reformers are committed to causes and they have no obligation to live up to abstract definitions of themselves. They do what they think needs doing and say what they think needs saying, even though that may require moving back and forth between what we see as reform and radicalism.

"Radical" and "reformer" do have a shred of meaning left, nonetheless. No other words serve as well to make the necessary, if fuzzy, discrimination between people who want total change and those who want a better version of what they have. I use the terms as carefully as I can, well aware that doing so makes positions seem clearer than they were.

The difficulties do not stop with separating radicals from reformers. There is the problem of deciding what is a legitimate reform movement. Some scholars try to draw a line between genuine reformers, whom they see as wanting change to move in new directions, and reactionaries, whom they see as wanting change to move backward, toward old ways of doing things. There are times when that distinction is helpful, but antebellum reformers (and I think American reformers generally) mingled old and new solutions to problems. They were often driven by a desire to adapt traditional values to new situations, to restore an old order by building new structures. They could not be consistently classified as reformers or reactionaries. The course of least confusion here is to abandon the distinction and to define a reform movement simply as any collective, organized effort to improve society or individuals by achieving some well-articulated goal.

From a present-day perspective many of the causes discussed in this book do not look much like reforms. Even though alcohol is still a problem, as it was in the nineteenth century, few of us think the world would be a better place if we banned it (we did that once and the world was not a better place). Far fewer of us would agree with phrenologists that analyzing the shapes of skulls is the key to human progress. And yet temperance and phrenology both figure in the story of antebellum reform. They do because people who believed in them presented them as instruments of social and individual uplift and created an institutional structure to proclaim the message.

So it comes down, in part, to taking the reformer's word that what he or she is doing is really a reform. That is not completely satisfactory, given the marvelous ability of people to misjudge and misrepresent themselves; but the alternative is worse. If we relied entirely on our own standards to decide whether a cause was a reform, we would put history at the mercy of present-day politics and we would lose sight of the meaning crusades in the past had for the people caught up in them. By taking that position, I am not saying we must suspend moral judgments altogether. It is possible to argue, for instance, that the Ku Klux Klan of the 1860s and 1870s was a reform movement because it had an institutional structure, a goal, and its leaders portrayed it as a means of "improving" the South. My inclination might be to accept that for purposes of analysis, and yet continue to state clearly that the Klan also was racist, violent, and life-denying. No one has to believe that all reforms are good.

Words like "reform" and "radical" are necessary abstractions. They have to be used and they ought to be explained. But I do not want to leave the impression that this is a book about abstractions. On the contrary, it is about vigorous, often flamboyant men and women and their strange, wonderful, and occasionally heroic causes, fads, and crusades. It is about the sisterhood of reforms that transformed Thomas Wentworth Higginson's life and the lives of thousands of other antebellum Americans.

R.G.W.

Contents

American Reformers
1815 – 1860

Introduction:
Patterns and Changes

Several things came together to produce antebellum reform, including important changes in what Americans believed. By 1814—the year the War of 1812 ended—a combination of theological and economic developments led many men and women to assume that the world did not have to be the way it was and that individual efforts mattered. Such notions are not terribly ancient; nor are they universal among human societies. They were, however, articles of faith for middle-class nineteenth-century Americans, with their confidence in progress and human will. The religious revivalism of the 1820s encouraged this optimistic and activist spirit by teaching that good deeds were the mark of godliness and that the millennium was near. Other significant new ideas, attitudes, and systems of thought jostled around in the public press and likewise encouraged reform. Some of these beliefs were scientific, a few were daring, many were foolish, and all helped nineteenth-century people think of novel solutions to ancient evils, as well as discover sins their ancestors never imagined.

Although antebellum reform emerged out of that cultural ferment, the real moving force behind it was a broad transformation of American society after 1814. Historians and economists grope for the correct term to describe what happened—"takeoff," "industrialization," and "modernization" have all been used. Scholars also endlessly debate how and why such dramatic changes occurred. But the

3

changes themselves touched the farthest corners of economic, social, and political life. They created the material conditions reform movements needed in order to exist and they jarred thousands of people into thinking about what had to be done to ensure the future glory of America and Americans.

The changes most easily measured were in territory and population. In 1815 there were eighteen states in the Union, none farther west than Louisiana; in 1860 there were thirty-three, including two, California and Oregon, on the Pacific coast. The land area of the United States in 1815 totaled around 1.7 million square miles. By 1860 the United States had reached its present continental limits, adding about 1.2 million square miles. Population growth more than kept up with territorial expansion: in 1814 there were 8,400,000 Americans; on the eve of the Civil War there were 31,443,321 of them, a rate of growth averaging over 33 percent per decade. Quite remarkably, Americans increased and multiplied enough to expand urban areas while simultaneously settling an agricultural frontier (about 38 percent of the population in 1860 lived in the newer states and territories of the Midwest and West).

The manner in which the population grew had as many implications for reform as did the growth itself. Reproduction, as usual, played the major role. But the antebellum birth rate, although high by present-day standards, declined steadily after 1800. That trend coincided with subtle but substantial alterations in family patterns, a matter of significance (as we shall see later) for understanding why reformers were so concerned about home life and why so many of them were women.

After 1820 increasing immigration, primarily from Germany, Ireland, and England, kept population growth high despite the downturn in the birth rate. During the 1830s around 600,000 people came to the United States, a fourfold increase over the 1820s. In the next decade the figure rose to 1,700,000, and then to 2,600,000 in the decade of the 1850s. The census of 1860 revealed that there were slightly more foreign-born residents—4,138,697—than there were slaves, a rise of nearly 2,000,000 since 1850. Many of these new Americans were hostile to reform crusades, particularly to temperance, and a large number of them were Catholic. For reformers, these hordes of poor, religiously suspect aliens were one of several indications that America was changing rapidly and that decent men and women had to act quickly to keep it on a morally true course.

Even more spectacular evidence of change came from the performance of the American economy after 1814. Precise figures are impossible to give, but it is clear that the standard of living for most free Americans was improving and that the scale and location of industry were altering dramatically. The proportion of the work force in agriculture declined while that in manufacturing and commerce rose. Much of the production of goods moved out of the household and into shops and factories using water or steam power. New cities sprang up and old ones boomed after 1820. In 1810 there were 46 "urban areas" (defined as places with 2,500 or more population). In 1860 there were 393, including two cities, New York and Philadelphia, with over half a million residents. At the close of the War of 1812 transportation was relatively slow and difficult. On land it was by paved turnpike at best, rutted trail at worst. On water it generally was easier, although occasionally risky to life and limb, thanks to the steamboat, then making its appearance on the rivers of the interior. An era of canal building would soon begin, the capstone of which would be New York's Erie Canal, started in 1817 and completed in 1825. Even so, in 1815 it was costly for most Americans to move themselves or their goods any distance, unless they were fortunate enough to be near a navigable waterway.

That soon changed. Generous amounts of public and private money went into "internal improvements" of all sorts and in 1828 Americans began construction of the most crucial element in their transportation system, the railroad. By 1860 its tracks stretched across 31,000 miles of the countryside, taking people and products where canal barge and steamboat could not go. This "transportation revolution" diffused economic change throughout the United States, as cities in the West like Pittsburgh, Cincinnati, St. Louis, and Chicago used their locations on rivers (or, later, on railroad lines) to develop into important manufacturing and distributing centers.

Present-day economists quarrel over such difficult questions as rates of growth in per capita income or in "value added by commodity output" in the antebellum period, but anyone born in 1800 and still alive in 1860 would have been very certain that *something* had happened. Proof was no farther away than the whistle of a distant locomotive or the smoke of the nearest factory.

America's economic development provided reformers with problems in need of solutions. Troubled by the pains and dislocations of sudden expansion, the cities were especially ripe for moral crusades. Reformers regarded them—with only a bit of exaggeration—as dismal swamps of vice, disease, and misery. Urbanization and industrialization also helped turn the attention of reformers toward slavery after 1830. Northern and Southern ways of life became more distinct and abolitionists (and others) came to see the South's "peculiar institution" as a relic of barbarism while the North's mixture of farming, commerce, and industrial growth appeared to represent the course of civilization and progress. In this case, economic differences between the sections strongly reinforced moral judgments.

There were other, less direct, ways in which the transformation of the United States helped foster antebellum reform. Prosperity meant that there were numerous middle-class men and women with education, income, and leisure to devote to social causes. New technology, moreover, put powerful weapons in the hands of such people. The same transportation revolution that brought goods to distant markets also carried lecturers to widely dispersed audiences they could not have reached a generation before. Innovations in printing reduced the cost of producing propaganda to the point where a person could make a living editing a reform newspaper or writing books and pamphlets for a limited, but national, readership. By the 1830s, it was simpler in every respect to cater to scattered groups of like-minded Americans, and to support one's self while doing it.

Changes in the nature of politics had almost as much significance for antebellum reform as did the economic transformation of the United States. If nothing else served to indicate that there was political turmoil between 1815 and 1860, the ebb and flow of partisan organizations would tell the story. The War of 1812 was the death-blow to the Federalist Party, which had once claimed George Washington, John Adams, and Alexander Hamilton among its leaders. Even before 1812 it had virtually been reduced to a New England remnant, thanks to the rise of Thomas Jefferson and his supporters, called Republicans or Democratic-Republicans. For several years after the war, most national political conflict took place among Democratic-Republicans rather than between two distinct, well-identified parties. That began to change after 1824 when John Quincy Adams, one of four Democratic-Republican presidential candidates, defeated Andrew Jackson. By 1828, when Jackson triumphed over Adams, the factions were becoming more sharply defined. Jackson, now under the label Democratic, had a superb ability both to unite his supporters and to create enemies. By the time he left office, his protégé and successor, Martin Van Buren, was confronted with a well-organized opposition, the Whig Party. Whigs and Democrats fought it out on fairly equal terms for more than a decade, but after 1848 the former disintegrated over the issue of slavery. The Democrats held together—often tenuously—until 1860, when they, too, split apart. After 1854, however, they faced a formidable challenge from the Republican Party, whose candidate, Abraham Lincoln, captured the presidency in 1860. This brief catalogue of political flux, complicated though it may seem, leaves out such ephemeral smaller parties as the Anti-Masonic, Liberty, Free Soil, and Know-Nothing, some of them having made respectable showings in local, state, and even national elections.

Reformers disagreed among themselves on political questions and could be found in every one of the major and minor parties, although more in the Whig and Republican than in the Democratic. Their numbers even included many men and women who rejected parties altogether. It was partisan conflict, rather than any particular political organization, that most influenced their actions.

A new style of political warfare began to emerge after 1800, as politicians learned how to court an expanding electorate. By 1810 a majority of states had lowered franchise requirements to the point where most adult white males could vote. When Jackson made his first run for the presidency in 1824, only three states restricted suffrage for white men in any meaningful way and in many areas even recent immigrants found it easy to cast ballots. This may have been democracy, but it also permitted anyone, including the worst sort of rascals, to help select the nation's leaders. Reformers complained that a degraded and sinful majority, manipulated by political machines, had more of a voice in the nation's affairs than they, the godly minority, did.

Politicians disgusted reformers by seeking the electorate's lowest common denominator. No promise was too extreme, no spectacle too extravagant, if it got votes. The political system, reformers thought, rewarded those who appealed to the rabble and who pretended to be common folk rather than appear superior in morality and intellect. The results were horrifying to right-minded men and women: high offices bestowed on the likes of Andrew Jackson, a duelist who married a divorcee, or Richard M. Johnson, Van Buren's Vice-President, who lived in sin with a black mistress. All around them reformers saw a frightful decline from the days of the Founding Fathers, when great men walked the earth and when wisdom and virtue had a place in government.

Yet reformers could not, and did not, entirely reject politics. The Jacksonian political system itself made their propaganda effective by creating a close link between "public opinion" and governmental action. Many reform crusades, moreover, were designed to have political consequences. If everything worked according to plan, temperance, Sunday schools, and public education, for instance, would produce a morally responsible electorate. In far more direct ways reformers engaged in political action. Evangelical Protestants lobbied Congress in 1828 to stop postal employees from working on Sunday (an effort to improve public morality); and in the next decade abolitionists mounted a petition campaign urging Congress to take stands against slavery. A faction within their movement began to run its own candidates for office in 1840. Temperance workers likewise became involved in political campaigns, winning significant victories in the 1850s and making alcohol a major issue for the next eighty years. Quite obviously there were times when reformers went beyond the powers of persuasion and sought to use the government to make people behave. In the process they dipped their toes, and sometimes a great deal more, into the muddy waters of democratic electioneering, despite their contempt for its mindless excesses.

The ambivalence reformers had toward politics is revealing, even if it was not absolute. America was becoming a strange and different place in the antebellum period and partisan warfare symbolized the change just as surely as did territorial expansion, alterations in family patterns, and the appearance of immigrants, cities, and factories. But politicians held out no promise of leading the transformation of the United States in a virtuous fashion; that task fell to reformers, almost by default.

There were, naturally, many ways of responding to change besides becoming involved in a moral crusade. Although it may seem like a detour, it is worth examining some of the alternatives. Otherwise it would be easy to make the mistake of thinking that reform was unique. On the contrary, it was one of several means by which antebellum men and women attempted to impose moral direction on social, cultural, and economic turmoil.

In September 1826, a prisoner named William Morgan was kidnapped from an upstate New York jail. His disappearance prevented him from carrying through on his plan to reveal the secrets of the Masonic lodge. Morgan's fate—he was presumed murdered—seemed to confirm suspicions that a sinister conspiracy was afoot and it precipitated a crusade against the Masons. In several states—New York, Pennsylvania, and Vermont, especially—Anti-Masonic parties became a significant force. Elsewhere in the Northeast antimasonry remained an issue, if not a political movement, for several years.

About the time it was declining, a professor at William and Mary, Thomas R. Dew, put pen to paper. In 1832 his *Review of the Debate in the Virginia Legislature of 1831 and 1832* defended slavery and sought to discredit the last shred of Southern abolitionism, the idea of resettling all black people outside of the United States. Dew's work was the beginning of a three-decade campaign of proslavery propaganda, pursued in periodicals and in lengthy treatises by Southern nationalists.

Two years after Dew's *Review* a mob gathered at a convent in Charlestown, Massachusetts, and burned it to the ground. Mobs were not at all unusual in the 1830s—one scholar tabulated 157 of them between 1834 and 1837—but the target of this one deserves notice. It was Catholicism. From 1834 on there would be acts of violence against Catholics and, increasingly, political campaigning against them and immigrants (especially against the Irish, who were both). The high tide of nativism came between 1853 and 1855, when the Know-Nothing Party was the fastest-growing political organization in the land, running on its principle that *"Americans must rule America."*

What we have here are four things—antimasonry, proslavery, mobs, and nativism—more or less unrelated to each other. They also seem only distantly related to antebellum reform (although antimasonry and nativism did attract many reformers). Yet each of the four, in common with one another and with reform movements, represented an assessment of what was wrong with America and of what needed correcting. Each, also like reforms, focused upon a supposedly disruptive element in American society: Masons, the North, whoever angered rioters, and foreigners. Reformers, naturally, had different lists of villains—heathenism, the competitive impulse, slavery, war, alcohol, ignorance, and so forth. But the thought was the same: old values were being lost and something or someone was to blame. Whatever was at fault had to be eliminated or controlled if America was to fulfill its destiny.

Behind that reasoning was an innately suspicious mentality which characterized many antebellum reformers as well as non-reformers. It blamed the nation's troubles on conspiracies of one sort or another—by the Slave Power, liquor dealers, Masons, the Catholic Church, or politicians and clergy serving special interests. Some historians have taken to describing that rhetoric as part of a witch-hunting "paranoid style" reappearing at certain periods in American politics.

The label is overly melodramatic when applied to antebellum conspiracy theories. To believe that plotters were responsible for what was happening to the country was wrong; but it was a part of a quest, going back to the eighteenth century, to find non-religious terms in which to analyze politics and social change. Rather than seeing the hand of God moving events, many antebellum Americans saw the hands of sinister men. That may not have been accurate, but it was about as good as any other explanation available in those days before Marx and modern social science. And it could serve the cause of reform as well as that of repression.

Besides being secular (if simple-minded), the "paranoid style" was anti-elitist. It raised doubts about established authorities and leading citizens. Ministers, politicians, and "gentlemen of property and standing" all were fair game—they were the ones plotting against the liberties of the people. In addition to venting class hostilities, such charges were entirely consistent with an ancient concern in Anglo-American political thought: a fear of power. Like their ancestors in the Revolutionary era, many antebellum Americans firmly believed that power corrupted people who had it. For abolitionists that view expressed itself in hatred of slavery; for other kinds of people it appeared in a conviction that selfish men (Masons, rum sellers, Jesuits, congressmen, or whoever) were secretly conniving against the interests of decent common folk. Fear of power can be crabbed and selfish—the ideology of a class that wants to be left alone to do as it pleases—but in antebellum America it did make men and women sensitive to many different issues, a few of which were silly but others of which, like slavery, were quite serious.

Mistrust of politicians, furthermore, can be healthy rather than "paranoid." That is especially true when disgust with old leaders brings new ones to the fore and raises the level of political participation. Reform movements, antimasonry, mobs, and nativism did precisely that. They drew people into the public arena who previously had not been involved in social action. Such men often gloried in *not* being members of the establishment and indulged in a kind of politics of anti-politics. In some instances that took the form of a literal rejection of political means, as when abolitionists refused to vote or when mobs enforced their own "justice." At other times it was not much more than simple contempt for officeholders. Yet even the crusades that seem exceptions to the antipolitical rule actually fit it. The antimasonic and Know-Nothing movements, for example, produced parties, but these did best when they attacked professional politicians and appeared to be under the control of fresh, inexperienced leaders. When political hacks and chronic office seekers climbed aboard the bandwagon, the movements lost credibility and support. Their temporary success and long-run failure is a sign that much of the electorate, not simply reformers, was uneasy with the increasingly party-oriented political system of Jacksonian America and responsive to people and organizations having a moral detachment from it.

Antimasonry, proslavery, mobs, and nativism had still other characteristics of true reform movements, but each lacked a crucial element. Mobs, obviously, were not movements. They were spontaneous and sporadic. They had neither institutions nor clear, long-range goals. Antimasons and nativists had reformers in their ranks and supported many reform objectives, but they were fuzzy about what sort of social order they wanted, once they purged America of sinister conspiracies. Proslavery writers often criticized Northern and Southern ways of life and presented alternative visions of society (and in that sense were reformers), but they did not have a distinctive organizational structure to spread their ideas and to channel the energies of the faithful. Instead of building a movement, they used publications and existing political bodies to carry the word.

The point of the comparison, however, has not been to argue that antimasonry, proslavery, mobs, and nativism were reform movements. It has been to demonstrate that reformers were more representative of their period than they seem to have been at first glance. They were Americans responding to change in a manner their society and culture allowed. Whether a person became a reformer, a nativist, politically active, a member of a mob, apathetic, or anything else was a matter of social position, upbringing, and events. The decisive factor was how the transformation of America played upon the individual's life history. For some the path led to reform; for others it led to different modes of behavior.

To say that is to disagree with many reformers (who thought of themselves as standing above and beyond their era), but it does not diminish the significance of reform. The antebellum variety *did* have an impact, although a difficult one to assess fully. From a present-day perspective, moreover, antebellum reform serves as a good indicator of tensions within its society and of the possibilities within its culture. It consisted of men and women trying to shape modern times with some—not all—of the moral and intellectual tools available to them.

How reform helped people to respond to a changing world varied with the particular crusade. At one extreme there were causes such as health reform and temperance, which were primarily significant for assisting people in achieving self-mastery and individual dignity. At the other extreme were antislavery and school reform, which acted more as explanations of what had to be done to society. Communitarianism played both roles. But important as the nature of a reform was, the position it held in a person's life depended greatly on whether one was a leader or a follower.

Leaders found a career that had not existed two or three generations earlier. Before 1800 very few people had been able to give themselves over entirely to moral or social causes. Full-time gadflies like Tom Paine were rare and most of them in the eighteenth century were religious itinerants, like the great Quaker abolitionist, John Woolman. Before the 1820s, reform more commonly was a sideline for men, and some women, who had social position, or at least gainful employment. The archetype of such a reformer was Ben Franklin, who included good deeds among his other activities. Only with the technological and social changes of the nineteenth century did it become possible for large numbers of Americans to make a livelihood out of agitation. To be sure, some leaders of antebellum reform did hold other jobs, as clergymen and even in business, like Arthur and Lewis Tappan. But many either rejected conventional occupations (including a fair proportion of onetime or would-be ministers) or else kept halfheartedly at other work while giving much income and emotional energy to a cause. A life such as William Lloyd Garrison's, which for thirty-five years consisted primarily of editing a reform newspaper, would have been unthinkable in Franklin's day.

Reform was a demanding profession, with poverty and violence among its dangers; but it had its rewards. For women it was virtually the only way to have public influence; to men it offered a kind of moral authority that law, politics, business, and (in some circles) the ministry no longer had. The greatest satisfactions, however, were personal, as reformers often acknowledged. Reform, they declared, transformed them in much the same manner as a religious conversion would have. Lydia Maria Child described it well. In the 1830s and already a successful author, she met Garrison, who "got hold of the strings of my conscience and pulled me into reforms." The encounter changed "the whole pattern of my life-web." Mrs. Child would have seasons of doubt and unhappiness afterward, but she found a meaning in antislavery she had not discovered in religion or writing fiction. For her and hundreds of her colleagues, reform was more than just another job. It was an important part of one's self.

Most people involved in reform were not leaders. They were obscure men with regular employment, single women, or women with family responsibilities. They drifted out of reform after a few years, or at most stayed on the periphery of it throughout their adulthood. Although their participation, dues, and consumption of propaganda kept reforms alive, they made little mark in the historical record.

There were hundreds of thousands of such people engaged in various causes, and the experiences of one of them, Henry Cummins, may have been more typical than were those of a celebrity like William Lloyd Garrison. A teen-ager in Eugene, Oregon, in the 1850s, Cummins described himself as "reformatory all round." His commitment to health reform gave him pride and self-discipline—as an eighteen-year-old he noted with satisfaction that "the cravings of my appetite, on account of my rigid abstemiousness, are fast subsiding." (It is not entirely clear which appetite he meant: the previous month he read Dr. Russell Trall's *Home Treatment for Sexual Abuses.*) Important though control of his bodily urges was, Cummins gained most from the social network his enthusiasms spun for him. From what was then a small town, distant from the cultural centers of the land, he corresponded with friends throughout Oregon on reform matters and inquired about the possibilities of going East to study phrenology or the water cure. Cummins was dedicated to reforms for years, but many of his acquaintances passed through them as a brief stage in life. "Most of the young men who commence the study of Phrenology, in Oregon," a friend noted, "have finely [finally] turned out Preachers or Merchants or drunkards." (That correspondent gave himself two more years as a phrenological lecturer, after which he planned to "study medison," which he thought "will not take me long with my knowledge.")

Antebellum reform was not entirely a movement of lonely youth, but much of its significance among the rank and file does appear to have come from the self-control, intellectual stimulation, and social contacts it provided young people like Cummins. (The surviving minutes of some small-town temperance societies deal less with the evils of drink than with costumes, rituals, and meetings with members of the opposite sex.) It does not demean reform to say that it did a great deal for reformers. It was no small blessing for individuals to have been able to put their lives in order and do some good in the process. A reform commitment inevitably depends on a peculiar resonance between the situation of the reformer and a broader problem.

Antebellum reform had its place in history, just as it did in the lives of individuals. In some respects it looked backward to traditions long predating it. The obvious instances were its evangelical Protestant imagery and its use of the rhetoric of the American Revolution. Less apparent debts to the past were the belief in conspiracies and an insistence that freedom was the right of human beings to buy and sell in the marketplace with a minimum of interference—both of them habits of mind going back to the eighteenth century and beyond. The latter view could be radical when directed against restrictive laws and entrenched privilege, as it was during the American Revolution. But by the end of the nineteenth century it became conservative dogma, ending up as little more than a rationale for allowing Americans to exploit their land and each other without having the government do anything about it. Yet such a definition of freedom still had much of its egalitarian thrust when it appeared in antebellum reform. A few people (communitarians, most notably) did challenge it and attempted to substitute an ethic of cooperation and harmony. The idea of laissez-faire, nonetheless, predominated among reformers and gave a critical edge to their analyses of tyranny, particularly to the abolitionist argument that the slave rightfully owned his or her labor.

Despite the significance of what was old in antebellum reform, many things were new about it. The prospect of making a career out of reform was one of them. Another was the matter of how people believed problems ought to be solved. Eighteenth-century reformers generally took human betterment—the limited amount of it they thought possible—to be something for members of the elite to determine and implement. It was the responsibility of those with moral and financial advantages to do their part to ameliorate suffering. That was to be done without any expectation that the millennium was at hand or that social relationships would be changed in the least. Antebellum reformers saw things differently. Some men and women, consistent with their evangelical Protestantism, insisted that change could be total, for people and for society, and that it began with the individual, no matter how lowly. Making a sinner's heart yearn for good behavior, not imposing morality by force or giving charity, was the task of reform. Reformers, of course, were not of a single mind about that. Temperance advocates were especially committed to legislating morality and there were others who swam against the individualistic and voluntaristic currents of antebellum reform. The most important of them developed quite innovative forms of coercion—schools, asylums, and assorted institutions to uplift or cure mankind. But antebellum Americans broke with their eighteenth-century predecessors whichever course they chose, whether they tried to improve humanity through conversion or confinement.

And yet the greatest transformation of American reform lay ahead, after 1860, really after the 1870s. Signs of change began to appear as early as the 1850s, when many reformers lowered their goals and lost some of the evangelical fervor of the 1830s and early 1840s. The trend continued, at an accelerated pace after the Civil War, until by the 1870s a prominent faction of Northeastern reform, consisting in part of ex-abolitionists and their children, dropped its horizon to the point where it would have been satisfied with little more than civil service laws, honest elections, and free trade. That was less ambitious than wanting to save the world.

Some of the gloomier mood came from the bitter sectional conflict of the late 1840s and the 1850s and the Civil War. The majority of reformers were above the Mason-Dixon line and most were drawn to the Northern cause, willing to subordinate their programs and swallow their doubts in order to help it triumph. They had, moreover, to reconsider their belief that the individual could be a force in history. Despite acts of heroism, humans seemed irrelevant when huge organizations delivered men and material to the front lines and cared for the sick and wounded. It was a massive army rather than sanctified hearts that won the war.

It was not just the war that took the fire out of antebellum reformers. A bit of the change came about because of what had *not* been accomplished in decades of agitation. Sinners were harder to reach than anyone imagined; drunkards stayed drunkards, the insane were not made sane, and so it went. Reformers had been far too optimistic about what propaganda and moral suasion could do. If nothing else, fatigue and a lack of results began dampening enthusiasm by 1860.

When success did come, it proved to have as much a chastening effect as failure. The destruction of slavery in 1865 deprived reformers of their most emotionally compelling issue. Few white Americans could bring to the cause of civil rights for blacks the same passion they invested in antislavery. Certainly some abolitionists kept faith in racial justice down to the end of the nineteenth century, and most crusades persisted after 1860—temperance and woman's rights actually reached peaks much later. When people worked for causes after 1860, however, their objectives usually were more modest than those of antebellum reformers and their emotional pitch was lower. As hopes for humanity declined, so did participation in reform. Political corruption in the 1870s simply provided more reasons for morally sensitive people to retreat in disgust from social involvement: the most meaningful of wars ended with elected officials wallowing in the public trough. Perhaps human nature was fatally flawed and mankind was indeed beyond redemption in this world.

By the 1890s yet other styles of reform began to emerge, types more familiar to us, although they may also be passing. Their story is too complicated to tell except in outline, as further reminder that modes of changing the world change like everything else. Since the late nineteenth century, reform has largely been secular and (often) committed to science as a guide to managing human affairs. Only in rare instances has a religious tone been as prominent as it was in the early nineteenth century. But where God retreated, the state advanced. Beginning with the Populists of the 1880s, reformers have called upon the government to solve problems with a casualness that would have appalled their early-nineteenth-century counterparts. There was no precedent in antebellum reform for the zeal of Progressives and New Dealers to construct regulatory agencies to oversee social and economic matters. This bureaucratic impulse was directed toward setting fair terms for competition in the marketplace and protecting Americans from the worst hazards of the day. In desiring to do that, rather than striving to create a perfect world, latter-day reformers expected less than antebellum ones had. They were, nonetheless, more perceptive for recognizing that solutions to the evils of modern life have more to do with industries and cities than with the sinful hearts of individuals.

Yet differences were not absolute between antebellum reformers and their successors. Some individuals, of course, bridged the distance with their own careers. Wendell Phillips (to cite a notable case) began as an abolitionist and, after the death of slavery, spent many years involved in less individualistic, more secular crusades. In style as well as personnel the line between older and newer modes of reform often becomes indistinct. The use of law, institutions, and science to further social change, for example, began in the pre-Civil War period, even though it would be central to Progressivism. Millennialism and immediatism—characteristics of antebellum reform —continued to crop up after 1860. They reappeared in 1912 when Theodore Roosevelt's followers stood at Armageddon and battled for the Lord (they lost) and again when "Freedom Now" became the rallying cry for the Civil Rights movement of the 1960s.

Still, much has changed since 1860 and many twentieth-century Americans have found it hard to be sympathetic to antebellum reformers (with the exception of the abolitionists). They seem quaint for their follies, their naïveté about evil, and their hostility to sex, drink, and rich food. We are battle-scarred by developments they could not even imagine; we are not so optimistic about progress and many of us are more at peace with our bodies. But perhaps we can admire antebellum reformers for the nobility of their greatest vision, or at least feel a bit of guilt for being so cynical about it. In their best moments they believed in harmony and human unity. They thought the glorious and perfect time was near when sin would vanish and men and women would behave morally because they wanted to, not because they were forced to. Instead, as we know and antebellum reformers could not, industrialization, imperialism, and war were advancing upon the modern world.

1. The Missionary Impulse

The report on a Kentucky girl in 1801 was dire: "She was struck down fell stiff heer hand and arm also became as cold as Death heer fingers cramp'd recov'd heer speech in 2 hours and was haled home on a sled continues in a state of despare which has lasted 3 weekes." The girl was not ill. She was having a religious experience. Hers was more extreme than most, although not unusual for Kentucky in 1801.

Between the late 1790s and the Civil War countless Americans like the Kentucky girl were caught up in outbursts of intense religious excitement. Few people outside the West had her kind of physical reaction, but men and women, girls and boys, became convinced of their own sinfulness, went through intense emotional turmoil, and emerged with a belief that they had been saved. Whether it came in special camp meetings or from the pulpit of the local church, the evangelical message was proclaimed across the land and the public responded with explosions of spiritual zeal. These bore a special relationship to the reform movements of the antebellum decades.

Revivals in the early nineteenth century were so frequent and widespread that historians sometimes apply the phrase "Second Great Awakening" to the entire period from 1795 to 1837. (The first Great Awakening had crested in the 1740s.) Within that long span of years there were, naturally, times and areas of greater and lesser enthusiasm. Between 1795 and 1810 most of the action was in Kentucky and Tennessee, in rowdy revivals presided over by Methodists, Presbyterians, and Baptists. There were more sedate awakenings in New York and among New England Congregationalists, but the vigor was in the West. From 1810 to 1825 the focus of revivalism shifted to the East, where influential clergy—Lyman Beecher prime among them—began preaching the gospel in revivalistic fashion while making important, often unacknowledged, modifications in New England theology. After 1825 evangelism reached its peak in the antebellum years in the work, largely in the West, of Charles G. Finney. His impact on reformers and reform, like Beecher's, would be great.

In 1821, the twenty-nine-year-old Finney went through a typically agonizing conversion, after which he gave up a promising law practice in rural New York to study for the Presbyterian ministry. Although he dissociated himself from "ignorant" Methodist and Baptist evangelists, he had less patience with creeds and formal theology than Beecher and the New Englanders. His forte was using common sense, everyday language, the Bible, and theatricality to drive his hearers to seek salvation. Soon after his ordination he was presiding over remarkable revivals in western New York and was well on his way to becoming the dominant force in evangelical Protestantism. In 1832 Finney came to New York City to assume the pastorate of the Second Free Presbyterian Church, newly situated in a former theater. His arrival symbolized a closing of the gap between Western and Eastern, and rural and urban, revivalism.

That is not to say Finney's triumph, or revivalism's, was complete. He and other evangelicals faced many critics, both from sects like the Unitarians and from within their own denominations. Finney eventually left the Presbyterians, and Beecher, at first a Congregationalist, joined their ranks only to be put on trial by the Cincinnati Synod for heresy. He survived the ordeal but the Presbyterian Church—the largest sect in the nation—split into pro- and anti-revival groups two years later, in 1837.

The evangelicals also battled each other. In 1827 things reached such a bad pass between Western evangelists, led by Finney, and Easterners, clustered around Lyman Beecher, that they held a nine-day peace conference. It failed. With his customary vigor, Beecher warned Finney not to enter Massachusetts. He recalled saying, "As the Lord liveth, I'll meet you at the State line, and call out all the artillerymen, and fight every inch of the way to Boston, and then I'll fight you there."

Despite hostility and despite dissension in its own ranks, revivalism was the core of antebellum Protestantism. It was the faith of people as far apart socially and geographically as rude Kentucky backwoodsmen and wealthy New York merchants. It flowed across denominational lines and appeared in all the major Protestant sects, thoroughly muddling the usual distinctions between them. In times of awakenings, for example, Baptists, free-will Methodists, and predestinarian Presbyterians forgot their disagreements—if they ever understood them—and became brothers and sisters in spirit. Laymen and clergy changed from one denomination to another, without effort or guilt. What counted more to believers than creeds and doctrines was whether a church was for or against revivals: and far more people belonged to revivalistic than to non-revivalistic churches. In some guise or another, evangelical Protestantism was the religion of most Americans.

Connections between revivalism and reform were obvious at the time and have been much emphasized by historians ever since. Evangelical clergy and laymen engaged in moral crusades of their own and appeared in the lead of secular ones like temperance and antislavery. Such revivalistic institutions as Lane Seminary and Oberlin College were breeding grounds for reformers, many of whom had been inspired by Beecher and Finney. In regions like the Western Reserve of Ohio and the "burned-over district" of New York reform movements followed close on the heels of hellfire preaching. Even voting statistics bear out the correlation, with, for instance, the abolitionist Liberty Party doing best in areas where religious enthusiasm had run high.

Still, it is possible to make too strong a link between revivals and reform. Of the hundreds of thousands of Americans converted between 1800 and 1860, only a small minority felt compelled to social action and a few were to be found on the anti-reform side of all questions. Not only that, many causes had strong support from such non-evangelical sects as the Quakers and Unitarians. Some crusades, notably communitarianism and spiritualism, were especially attractive to freethinkers and atheists. Deism, with its mechanistic God and skepticism about doctrine and clergy, had a following in labor reform, where an eighteenth-century tradition of artisan radicalism and rationalism remained vital. Even among evangelical reformers, Christianity was not the only source of intellectual and emotional stimulation. Many of them looked to science and natural law as well as the Bible for inspiration and struggled to break out of the cultural and institutional limitations of evangelical Protestantism. All reformers buttressed their arguments with enlightenment humanitarianism, the democratic rhetoric of the American Revolution, the sentimental conventions of the day, and Scottish philosophy. Yet when everything is said and done, it was evangelical Protestantism that provided most of the ideological and organizational foundation for antebellum reform.

Beginning in the early twentieth century, popular critics of revivalism like H. L. Mencken made it seem utterly simple-minded, the very epitome of anti-intellectualism. In fairness, religious fundamentalists provided critics with all the evidence they needed by waging war against every interesting concept to emerge in modern times. The gulf between intellectuals and revivalism in this century, however, makes it easy to forget the complex and sophisticated role evangelical Protestantism has had in the history of ideas. It grew out of—and produced—impressive theological debates and permeated much eighteenth- and nineteenth-century social, moral, economic, political, and scientific thought.

That is by way of a reminder that there were ideas of substance behind antebellum revivalism. Yet important as they were to theologians, what mattered most for reform was a handful of highly generalized beliefs, held in one form or another by all evangelicals. These usually were not formal doctrines (although they could be); more often, they were half-articulated assumptions about the future and about human beings.

The Second Great Awakening raised expectations that the Kingdom of God on earth was imminent. Similar notions appeared during the first Great Awakening and had surfaced throughout the centuries, but the quickening of religious fervor after 1800 seemed a sure sign to many Americans that the new day was dawning. One variety of these beliefs, properly called millenarianism, held that there would be a literal return of Christ, a Day of Judgment, and an end to history. Its most numerous exponents in the antebellum period were followers of a New England Baptist preacher named William Miller, who set the year of Christ's arrival as 1843 (it was postponed to 1844, then indefinitely). Several prominent reformers became Millerites—one of their leaders was an ex-abolitionist—but millenarians usually had an anti-reform cast of mind. They generally maintained that times will inevitably get worse until the reappearance of Jesus and that godly people must withdraw from the sinful world and passively await the Judgment.

There was another way of thinking about the Kingdom of God, commonly labeled millennialism. It was more optimistic than millenarianism and of much greater significance in antebellum reform. Millennialists disagreed over whether the reign of God was near or far, whether it would come gradually or swiftly, and whether it would begin with a cataclysm or quietly. But they agreed that it would be a real historical era occurring before the final Judgment—a thousand years of peace, prosperity, harmony, and Christian morality. That was a vision of the ideal society, and it was an important one for reformers to have: the imperfections of their own day were stark by comparison with a time of God's justice. Millennialism assured them that a better world was possible (people have not always thought that to be the case) and let them hope they might live to see it. Belief in the approaching Kingdom of God stirred dissatisfaction with earthly kingdoms while spurring antebellum crusaders into action.

In yet other respects millennialism was congenial to reform. It fostered a foreboding about the period before God's rule began, a dire conviction that the forces of light and dark would engage in a terrible final battle. But it also broadcast the ultimate glad tidings: God will triumph. In these extremes of apprehensiveness and joy, millennialism gave reformers a mechanism to express conflicting feelings about the direction in which the United States was heading.

The troubled mood matched their fear of immorality, mobs, irreligion, political turmoil, sectional conflict, and similar signs of disorder and decay. The promise of a perfect future, on the other hand, embodied reformers' expectations that everything would turn out for the best.

That millennial optimism was particularly strong because it interacted with other common attitudes. It merged with a belief that the United States was chosen by God to fulfill a great mission, an old notion given new life in the antebellum period by territorial expansion and religious revivals (sure marks of divine favor). This idea of national destiny was simultaneously accepted and used by reformers. They claimed that America's special place in God's design meant that its sins were more heinous than those of other countries and that their reforms were urgently needed. The divine plan—the millennium—depended upon it. Whatever the merits of the argument, it neatly confused religious and patriotic fervor to make a case. In much the same fashion, millennialism converged with prevalent attitudes toward economic development. It was easy for reformers (and many other Americans) to feel that a new era was beginning in the antebellum years. Evidence of God's favor was not just in revivals or addition of territory to the Union: it was also apparent in a rising standard of living and in scientific and technological advances. (At some points millennialism became almost indistinguishable from the secular idea of progress, that bourgeois Victorian faith that Civilization was marching onward and upward.)

In spite of its ability to adapt and survive, millennialism would not have been so influential in the antebellum period if clergymen had not told mankind it could help God usher in his kingdom. Very much in tune with the activist spirit of their age, millennialists argued that people need not sit idle in anticipation of the glorious new day. Good deeds and improved public morality were omens of its approach and might well hasten it along.

When nineteenth-century preachers made this claim that human effort could bring about the millennium, they were abandoning a line of theology stretching from John Calvin through early American Congregationalism and Presbyterianism. Calvin and Calvinists maintained that human beings were innately sinful and could, of their own free will, do nothing pleasing to God. Salvation came only as an arbitrary, predestined judgment from an omnipotent deity. By the end of the eighteenth century Methodists and a few other sects in America had repudiated those propositions, preferring to think that people might be able to assist themselves in being saved. As early as the seventeenth century, even Presbyterians and Congregationalists had been finding ways of mitigating the harshness of their theology without going over to the "free will" position later taken by Methodists. Beecher's generation softened Calvinism still further and Finney, nominally a Presbyterian, overthrew it.

Among the means he used was the concept of "disinterested benevolence," which he saw as the sum of all "holiness or virtue." The phrase itself had an honorable history in American Protestantism, going back to Jonathan Edwards in the eighteenth century. Finney, however, took any trace of Calvinist hellfire out of it and turned it into an inspiration for reformers. Edwards had believed humans were incapable of disinterested benevolence while in their natural, sinful state. Like any other good thing, it was one of God's gifts to regenerate (if undeserving) individuals. Finney was more concerned with results than metaphysics. Where Edwards' universe revolved around God, his centered on what the believer did; and he was certain people could act virtuously if they wanted to. In a thoroughly practical manner he tried to persuade them of the "utility of benevolence." Often his reasoning was more reminiscent of Ben Franklin than John Calvin (as when he declared that "if we desire the happiness of others, their happiness will increase our own"), but there was a moral earnestness to Finney. He insisted that men and women not only could but should "set out with a determination to aim at being useful in the highest degree." So much the better that being useful would make them happy and please God in the bargain —Finney's call for benevolent action was more effective for having a greater degree of self-interest than disinterest to it. His theology may have been muddled, but its message was firm. Of true Christians, Finney wrote: "To the universal reformation of the world they stand committed." It is little wonder that his preaching spawned converts to antislavery, temperance, and other crusades, as well as to the gospel.

Finney (and most of his critics, for that matter) had revised dramatically upward the old Calvinist estimate of human nature. The problem was deciding where to stop. Was it just that people could do good deeds on their own volition, even though remaining essentially sinful? Or might human beings become completely free from sin while on earth? The Bible, after all, commanded: "Be ye therefore perfect even as your Father which is in heaven is perfect."

In that passage lurked a doctrine—perfectionism, or the notion that individuals could become sanctified while on earth. Finney himself, although growing more sedate with age, arrived at a version of perfectionism in the 1830s and helped spread it among his peers. He and the great majority of evangelicals, however, accepted a moderate form of the doctrine while staunchly rejecting a dangerous implication in it—the possibility that sanctified persons could do no wrong. That would have freed believers from all worldly laws, a horrifying prospect to Calvinists and anyone else who recognized the villainy pious men and women can perpetrate. A few perfectionists did believe that whatever they did was not a sin (we will meet some of them later), but the great majority, including Finney, avoided that radical conclusion.

The significance of perfectionism here is not the forms it took—which were many and strange—but rather the fact that it existed in all branches of evangelical Protestantism. Although it could be egocentric, with no social content whatsoever, it also could become an energizing principle, giving inspiration to people who wanted to impose absolute moral integrity upon their own lives and upon a changing world. Perfectionism helped create an "ultraist" mentality which insisted that anything short of millennial standards should not be tolerated, a cast of mind common among antebellum crusaders. It was manifested in such things as utopian efforts to construct a new social order, calls for slavery to end immediately, a belief that any alcohol was evil, and an unwillingness (at least in the 1830s and 1840s) to compromise. Unlike their eighteenth-century counterparts, antebellum reformers seldom wanted merely to improve conditions. They wanted to make things *right*.

The crucial doctrines of evangelical Protestantism, including perfectionism, were things people felt and acted upon, rather than analyzed carefully. Evangelicalism was a religion of the heart, not the head. It asserted that salvation was an internal conviction, an experience, not something arrived at through study and contemplation. Theodore Dwight Weld, abolitionist and onetime student at Lane Theological Seminary, phrased it well when sympathizing with a friend who was puzzling his way through "mere *intellectual theories* of religion." Weld's advice was for the man to give up, turn "to direct communion with God," and bring his "spirit simply and utterly in contact with infinite purity and love." Weld was not repudiating all intellectual activity, in the manner of some twentieth-century revivalists, but he was calling for a religion of emotion rather than dogma.

That evangelical faith in the heart was extremely significant. Like Finney's disinterested benevolence and perfectionism, it belonged to the nineteenth-century repudiation of Calvinism. In practical matters, it was a proclamation that everyone, not just professors of divinity, could understand what was important to know, a doctrine as egalitarian as anything put forth by Jacksonian politicians. In common with much of evangelicalism, it joined easily with secular currents, including a democratic faith in the people and a romantic trust in feeling and intuition. More important for reform, it was part of a Protestant network of assumptions that encouraged individuals to believe things were wrong with their situation, and yet have confidence they could make it better.

Christian benevolent activity was not new in the nineteenth century. Cotton Mather, in 1710, published *Bonifacius: An Essay upon the Good*, which was reprinted off and on for decades. Mather influenced many people (including Benjamin Franklin) with his call for "REFORMING SOCIETIES," separate from, but allied with the churches. These anticipated later voluntary organizations, but nothing in the eighteenth century came close to matching the size and range of benevolent groups that sprang up after 1800. It took westward expansion and loss of position in the Eastern states to push evangelicals into making their real contribution to the organizational, as well as intellectual, structure of antebellum reform.

Movement of population into upstate New York, Vermont, and

the Ohio Valley meant that after the Revolution there were thousands of souls scattered along the frontier, ripe for harvesting. The Methodists and Baptists, who had circuit-riding ministers and a tradition of evangelizing, were in a better position to provide religious services than were the older New England denominations, with their settled clergy. Aware of the deficiency, Presbyterians and Congregationalists developed techniques to proselytize Westerners. Among the devices they came up with was the Connecticut Missionary Society, which, by the 1790s, was busy spreading the gospel according to New England. The society was run by a committee, on which laymen had equal representation with clergy. With impressive efficiency, it raised money, supported agents in the field, and produced propaganda. Its methods could—and would—be adapted to serve any number of religious and secular causes.

Heathenism in the West was not the only enemy. New England and New York Protestants also had to mobilize against challenges on the home front. By the end of the Revolution few states still had a legally privileged, established church. In parts of New England, Congregationalism did retain a special status under law until after the War of 1812; but even there the handwriting was on the wall much earlier. Baptists, Methodists, and—more disturbing—Unitarians (who denied the Trinity) and Universalists (who believed all would be saved) were growing in influence. It was only a matter of time before they overthrew the "standing order" in religion. No longer able to count on the government to preserve their dominance, Congregationalists and their Presbyterian allies launched a counterattack. Evangelism was a part of it, but so was reliance on voluntary organizations much like the Connecticut Missionary Society. Some were reform societies, others were not; all of them, nonetheless, provided models and personnel for every other antebellum crusade, including the least religious ones.

Most of the earliest nineteenth-century Protestant voluntary organizations clustered in New England and the mid-Atlantic states. A few of them aimed at specific sins. The name of the Anti-Duelling Society, for instance, revealed its purpose. (It was begun in 1809 and Lyman Beecher was a strong supporter.) But many of the first organizations were quite general in scope, much as Cotton Mather had suggested a century before. Although important for its anti-liquor stand, the aptly titled Connecticut Society for the Reformation of Morals (1813) sought to suppress a multitude of evils (among which its founders included the Democratic-Republican Party). The mandate of a similar organization—the Andover South Parish Society for the Reformation of Morals—was typically broad. Its members were "to discountenance immorality, particularly Sabbath-breaking, intemperance and profanity; and to promote industry, order, piety, and good morals." Such groups drew upon local clergy and pious laymen, and very likely served both useful religious and social functions. They released the Protestant energies of parishioners in a sustained fashion, in contrast to revivals, which were sudden and sporadic. Moreover, they acted as a kind of moral police, pointing out immorality and lawbreaking that elected officials might prefer to ignore.

Though such work was important to people involved in it, the largest Protestant voluntary associations were dedicated to missionary activity rather than to harassing local wrongdoers. The first national one was the American Board of Commissioners for Foreign Missions, begun by Congregationalists in 1810, with Lyman Beecher among the founders. It owed something to the example of the British, who had long been spreading the gospel to remote and uncivilized lands, including North America.

Inspiring though that task was, evangelicals quickly recognized that there were threats enough to deal with in the United States: most especially, Unitarianism, Universalism, Catholicism, and irreligion and vice on the frontier. To fight them, evangelicals developed formidable instruments of propaganda. The American Bible Society came into existence in 1816, with a goal of putting the scriptures into the hands of every family in the nation. The American Sunday School Union (1824) aimed its efforts at children and printed books, pamphlets, and periodicals for them. Probably the most significant of all was the American Tract Society, formed in 1825; it had up-to-date presses at its disposal and no shortage of manuscripts. By 1830 these voluntary associations and lesser ones covered the land with the printed word and had thousands of auxiliaries contributing their mite to the cause. The message they proclaimed was firmly revivalistic and—less firmly—reformist. Temperance and other moral causes were preached along with diatribes against heresy and lack of faith. The American Tract Society eventually went so far as to distribute antislavery material.

The missionary societies generally made a point of claiming to be national in scope. That was not entirely accurate—leadership and support tended to concentrate in New York, Pennsylvania, and New England. Yet most of these organizations did represent a consolidation of prior state and local efforts, sometimes after much resistance. (Massachusetts and Pennsylvania groups, for instance, tried to obstruct the formation of the American Bible Society.) It was a considerable accomplishment to impose some central control over missionary enterprises (or over anything else in antebellum America). Being able to do so depended on several factors, the most obvious of which were improvements in transportation and in communication after 1815. Also playing a part was a rising sense of nationalism, fueled both by revivalism and by economic and political developments following the War of 1812. None of these large-scale missionary ventures would have been possible if evangelicals had not been able to look beyond the borders of their communities and regard a sin in one part of the Union as a matter of concern for all Americans.

In order to reach a far-flung audience, and to hold their organizations together, evangelicals developed institutions and tactics that were impressive by antebellum standards. Details, of course, varied, but the usual arrangement was for the national society to have local affiliates, sometimes a great many of them—the Tract Society claimed 3,000 in 1837. These auxiliaries collected and spent funds, passed out propaganda, and engaged in work of their own. Connections between them and the parent society were often quite loose, and disharmonious. ("Ideas of state-rights and state independence," an abolitionist noted, "determine the character of even our benevolent operations.") Annual conventions brought together members from throughout the Union, where they proposed resolutions, listened to inspiring oratory, elected officers, and quarreled. For the rest of the year most of the national society's affairs were left to a board of managers or an executive committee. It oversaw production and distribution of printed material, tried to meet expenses, and, in some instances, supervised paid agents who traveled about on the society's business. Almost all the devices necessary for any kind of agitation were refined by the Protestant ventures begun between 1810 and 1825 and were copied wholesale by later reform movements. When Justin Edwards shifted from tracts to temperance in 1826, and when the Tappan brothers helped build the American Anti-Slavery Society in 1833, they had only to draw upon their experience in evangelical crusades.

By 1830 Protestant voluntary associations constituted a loosely interconnected "benevolent empire." Although formally distinct from each other, the evangelical organizations propagated the same world-view, tapped the same financial resources, and had many of the same men on their boards of directors. They often held their conventions at the same times, in the same cities. These linkages permitted a measure of coordinated action, as when, in 1829, the benevolent societies mounted an especially energetic campaign in the West. (Reports had been coming in of appalling moral and theological degeneracy there, and Eastern evangelicals feared for the safety of the nation.)

The agencies of the benevolent empire had other things in common besides ideology, members, and sources of revenue. Many of them were interdenominational in ways that went well beyond the usual cooperation between Presbyterians and Congregationalists, who had engaged in joint ventures since agreeing to a Plan of Union in 1801. The managers of the Sunday School Union and the Bible Society, for example, included Presbyterians (the largest single group), Congregationalists, Methodists, Episcopalians, Baptists, Dutch Reformed, and even a stray Moravian and Quaker or two. (Unitarians were conspicuously absent.) The American Board of Commissioners for Foreign Missions was thoroughly Congregational, but its managers showed a sense of guilt about that—an 1860 publication they sponsored headed a section with the caption "The Board ceases to be Denominational." (It meant combined efforts with Presbyterians.) Cooperation across denominational lines sometimes broke down, but it was part of the evangelical spirit and it foreshadowed later secular reforms, such as antislavery and temperance, where there was a determined effort to keep the cause from becoming the property of any particular sect.

Another feature of the missionary organizations, likewise to reappear in antislavery and temperance, was the crucial role played by the laity. Clergy, of course, were never absent. What is striking, nonetheless, is the time, money, and administrative skill contributed by laymen. The driving forces of the benevolent empire were people like Arthur and Lewis Tappan, wealthy New York merchants who were at the center of nearly every one of the greatest religious and secular reforms of the day.

It would seem difficult to have opposed the activities of the benevolent empire. To have done so would have been to go against God and Christian morality. Most of its work did, indeed, meet with a fair measure of public approval, at least until leaders like Arthur Tappan got mixed up with antislavery. Still, the managers and agents of the various societies have always had enemies. These included, at the time, reprobates, skeptics, Unitarians, and anti-mission elements within the revivalistic denominations themselves. Politicians—Jacksonian Democrats especially—railed against the repressive goals of evangelicals and warned darkly about an alliance of church and state (neatly playing upon traditional American political values and, simultaneously, appealing to the fears of Catholic voters).

The most recent critics are historians who charge the evangelicals with serving their own narrow interests rather than truly aiding mankind. Their real ambition, supposedly, was "social control," which is a way of accusing them of imposing their authority and their standards upon poorer folk, at the expense of diversity and freedom. The Protestant voluntary associations, in the words of one scholar, were little more than "means to make people obey their [the evangelicals'] will."

That argument, to an extent, rests on knowing the motives of the people who founded the associations—and it is difficult to find out what went on in the hearts and minds of long-dead human beings. The evidence we do have does not entirely absolve evangelicals of self-serving and bigotry, but it indicates that there was more to the benevolent empire than social control. The first antebellum efforts—the Connecticut Society for the Reformation of Morals, for instance

—came closest to supporting the accusation. They had an air of truculence about them: a dislike of deviance from the strict New England way and a determination to make unruly elements behave properly. Yet there were less surly and repressive aspects to evangelical benevolence, especially after the mid-1820s, when millennialism became more pronounced and Finney and perfectionism entered the picture. Mixed with the rhetoric about moral decline and heathenism was a genuine belief that things could improve, that people could and should be helped, and that a better world would be the result. There was, moreover, a capacity for growth in many of the supporters of missionary activity. Some of them did shed a few sectarian prejudices after working with godly men and women in other denominations. They also saw that their own successes were not enough: getting the Bible and the Word to the public did not make America a Christian nation. That recognition led a number of people, including Arthur and Lewis Tappan, into antislavery and temperance and out of the more restricted religious concerns of the benevolent empire.

Evangelicals were uneasy about change and committed to a traditional morality, but that does not necessarily make them reactionaries. Rather than simply endorsing or opposing change, humans can want to guide it in what they believe to be a constructive manner, which is what the benevolent empire was intended to do. In a very loose use of the term, "social control" may be what that was. But it was not sinister, even in cases where it was shortsighted and intolerant. There were worse ambitions than hoping Americans might behave better toward each other and lead more moral lives.

Evangelical Protestantism released people from some of the old Calvinist suspicions about human nature and gave them an outlet for emotional and reformist enthusiasm. But like any liberating ideology, it could be taken to extremes that appalled its first supporters. As early as the 1830s even Finney, once attacked for unorthodoxy, was disturbed by what people were making of revivalistic techniques and impulses. His own theatrical style was imitated into absurdity by unscrupulous evangelists. Others fell into theological unorthodoxy too bizarre for Finney and most of the Christian world to stomach.

A few preached, and more practiced, scandalous sexual doctrines. In 1844 Theodore Dwight Weld reported that "within the last four years not less than thirty ministers of evangelical denominations have been guilty of the most flagrant licentiousness."

Reform urges had also begun to take on a life of their own, separate from evangelical Protestantism, and to grow in ways that caused problems for revivalists like Finney, who had done so much to stimulate social action. Finney endorsed temperance, health reform, abolition of slavery, and other worthy causes; but he insisted that revivalism came first. In common with most evangelists, he believed that excessive reform agitation alienated potential converts and diverted the enthusiasm of believers away from religion. He was not vocal about his own social views and he used his influence to discourage revivalistic publications and divinity students from taking controversial stands. That caution sometimes irritated influential laymen who believed reform was a sacred obligation (had not Finney said as much?) and that it should not be sacrificed to expediency.

As time went on, many reformers became increasingly disappointed, not just with Finney, but with revivalism generally. It appeared to have become mechanical, without real conviction behind it—Finney himself denied that revivals were miracles and gave instructions on how they might be produced (virtually a "do it yourself" manual for evangelists). There was mounting evidence that converts attracted by those methods did not engage in good works, as evangelical teachings said they would. Slaveholders saw the light but kept their slaves; tipplers went through a change of heart, but continued to drink. To make the situation more puzzling, it was obvious that there were many decent, reform-minded people who were not evangelicals (some were Unitarians and Universalists!). Perhaps the proper way for evangelicals to judge them was not by their theology, but by their actions. On that scale they came out better than any number of revivalistic preachers.

Some evangelistic reformers kept their faith and preserved their sectarian prejudices. But even those men and women gave reform a high priority and little trusted fellow evangelical Protestants to do the right thing. (Arthur Tappan, for instance, virtually bribed Western churches into temperance by giving donations to non-drinking congregations.) Many other reformers became less concerned about religious matters after years of crusading, and a few drifted into unorthodoxy. In some cases they did so in protest against the failure of churches to take stands on moral issues (generally slavery) ; in other cases they acted out of a feeling—itself a product of the revival—that a good heart and good deeds mattered more than religious formalities. For such people (and they included former clergymen) reform itself became a religion. Looking back on her career as an abolitionist, one woman wrote, "That is the only true church organization, where heads and hearts unite in working for the welfare of the human race." Her words were echoes of others, spoken over the decades by men and women who transferred their zeal from religion to reform, and from individual to social salvation. The irony is that when a cause like antislavery or temperance became a church, it was many of the things evangelical Protestantism was at its best: passionate, interdenominational, and committed to improving the human situation.

All reformers, including non-evangelicals and ones who left their churches, owed much to revivalism. Their language was filled with its rhetoric of sin, damnation, and salvation. It gave them a way of viewing the world—even the most secular of reformers talked of "progress" and "civilization" in tones harking back to millennialism and perfectionism. Evangelical techniques and enterprises, finally, showed how crusaders could organize and propagandize on a national scale. Yet evangelical channels were too narrow to contain all reform energy. By the 1830s communitarianism, antislavery, temperance, and various social causes and pseudo-sciences were redirecting, as well as drawing upon, religious impulses.

2. Heaven on Earth

"Since the war of 1812–1815," John Humphrey Noyes declared in 1870, "the line of socialistic excitements lies parallel with the line of religious Revivals." Even when Noyes wrote, his use of the word "socialistic" was beginning to sound antiquated. He did not mean Marxism or the kinds of socialism familiar in the twentieth century. He had in mind the bold experiments of small bands of antebellum men and women who gathered together in their own ideal communities, as Noyes and his followers had done at Oneida, New York. These were little utopias carved out of the American countryside, dedicated to one or another social or religious theory, and designed to serve as models for the rest of the world to imitate. Noyes deeply regretted that the people who constructed these communities had not seen the "parallel" and joined forces with evangelical Protestants. Each sought what the other needed for success: revivalists "failed for want of regeneration of society" and utopians "failed for want of regeneration of the heart." The unwillingness of communitarians and evangelicals to unite "their two great ideas" was all the more tragic since the groups had so much in common. They shared a faith in the perfectibility of mankind and a belief that the millennium was at hand. Both desired "to bring heaven on earth." Utopianism and revivalism, Noyes insisted, "are closely related in their essential nature and objects, and manifestly belong together in the scheme of Providence, as they do in the history of this nation." Noyes was perceptive.

39

No one knows exactly how many communitarian societies were built in the nineteenth century, but over a hundred were founded between the Revolution and the Civil War. The greatest wave of enthusiasm for utopian ventures came in the 1840s, in the aftermath of the revivals of the 1820s and 1830s (a fact Noyes stressed). Most communities lasted no more than a few years, some only a matter of months. Yet there were long-lived ones as well: the Shakers began in the eighteenth century and died out in the 1970s. Two others, Oneida and Amana, still exist as business enterprises.

Utopian societies, if one counts active members, were among the least popular expressions of antebellum reform and radical sentiment. At their height in the 1830s the Shakers numbered around 6,000, divided among several locations. All other communities were far smaller and many consisted of no more than a few dozen people. At that, there was no other period in our history, except possibly in the late 1960s, when such a large proportion of Americans joined communal societies.

The importance of these, however, goes far beyond the number of people involved in them. In some respects communalism was an exception in the midst of antebellum reform. It was genuinely radical —communitarians aimed at creating a totally new order rather than improving the old one, as reformers sought to do. Some communitarians, moreover, emphasized the influence of environment in shaping the character of human beings. In that, they disagreed with most antebellum reformers, who gave greater attention to the human heart than to the material world. Yet communitarianism also was the extreme that proved the rules of antebellum reform. As Noyes recognized, it was the ultimate expression of perfectionist and millennialist logic. In that, and in numerous other ways, communal ventures played out themes or tensions characteristic of reform and of American society generally.

It is difficult at first to see much coherence in anything so varied as antebellum communalism. The communities themselves ranged from highly structured to utterly unstructured, from theological to freethinking, from celibate to "free love." To make sense out of that diversity, historians and sociologists have developed several systems for classifying utopian communities. The simplest merely divides them between those that were primarily organized around religious doctrines and those that were primarily secular. That distinction is helpful enough to be worth following, but it requires a word of caution. Like many ways of classifying things, it is most interesting when it breaks down. As we shall see, and as Noyes grasped, one of the significant things about antebellum communalism was the manner in which it fused religious and secular impulses.

Some of the largest and most stable utopian societies in antebellum America were neither antebellum nor American in origin. These ventures represent a particular kind of religious communalism, best labeled "pietistic." All such groups formed around a strong and magnetic leader whose unorthodox theological teachings gave the community its reason for being. The communities themselves were in the United States but not especially of it. Several traced their ancestry to German sects, the rest to other seventeenth- or eighteenth-century European religious splinter groups. The most notable of the German-speaking communities—Ephrata, Harmony, Zoar, and Amana—were especially adept at keeping their Old World character in the midst of a rapidly changing new world.

Ephrata was not quite the first, nor was it the largest utopian society in North America; but by the antebellum period it was the oldest. Ephrata's founder, Conrad Beissel, left the Palatinate in 1720, apparently with the idea of joining the Woman in the Wilderness, a mystical community of German pietists who gathered in the Pennsylvania forest to await the millennium. By the time Beissel arrived most members of the Woman in the Wilderness had scattered or died. Beissel remained and spent much of the next twelve years in hermit-like spiritual contemplation. In 1724 he joined the Dunkers, a German sect, but in 1728 he published a work contradicting some of their doctrines. He attracted a few followers and in 1732 Ephrata, located near Lancaster, Pennsylvania, began as a communitarian society, or "cloister."

Those who lived within it were in no danger of being corrupted by luxury. Their days were filled with work and worship; their diet was sparse and vegetarian; their dress was homespun. Men lived in one large building, women in another. Little in those dwellings distracted them from spiritual thoughts. The passageways were exceedingly narrow; the rooms were small and spartan; and the residences were constructed and furnished without the use of metal, in imitation of Solomon's temple.

For all its plainness and religiosity, Ephrata did not have absolutely rigid rules on two matters quite crucial to later communitarians—sexual relationships and private property. Beissel did not insist upon chastity, although he encouraged it and most of his followers were celibate in the mid-eighteenth century, when their numbers may have reached three hundred. The community punished "the untimely intercourse of some of the brethren and sisters with each other," but over the years there was a decline in celibacy as well as in membership. By 1900 most of the seventeen remaining Ephratans were married. Beissel also did not demand that all property be held in common, although the community as a whole owned whatever was donated to Ephrata or produced by residents. Those who valued worldly goods (or sexual intercourse) simply left the cloister, took housing nearby, and became "outdoor" members, over whom Beissel and his successors exercised less rigorous discipline.

Nineteenth-century communitarians sometimes faulted Ephrata for its mystical theology, its isolation from the world, and its equivocation on marriage and property. That was to miss the point: spiritual contemplation was the essence of Ephrata and of the pietistic communities. Unlike later communitarians, Ephratans (and most pietists) never intended to provide the rest of humanity with models of such mundane things as relationships between the sexes and ownership of property.

By the early nineteenth century Ephrata was a relic. Beissel died in 1768. Peter Miller, his successor, survived him by twenty-eight years, leaving no one with his or Beissel's intellect and personal power to carry on. Ephrata inspired interest and at least one imitator in the nineteenth century, but by then it was not even the most vital of the German pietistic communities, an honor which more properly belonged to George Rapp's Harmony Society or (after 1847) to Amana.

In 1791 Rapp, a thirty-three-year-old German farmer, told an official investigating his religious beliefs, "I am a prophet and called to be one." Prophet or not, Rapp had been in conflict with the established Lutheran Church of Württemberg at least since 1785. He would remain in conflict until he left Germany in 1803 to find a New World home for his several hundred disciples. In December 1804 he purchased land in western Pennsylvania, and in February 1805 he and some supporters formally incorporated the Harmony Society.

Although living conditions were primitive at first, the Harmonists were steady and industrious. In a decade they cleared and cultivated over two thousand acres of land. As early as 1807 they were selling goods to the outside world, including 3,000 gallons of whiskey. They soon constructed several mills and a town. Dissatisfied with the climate, the soil, and the difficulty of getting their products to market, the Harmonists sold their Pennsylvania property for $100,000 (less than its real value) and moved to Indiana in 1815. The Harmonists—of whom there were now about eight hundred—again prospered. In 1824 the society advertised its holdings as consisting of numerous buildings (among them a cotton and woolen mill, a distillery, and a tavern) and of 20,000 acres of land on a navigable portion of the Wabash River. For reasons that are not altogether clear, the society again decided to move. In 1825 it sold everything to Robert Owen, the wealthy British social theorist, and returned to Pennsylvania, to land north of Pittsburgh. This, the society's third home, was named Economy. The Harmonists did well, despite a slow drop in their population. By 1874 they had closed several factories on their own land for lack of a labor force, but they kept flourishing ones on the outside. In that year a visitor marveled over their cutlery shop at Beaver Falls, Pennsylvania, which he described as "one of the largest in the world, where of late they have begun to employ two hundred Chinese." By 1900 the society had fewer than ten members—and substantial investments in petroleum and railroads.

Harmony was a more worldly place than Ephrata, yet the two had some similar characteristics. Each was the creation of a vigorous and compelling founder—Rapp's control over his followers, although occasionally challenged, remained firm until his death in 1847, at ninety. Each community was millennialistic—Rapp informed an inquirer in 1822 that Harmonists "believe without doubt that the kingdom of Jesus Christ [is] approaching near." If anything, Harmonists were more consistent in banning private ownership of property than Ephratans had been. By the terms of the "Articles of Agreement" of 1805 members signed over to the society all their earthly possessions.

Like the Ephratans, Harmonists generally remained celibate. Rapp had advocated sexual abstinence as early as 1791 (and probably practiced it as early as 1785), but he did not initially insist upon it. His own son, John, was married just before the society's ban on intercourse took place. Celibacy became policy in 1807 at the urging of members caught up in a new wave of religious enthusiasm sweeping the society. Apparently there was a brief relaxation of the rule around 1817, when several marriages were performed, but by the time Charles Nordhoff visited Economy in 1874 the residents assured him that they were celibate. Indeed, they attributed their long lives and good health to it. Be that as it may, celibacy and unwillingness to proselytize non-Germans had the same effect on the Harmony Society as on Ephrata: the membership grew old, died, and left none to keep the faith.

These were not the only German pietistic societies. Some others were schisms from the more famous ones—Harmony spawned settlements in Missouri and Oregon—and there were also several significant ventures originating independently of Ephrata or Harmony. The latter included Zoar in Ohio (1817–98), Amana (1843–1933), and Saint Nazianz (1854–96), a Catholic community in Wisconsin. The Germans, moreover, were not the only European people to form pietistic societies in America. A Swedish settlement at Bishop Hill, Illinois, may have had as many as 1,500 members in 1854. (It also had an extraordinarily turbulent history, punctuated by a cholera epidemic, extravagant speculation in land and businesses, and the murder of its founder in a courthouse shooting in 1850.) Colorful as Bishop Hill was, neither it nor Harmony was the largest and most influential pietistic community in the antebellum period. The Shakers were, probably because they were British in origin and thus, almost alone among pietistic communities, were effective in recruiting English-speaking members in the United States.

The American career of the Shakers was rooted in the spiritual experiences of Ann Lee, the illiterate daughter of a Manchester blacksmith. Her life, like her theology, was plain and demanding. Born in 1736, she took to factory and menial labor at an early age. While still a young woman she married Abraham Stanley (or Standerin), a blacksmith like her father. It was an unhappy match. Ann Lee apparently felt repugnance at sexual intercourse and, in any case, suffered through the birth and loss of four children, each of whom died without reaching maturity. Before marrying Stanley, she had joined the Shakers, a small sect tracing its lineage to seventeenth-century France and so named for the convulsive dance that was part of their ritual. Fired with zeal, she preached, prayed, and went into trances. She also was persecuted by mobs and by the authorities, who occasionally threw Ann Lee and fellow Shakers into prison. While in jail in 1770 she had a particularly powerful revelation and upon her release began to attract followers, who accepted her as "Mother in Christ." In 1774 another revelation directed her to take passage to America, which she did, accompanied by eight others— her husband among them. He deserted her in New York.

Mother Ann lived apart from her tiny flock for nearly two years but by 1776 she rejoined them at what is now Watervliet in upstate New York. They endured difficult times, both because of the hardships of making a living and because of the hostility of neighbors, who disliked their practices and suspected them of pro-British sympathies in the Revolution. Although Mother Ann was central to Shaker theology, she died in 1784, three years before the sect formed its first true communal settlement in Mount Lebanon, New York, and well before it entered its period of greatest expansion.

The Shakers began to grow after 1779, when a Baptist revival swept the country around Mount Lebanon. In what would prove to be a persistent pattern, they gathered in men and women who had been awakened by evangelical preaching but not satisfied by it. In 1805 the Shakers similarly took advantage of revivals going on in the West by sending out preachers of their own. The result was another rich harvest of converts and formation of a half dozen new communities. Still later the Shakers received people jarred from their spiritual moorings by Finney's great revivals of the 1820s and 1830s.

The sect also owed some of its success after Mother Ann's death to the ability of her successors. In 1787 Joseph Meacham and Lucy Wright, both skillful organizers, became the first American-born leaders. Wright presided over development of settlements throughout New York, New England, Ohio, Indiana, and Kentucky. In 1830, nine years after Wright's death, Frederick W. Evans joined the Shakers; in 1836 he became an elder, a position he held for fifty-seven years. While in his native England, Evans had been a free-thinker and a believer in Robert Owen's schemes of social reorganization; upon his arrival in the United States he became involved in labor reform. He had come upon the Shakers, in fact, while searching for a place to locate an Owenite community in New York. He proved to be an effective administrator and propagandist for the Shakers, serving them well from their high tide in the 1830s and 1840s into their decline after mid-century.

For all the ability of Meacham, Wright, and Evans, much of the strength of the Shakers was in their distinctive and compelling way of life. Mother Ann Lee had taught that God was both male and female in nature, with Jesus representing the masculine side. Since Mother Ann represented the feminine side, her coming (according to her followers) marked completion of God's revelation and the beginning of the kingdom of heaven on earth. This was a variety of millennialism and an assertion of the spiritual equality of men and women. Both sexes shared authority throughout the sect's hierarchy, from its "Head of Influence" at Mount Lebanon to the "families" (or smaller groups of men and women) that were the basic unit within each community. "Each brother," one visitor reported, "is assigned to a sister, who takes care of his clothing, mends when it is needed, looks after his washing, tells him when he requires a new garment, reproves him if he is not orderly." Such wifely chores aside, there were few places in American society where females were so emancipated from their usual roles as wives and mothers and granted so much genuine influence. It is no accident that by the middle of the nineteenth century, probably even earlier, women were a majority among the Shakers.

Shaker men and women lived in chastity as well as relative equality. Mother Ann made "Virgin Purity" a pillar of her faith and insisted that her followers be celibate (very likely recalling her own sad marital career). Shakers believed that sexuality was an "animal passion" belonging to a lower, less spiritual order of existence. Even though many non-Shakers shared that belief, few antebellum Americans went to the extreme of trying to ban sexual intercourse altogether, and Shakerism struck many observers as being cold and contrary to human nature.

Yet one of the secrets of Shakerism's appeal was the way it alternated self-denial with emotional release. Much of a Shaker's day was spent in silence, hard work, and emotional restraint. Various rituals, however, provided moments of sheer ecstasy. The most curious of these, and the best known, was the "dance" that was part of Shaker services. In reality, the "dance" and its accompanying music changed over time; but it always was a performance in which both sexes participated, parading in what visitors described as odd, regimented movements, sometimes dignified, sometimes spasmodic. The Shakers also went through periods of special enthusiasm, as in the late 1830s and early 1840s, when each of their communities was swept by spiritualism, mystical experiences, and speaking in tongues. Those outbursts and the "dance" help explain why Shakers were so good at gathering in men and women who had originally been converted by revivals in the outside world. The Shakers gave regular expression to evangelical Protestant emotionality, and made it all the more intense by mixing it with Protestant asceticism.

Bizarre as their customs seemed to some commentators, the Shakers gained the admiration of such non-Shakers as John Humphrey Noyes and Robert Owen, each of whom considered them a precursor of more "modern" communitarianism. On the matter of private property the Shakers were indeed among the most radical of utopians. They did away with distinctions in "temporal blessings" about as completely as any American commune ever has. But theirs was "Christian Communism," not the modern, secular variety. They shared their possessions because they did not value them much: their eyes were on heaven. That otherworldliness marks Shakerism as (in Noyes's phrase) one of the "antique religious Communities."

Most of the pietistic societies, including the Shakers, were European as well as "antique"—the significant exception was Jerusalem, established in New York in 1788 by a Rhode Island woman, Jemima Wilkinson. What European pietists found in America was toleration for their practices, inexpensive land, and economic opportunity. Most also discovered that they could remain European if they wished—only the Shakers recruited Americans successfully.

Although pietistic societies were beginning to fade as early as the 1820s, Noyes and Owen were right to think that they had lessons to teach later communitarians. The pietistic communities had begun the process of breaking away from conventional notions of family relationships and private property, both of which generally proved destructive to utopian ventures. In that, and in their pacifism, millennialism, and ability to survive, they were a model and an inspiration to other antebellum utopians.

But they were a deceptive model. Antebellum communitarians saw the durability of Ephrata, Harmony, and the Shakers as evidence that communal living was possible. What they did not see was *why* it had been possible. Many of the German pietists were bound by Old World ties of kinship and friendship, or simply by the experience of speaking the same language in a foreign land. Also, they were peasants for whom farming, simplicity, and hard work were second nature. Virtually all pietists, moreover, subordinated themselves to authoritarian leaders like George Rapp or to an exacting regimen like those of Ephrata or the Shakers. In contrast, most communitarians after 1825 were Americans who lacked a peasant tradition, or even much skill at farming. They were individualistic, self-assured, and intellectually restless—characteristics that made them chafe at the discipline of communal life. They were too impatient to await and contemplate the arrival of heaven on earth in the manner of the pietists. They could be ferociously dogmatic, but unlike the pietists, they did not completely accept the truth as given. They debated it among themselves and sought it in an even grander debate between ideology and experience.

American communitarians after 1825 generally operated within the Christian tradition, just as eighteenth-century pietists did; but each took different components from it, which, in turn, led to different modes of behavior. The pietists drew upon the communalism, monasticism, and mysticism of the primitive church. Later utopians lived out a social gospel, bringing Protestant principles to bear upon the wider world around them, as well as within the community. Nowhere was the divergence in styles of religious communalism more apparent than in the contrast between the old pietistic societies and Hopedale and Brook Farm, two of the most important New England communities of the 1840s.

Hopedale's founder, Adin Ballou, characterized it as a missionary, temperance, antislavery, peace, charitable, woman's rights, and educational society. True to his word, he and members of Hopedale regularly sallied forth from their Milford, Massachusetts, home to participate in those causes and others. While guiding Hopedale, Ballou lectured for temperance and for the American Anti-Slavery Society and he served as president of the New England Non-Resistance Society, an offshoot of the peace movement and a forum for Christian anarchism. At that, some disaffected residents charged Hopedale with being too isolated from the reforms of the day.

Ballou and his followers were religious enthusiasts and zealous reformers, but on a number of issues they were among the least daring communitarians and were far more moderate than their doctrines implied. Ballou was a Universalist minister and believed that all humans were destined for heaven (he did feel that some would need a period of probation and punishment first). He also held to the nonresistant faith that human relationships should be free of coercion, including coercion by man-made governments. Yet he did not push those doctrines (as some did) to the point of denying human sinfulness or arguing that individuals should be free to do whatever they want. Hopedale elected "official servants" who used the power of persuasion rather than force to get members to behave properly. In order to perform some community functions, Ballou even organized residents into an "Industrial Army" (the name was quickly changed to the less military-sounding "Industrial Union"). Ballou's "Army" was a far cry from the regimentation of the Shakers, whom he thoroughly repudiated, but he likewise had no use for virtually ruleless communities such as several founded by a more consistently anarchistic contemporary, Josiah Warren.

Ballou was equally moderate on the matter of private property and he was downright conventional when it came to marriage. Hopedale was organized along the lines of a joint-stock company, with provisions for dividends and for repurchase of shares held by dissatisfied investors. It also permitted members to work at their own businesses and to maintain property separate from that of the community. The looseness of Hopedale's economic arrangements was a major, but understandable, weakness. Ballou was primarily a moralist, concerned above all with the relationship between an individual and God, not with relationships in the marketplace. He was appalled at "revolting extremes of wealth and poverty," but he saw avarice and exploitation as rooted in the human heart, not in the economic structure. Ballou was equally moralistic in his views on matrimony, which he regarded as "sacred," and on family life, which Hopedale encouraged. He was horrified when a case of marital infidelity occurred in the community and he thought it appropriate that the offending couple departed for Modern Times, one of Warren's ventures. There, he noted disapprovingly, leaders advocated "promiscuous cohabitation."

Despite his prudery, Ballou was morally earnest, gentle, and charitable; Hopedale was pleasant, and, for a time, reasonably prosperous. In the words of a man who disagreed with Ballou on many issues, Hopedale was "one of the most distinctively American communities, and one meriting more complete success than it attained." Yet it met an abrupt, unique, and largely undeserved demise. Around 1851 Hopedale enjoyed a brief period of affluence. Ballou resigned its presidency in 1853, convinced that the community, then numbering over two hundred, was in good order. Its stock, meanwhile, had been passing into the hands of the Draper brothers, Ebenezer and George, who soon became majority shareholders. They threatened to withdraw their investment when Hopedale fell behind in meeting its obligations, thereby forcing the community to turn over its assets to them. In 1856 they incorporated its property into their other business enterprises. That was the end of Ballou's dream.

Brook Farm, located in West Roxbury, Massachusetts, was—like Hopedale—thoroughly a product of New England culture, but of a slightly different strand. Hopedale derived from Ballou's non-resistance, reformist impulses, and Universalism. It was firmly committed to a code of Christian ethics. Brook Farm was not as infused with reform zeal and was, if anything, more individualistic. But it also was religious in inspiration, although it appeared less so to contemporaries. Elizabeth Peabody spoke of an early plan for it as "Christ's Idea of Society," and it originated in conversations between two Unitarian ministers, William Ellery Channing and George Ripley, in 1840 and 1841. Issues raised by Channing spilled over into discussions of the "Transcendental Club" (loosely organized gatherings of Boston-area intellectuals). Fired with enthusiasm, Ripley and some colleagues purchased land and began the community in the summer of 1841.

Brook Farm is sometimes characterized as a "Transcendentalist Utopia" but what it owed to Transcendentalism is not completely clear. Transcendentalism itself was not a coherent set of doctrines; it was more a sensibility and a set of attitudes about mankind and nature. From it, Ripley, the community's moving force, may have gotten a belief in the limitless potential of human beings, but other communitarians got the same belief from evangelical Protestantism, through its perfectionist strain. Transcendentalism may actually have contributed a destructive element to Brook Farm: a feeling that individuals ought to free themselves from the restraint of institutions. That could justify seceding from society in favor of a utopian venture or it could be taken to the more radical conclusion that individuals ought to avoid all organizations, including communitarian and reform ones. Most of the major Transcendentalists, except Bronson Alcott, usually followed the latter course. Ralph Waldo Emerson agonized over whether to join Brook Farm and finally convinced himself (as he commonly did) that he was more valuable preserving his autonomy and remaining unaffiliated. He visited and observed Brook Farm with the same detachment his fellow Transcendentalist Margaret Fuller displayed when she spoke of going there to watch "the coral insects at work." When the influence of Transcendentalism was felt at Brook Farm, it was often in the form of a thorny independence like Emerson's—and that weighed heavily against the discipline and authority essential to communal life.

Yet that was part of Brook Farm's charm. It had room for playfulness, for fads, for odd attire, for unfashionably bearded and long-haired men, and for sweet eccentrics like Burrill Curtis, who, according to one account, "had been a model for a portrait of Christ." The motive of the original Brook Farmers, according to Elizabeth Peabody, was to be "wholly true to their natures as men and women." Those natures were deliciously varied and more utopian than communitarian.

Although there was a frivolous side to Transcendental individualism, it did encourage serious self-development. George Ripley had hoped "to insure a more natural union between intellectual and manual labor than now exists." The community, accordingly, was organized so that all members not only worked with their hands but also had the means "for intellectual improvement and for social intercourse, calculated to refine and expand." Some were not enchanted by having to do farm chores (Nathaniel Hawthorne's confrontation with a manure pile is one of the less elegant moments in New England literary history). But many were enthusiastic about Brook Farm's blend of physical activity with literature, poetry, and the other arts. "The weeds," George William Curtis recalled fondly, "were scratched out of the ground to the music of Tennyson and Browning." Whatever the effect upon weeds, Brook Farm's cultural ferment was unparalleled among American utopian societies and produced two impressive things: the *Harbinger* and the community's schools. In 1845 the Farm took over publication of the *Phalanx*, a New York Fourierist periodical, renamed it the *Harbinger*, and made it into an important weekly journal. After Brook Farm's failure in 1847, ex-members moved the *Harbinger* to New York and continued it for nearly two years. The schools were well staffed and remarkably flexible for the times. They had a broad liberal arts curriculum, broke with the practice of rote memorization, and attempted to combine learning with doing. They were fun, as nineteenth-century schools went, and respectable enough to impress Harvard. Culture and students were Brook Farm's best crops.

They were not cash crops. From its beginning Brook Farm was economically marginal. It was organized more or less as a dividend-paying joint-stock venture, but it was too Transcendental to be profit-making. The founders hoped to make "the acquisition of individual property subservient to upright and disinterested uses." They nonetheless sought to "reserve sufficient private property, or means of obtaining it, for all purposes of independence." The result was a muddle of community and private interests, which would have been troublesome if Brook Farm had been prosperous. As it was, the real problem was making ends meet, not distributing profits.

In 1844 and 1845 Ripley and other leaders, newly converted to the secular socialism of Charles Fourier, reorganized the community into a "Phalanx" (Fourier's term). It did gain some needed structure: workers were divided into three different categories—Farming, Mechanical, and Domestic—with each being broken down into various groups, as Fourier taught. (Thus the Farming Series contained a Milking Group, a Haying Group, and so forth.) The system was cumbersome and the small community had about as many groups as members. No amount of reorganization, moreover, could solve the problem of finding a secure economic base for Brook Farm. Whatever chance it had disappeared in 1846, when a disastrous fire swept the expensive and uninsured new main building. The remaining property sold in 1849 for under $20,000, a paltry sum compared to the Harmony Society's holdings, and even much less than Hopedale's.

Brook Farm has enjoyed a fame all out of proportion to its success or its size, which never exceeded one hundred members. Nostalgia for it lasted into the early twentieth century, when William Hinds reported that "so cherished are those memories that a few survivors of Brook Farm and a score of kindred souls gather annually in the summer months . . . to live again in the Brook Farm life." To this day the community's reputation has a bittersweet air to it, a sense of having been a charming interlude too innocent to last. Much of Brook Farm's notoriety stems from the fact that it was put together by New Englanders who, unlike the German peasants at Harmony, wrote letters, articles, and books about their experiences. And then there was Nathaniel Hawthorne. He turned his brief sojourn at Brook Farm into the *The Blithedale Romance* (1852), a thinly fictionalized portrait of the community. It was this novel, more than anything else, that kept interest in Brook Farm alive outside New England literary circles. Hawthorne's perspective was complicated and ambiguous—but, on balance, unflattering. At one point, the narrator of the novel reflected on the youthful naïveté that had taken him to the community. "I rejoice," he declared, "that I could once think better of the world's improvability than it deserves." Such disillusion was common enough: when Ballou looked back on the failure of Hopedale he saw his "over-sanguine" faith in human beings as "a weakness." But there was more to *The Blithedale Romance* than that. Hawthorne showed an ugly side to the reform impulse. In the character of Hollingsworth, he portrayed "godlike benevolence . . . debased into all-devouring egotism." That was a powerful epitaph for the utopian spirit, no less influential on scholars for being largely unwarranted.

The problems with Brook Farm and Hopedale went deeper than egotism and beyond the need to find an economic base. Adin Ballou inadvertently put his finger on the difficulty when he tallied the virtues of a communitarian proposal he had made in 1840. "It exhibits a strong determination," he wrote, "to maintain unabridged individuality of personal rights and responsibilities, the integrity of the marriage and family relationship, and the great safeguards against communal tyranny and absorption. . . . It contemplates no unnatural, exclusive monastic retreat from society at large." The list is remarkable because it is generally accurate for Hopedale and Brook Farm and because it contrasts with the characteristics of the longest-lived, most successful pietistic communities. The latter subordinated individual conscience, autonomy, and property rights to the community. They altered family relationships. They drew sharp boundaries between the community and the outside world. Hopedale, Brook Farm, and two contemporary Massachusetts ventures, the Northampton Association (1842–46) and Bronson Alcott's Fruitlands (1843), lacked the authoritarian structure and unorthodox living arrangements of the older communities. Although they appeared odd enough to outside observers, they failed for being too moderate, too respectful of individual property and consciences. They were too conventional to attract a zealously committed membership, to isolate it from the world, and to hold it through hard times.

Being too conventional was not a problem with Oneida. It was, like Hopedale and Brook Farm, an offspring of New England theology.

Where Hopedale was shaped by Ballou's Universalism and non-resistance, and Brook Farm by Ripley's Unitarianism and Transcendentalism, Oneida was a product of evangelical Protestantism. Its founder was John Humphrey Noyes, a Vermonter by birth; a Dartmouth, Andover Theological Seminary, and Yale man by education; a lawyer and clergyman by training. He had what was probably the most original mind of any American communitarian and, above all, he was a believer in perfectionism.

Noyes was literal, logical, and extreme about it. While at Yale Divinity School he came to feel that once a person was saved, he or she became absolutely perfect, that is, incapable of sinning. (He achieved that state on February 20, 1834.) His theological notions cost him friendships, his license to preach, and his membership in the New Haven Free Church. By the end of 1834 he was a twenty-three-year-old perfectionist without a pulpit. For a time he wandered about, trying to meet Charles G. Finney, the great revivalist. Noyes then worked among the poor in New York City (where, according to rumor, he "lay dead *drunk* . . . by way of showing the perfection of his *flesh*"). During his travels he met William Lloyd Garrison, the abolitionist, whom he would strongly influence; and he acquired a growing reputation as a propagandist.

In 1837 he gave the first sign of the unorthodox sexual ideas that would take final form at Oneida. Abigail Merwin, an early convert whom Noyes loved, spurned both him and his doctrines, and married another man. Much grieved, Noyes wrote a follower that "when the will of God is done on earth as it is in heaven there will be no marriage." Noyes was not calling for Shaker-like celibacy. He meant that among those who had become perfect, all belonged to each other: there were no exclusive attachments. Merwin was his bride in spirit, even if she was another man's under law. "I call a certain woman my wife," he explained. "She is yours, she is Christ's, and in him she is the bride of all saints." The letter was published. It sounded too much like "free love" to sit well with the public and Noyes lost a substantial portion of his small band of followers in the subsequent furor. Despite the letter's scandalous implications, Noyes was not yet ready to abandon monogamous marriage. In June 1838 he wed Harriet Holton, a good and loyal woman who had been a

supporter and contributor since 1834. The couple settled in at Putney, Vermont, where Noyes's family lived. There Noyes's tiny con-
gregation of disciples (most of them relatives) printed his works and
developed the doctrines and practices that would distinguish Oneida.

Noyes became a communitarian only gradually. In 1841 the little
group at Putney began to organize more formally and to pool resources. Noyes, his brother George, and two of his brothers-in-law
created a financial partnership in 1844. Their assets were substantial, thanks to Harriet's generosity and to an estate left by Noyes's
father. After a year they reorganized into a corporation open to any
who invested money or labor. By Noyes's own account, he and his
followers had been reading communitarian publications, especially
the *Harbinger*. Although Noyes rejected Brook Farm's Fourierist
principles, the community impressed him and, with more sentimental-
ity than truth, he declared Oneida to be its direct successor. In any
event, by 1846, the year of the Brook Farm fire, the Putney perfectionists were evolving the legal and economic structure of a communal sociey.

They also were beginning the marital experiments that would
cause them to be driven from Putney. Despite the controversy sur-
rounding his letter in 1837, Noyes continued to insist—privately—
that what he called "communism in love" would eventually be part
of the practice of perfection. He nonetheless reproved a few who
were eager to start prematurely by sharing spouses. That changed in
the spring of 1846. Noyes and a follower, Mary Cragin, were powerfully drawn to each other. They quickly discovered that Harriet and
Mary's husband, George, were similarly attracted. Following a suitable period of discussion and contemplation, the four began the
system of "complex marriage," maintaining that it was not a sin for
any sanctified man and any sanctified woman to have intercourse.
Noyes's two sisters and their husbands joined the complex marriage
and by the end of 1846 the central members of the Putney group
declared themselves a community of persons as well as of property.
The word was soon out. Noyes's explanations and theological justifi-
cations did no good so far as the enraged townspeople of Putney were
concerned. By the fall of 1847 he fled to New York City to avoid
prosecution on charges of adultery. Shortly after, he and some of the

Putney group joined a communal settlement begun by fellow perfectionists in Madison County, New York. Together they formed the Oneida Association and Noyes would be its leader for over thirty years.

In addition to complex marriages, Noyes's sexual program at Oneida involved birth control and, eventually, planned reproduction. Within six years of their wedding, John and Harriet Noyes had five children, four of whom were stillborn. To avoid the uncertainty and the likely sorrow of another pregnancy, Noyes began to experiment with contraception. Of the few methods available in the early 1840s, he chose "male continence," or intercourse without ejaculation. From 1846 onward Noyes insisted that it be a part of complex marriage. He promoted male continence for various reasons, including health: it freed women from pregnancy and spared men the expenditure of seminal fluid, which Noyes, like many nineteenth-century Americans, believed to be debilitating. The perfectionists also had in mind a common-sense consideration. Had they not used birth control there would have been awkward problems determining the paternity of children. But Noyes added theological arguments to these practical ones. Male continence, he maintained, was part of God's design. It would "give new speed to the advance of civilization and refinement." With fear of pregnancy banished, sexual intercourse "became a joyful act of fellowship" among men and women, even among near relatives. In other words, with male continence intercourse became a religious ritual.

Religious or not, complex marriage and male continence were shocking doctrines in the nineteenth century and critics viewed them as nothing more than free love. Noyes, correctly and vainly, pointed out that any libertine who came to the community expecting casual sex was bound to be disappointed. Oneida accepted members only after close scrutiny to make sure their characters were properly sanctified. Sexual encounters were subject to a variety of rules and regulations. By the 1860s all requests for intercourse had to be made through a third party and were duly recorded in a ledger. The community leadership reproved individuals motivated by mere sensuality or couples having an "exclusive attachment" for each other. As for male continence, Noyes was fond of pointing out how demanding it was. He claimed that "licentious persons" treated it "with bitterness and scorn" because "the real self-denial which it requires cannot be adjusted to their schemes of pleasure-seeking." Its essence, he wrote (with much truth), "is self-control, and that is a virtue of universal importance."

As Noyes indicated, the effect of Oneida's sexual practices was not to unleash sexual impulses but to control them and give them cosmic significance. That was especially apparent in Oneida's ambitious experiment with planned reproduction, or "stirpiculture" (a word Noyes coined). The program began in 1869 and involved formation of a committee at Oneida to approve, even to suggest, "scientific combinations" of community members to become parents. Since Noyes believed moral characteristics were passed on to children, the men and women selected were supposed to be the most spiritually advanced in the community, although some attention was given to physical condition as well. During the next decade fifty-eight children were born at Oneida, thirteen conceived accidentally and forty-five as stirpiculture babies, nine of them fathered by Noyes, the most spiritually advanced member of all.

Noyes was not the only nineteenth-century figure to believe that extraordinary parents produced extraordinary offspring (although he was more literal-minded than most about getting "superior" people to reproduce). Noyes cited the biological works of Francis Galton and Charles Darwin to justify stirpiculture; yet despite his fancy references and his talk about "scientific propagation," the experiment was more an extension of his religious perfectionism than anything else. He felt that body and spirit were interconnected and that humankind could work toward perfection in both by following principles that were God-given and discoverable by rational analysis.

The community flourished in spite of the hostility its sexual practices aroused. As Noyes grew older he became interested in learning about the economics of communal life and, in retrospect, he attributed Oneida's endurance to what he came to see as two of the essential features of stable utopian societies: community ownership of property and an emphasis on manufacturing and commerce rather than agriculture. Oneida had a difficult period after its founding in 1848, but large contributions from its first members carried it through. It had greater capital reserves than most communal societies, a fortunate thing since the best estimate is that it invested over $40,000 before its enterprises turned a profit. Oneida's initial success came from the production of a superior animal trap, invented by a member; by 1875 that and other enterprises gave Oneida and a smaller satellite community at Wallingford, Connecticut, property amounting to $500,000. Prosperity showed in Oneida's buildings, which included a handsome Mansion House, a Turkish bath, and a theater to entertain its two hundred and fifty members. After the hardships of the first years, there was a generally pleasant style and pace of life at Oneida. Its demise as a community was not due to economic collapse.

In the 1870s Oneida's perfectionism became less theological and more secular. Younger members absorbed new ideas from the community's schools and through college education on the outside. Noyes himself showed an interest in social science and in secular "socialism." The result was an undercurrent of questioning of the old ways and a decline in religious fervor. Noyes's failing leadership was an even greater problem. He had exercised control firmly, but often indirectly, delegating responsibility to committees and depending on the community's "mutual criticism" sessions to reprove members who showed signs of falling by the wayside. Although Noyes clearly was the driving force of Oneida, he was often absent. In 1851 he went to London, despite a financial crisis, and he spent prolonged periods in Brooklyn or New York City watching over perfectionist publications. In 1875 he tried to impose his son Theodore, a Yale-trained physician, as head of the community. Theodore and Oneida balked. He finally succeeded in turning over much of his authority to Theodore and to a committee in 1877. That arrangement lasted until 1878, when Theodore, lacking sympathy with Oneida's religious principles and possibly ill, clashed with his father and left for New York City. Open rebellion against John Humphrey Noyes came the next year.

Appropriately enough, a sexual matter brought dissension into the open. It was the question of which male ought to act as "first husband" to virgin females in the community, a duty Noyes once had taken upon himself but which he had begun occasionally to pass along to others. Neither the factions nor the issue was clearly defined, yet the dispute was bitter enough to send Noyes into Canadian exile in 1879, fearful that his enemies would have him prosecuted for statutory rape. Like many other communal ventures, Oneida depended on the personal power of its central figure. It could not survive the erosion of Noyes's authority and his permanent departure from the community. With him gone, with the leadership divided, and with a group of local clergymen attacking the community, Oneida's governing council reluctantly decided that the system of complex marriage could no longer be administered and had to be abandoned. On January 1, 1881, Oneida ceased to be a community and became a joint-stock company. It would do well manufacturing silverware for generations of blushing brides.

Oneida, Brook Farm, and Hopedale represent a native American midpoint between two types of communitarianism originating in Europe: that of the German and Shaker pietists and the secular variety of Robert Owen and Charles Fourier, which would enter the United States between the 1820s and the 1840s. Like the pietistic communities, Hopedale, Brook Farm, and Oneida were religiously inspired; like Owenite and Fourierist ventures, they were more engaged in transforming society than in fleeing from it. But only Oneida had the greatest strengths of both communitarian traditions. It had the discipline of the pietists and their knack of giving theological significance to all aspects of communal life. It also had an experimental zeal and an interest in "science" and economics. Those, as we shall see, were characteristics of the Owenites and Fourierists.

3. Earth as Heaven

The common purpose of secular communitarian societies was to restructure social and economic relationships: their focus was on this world, not on the next. A few were quasi-religious but many were freethinking or ignored religion and let members believe whatever they wished. If they were not much given to theology, each was, nonetheless, organized around a philosophy, generally one taken from British or French utopianism. Some were based on detailed and rigidly structured bodies of ideas, like Charles Fourier's. In other ventures the central beliefs were loosely formulated or loosely enforced, as in Josiah Warren's communities, the most notable of which was Modern Times, located on Long Island (1851–66). Warren wished to establish "equitable commerce"—a system to give people the full value of their labor—but he otherwise sought absolute personal freedom, which meant, among other things, freedom to quarrel. The diversity of secular communitarianism notwithstanding, it was dominated in turn by two men, Robert Owen and Charles Fourier. Between them they were responsible for the greatest number of utopian societies begun in America after 1825.

Owen's was one of the success stories of the Industrial Revolution. He was born in Wales in 1771 and left home at the age of ten to become a draper's apprentice. Before he was thirty he was manager of the cotton mills at New Lanark, Scotland; under his charge they would grow to be the greatest in Britain. New Lanark was the primary source of the fortune Owen spent promoting his ideas, and was also the place upon which many of his theories developed. Sensitive to the prevalence of vice, ignorance, and misery among the workers, he found himself with a rare chance to shape their lives—in addition to managing the mills, he was a partner in the firm that owned the town. Seizing the opportunity his position gave him, Owen made numerous innovations at New Lanark and genuinely improved the financial security, living conditions, and educational opportunities of the townspeople. The experience in Scotland earned Owen a considerable reputation, left him with a sense of his own ability to alter social relationships, and confirmed him in his belief that the problems of his day required collective solutions. It did not, however, make him a communitarian. New Lanark was pleasant, in terms of what mill towns usually were, yet it was far from being a utopian society. It was a highly successful, profit-making venture.

After 1812 Owen turned his attention to broader industrial questions than those at issue in New Lanark. He presented proposals on national working conditions, unemployment, and poor relief to Parliament, which, by its failure to take them seriously, disillusioned him about the possibility of using governmental action to reform society. In the spring and summer of 1817 Owen took his case to the public in speeches, letters to London newspapers, and in documents printed at his own expense. These put forth "the peculiar advantages to be derived from the Arrangement of the Unemployed Working Classes into 'Agricultural and Manufacturing Villages of Unity and Mutual Cooperation.'" The villages were to contain no fewer than 500 and no more than 1,500 people (he later raised the upper limit to over 2,000). They were to consist of healthy living quarters arranged in a parallelogram, with good schools for children and useful, mixed employment for adults. Even though he first represented his plan as an alternative to poor relief, Owen quickly came to see it as the prototype of a new social organization in which humans would cooperate with one another, lead decent and prosperous lives, and enjoy the benefits of the machine age without its vices. This was the beginning of his communitarianism and it was of a forward-looking sort, with only traces of the yearning for an agrarian past found in some other varieties of utopian thought.

Owen's beliefs after 1812 are neither extraordinarily complex nor easily summarized. He wrote copiously in the forty-five years between his *A New View of Society* (1813) and his death in 1858. More a publicist than a philosopher, he neglected to analyze crucial concepts rigorously; he sometimes skewed his logic, shifted his emphasis, and changed his mind. Yet Owen's words and deeds excited American communitarians. What he truly meant to say was less significant to them than his ability to fire their imaginations with visions of a perfect, practical future.

Owen's most distinctive proposition was the hardest for American reformers to accept wholeheartedly. In his *A New View of Society* he declared that "the character of man, is, without single exception, always formed for him" by his surroundings. This was a blunt statement of environmentalism, the doctrine that human beings are creatures of circumstances. Environmentalism was not entirely new to Americans—some of them had been using it for decades to explain racial differences—but it was troublesome because it seemed to absolve individuals of responsibility for their sins. It rooted evil in a person's surroundings, not in his or her soul. Owen did not explore the logical implications of environmentalism and he occasionally hedged a bit, adding such factors as "constitution or organization at birth" as determinants of character. Yet environmentalism was central to his view of reform. It was the intellectual justification for his social engineering, particularly for its emphasis on creating a proper moral climate through education and an improved standard of living. Although most American reformers persisted in believing that change had to begin with the human heart, not with external circumstances, Owen forced them to consider social conditions more than they might otherwise have done. He presented a challenging alternative to the Protestant view that humans were to blame for whatever evil befell them.

Owen's greatest contribution to American utopianism, in fact, was the way he either departed from or modified Christian categories of thought. Where German and Shaker pietists, and even utopians of the 1840s like Ballou, Ripley, and Noyes, imagined a sort of Christian commonwealth, Owen rejected formal religion. He sought a new moral world based on "fundamental laws of nature" and the "science of man." This secular ideology was closer to Christian traditions than either Owen or his clergyman enemies realized, but it was an important addition to communitarianism. After Owen, American utopian societies could be based on "reason" rather than on the Bible or revelation.

Owenism also provided antebellum communitarians with a new way to treat equality and property. Contemporaries often saw Owen as a radical egalitarian. Indeed, he assured members of New Harmony that "there will be no personal inequality, or gradation of rank or station; all will be equal in their condition." He wished for laborers to receive the value of their work; he wanted the present "competitive system" to be replaced by cooperation. He was even bold enough to examine inequalities between men and women and to attack the family as an enemy of the communal spirit (accepting, in the process, such controversial practices as birth control and divorce). Owen, it should be said, was not always consistent: he preserved social distinctions in some of his plans; in none of his ventures did he get around to abolishing private property or effecting revolutionary changes in family patterns. Yet in spite of ambiguities and failures of nerve, Owenism was the beginning of a secular critique of capitalistic individualism. It promised American communitarians that by following a rational plan they could build a cooperative social order immediately, without revolution, without going through the conventional political process, and without God.

Some arrangements in that new order would have been novel to Americans, but other parts of it were consistent with commonly held values. It was egalitarian and devoted to ever-increasing prosperity. Its advocacy of education and cooperation likewise expressed American clichés. Even the size of Owen's proposed villages played to American prejudices. With a population of one to three thousand, they were not large cities (those havens of vice), but they were big enough to support both agriculture and industry. They combined the moral advantages of rural small towns with the material advantages of a mixed economy. And yet, despite these appealing aspects, Owenism had irritating features. It grated on the American devotion to private property and conflicted, somewhat unnecessarily, with

Protestantism—which partially explains why its life in the United States was brief and its communities ephemeral.

Word of Owen and his ideas reached America quickly. Owenism influenced a New York Society for Promoting Communities, founded in 1819, and a small group of Philadelphia scientists and intellectuals. But the real enthusiasm came with Owen's visit in 1824. For some time he had considered building his own community in Scotland or elsewhere in Britain—he firmly believed that once a model was constructed the rest of the world would rush to imitate it. His chance to find out came when the Harmony Society decided in 1824 to sell its Indiana property and move back to Pennsylvania. Although the price amounted to over half his fortune, Owen could purchase an already constructed community in a good location for a fraction of the cost of anything similar in Britain. Less than two months after being contacted by an agent of the Harmony Society, Owen set sail for the New World.

Landing in New York in November 1824, he circulated for nearly a month among a great variety of Americans—socialites, literary figures, businessmen, scientists, intellectuals, and a group of Shakers. It was not until mid-December that he arrived in Harmony to look it over and conclude arrangements for purchase. Two and a half weeks later he was owner of 20,000 acres of Indiana countryside and nearly two hundred assorted buildings, which he rechristened New Harmony. Journeying back to the Eastern states for the winter and early spring of 1825, Owen continued to stir excitement. He addressed Congress twice, the second speech being attended by outgoing President James Monroe and President-elect John Quincy Adams. Things were at such a fever pitch that Owen came to regard America as his most promising field (he later decided differently). He predicted that the Northern states would be converted to his theories by 1827.

He may have been too successful in kindling interest in New Harmony. When it opened for settlement under his auspices in May, it had over eight hundred members. There was housing for seven hundred.

Crowding was only one of the problems to plague New Harmony in its short, troubled history. From the outset the community suffered confusion in purpose and leadership. Owen was not clear about what property arrangements he expected to make with settlers —his son William claimed he first thought about the matter only a few days before purchasing Harmony. Owen likewise declined to state what form the community would take once it passed through a transitional stage as a "Preliminary Society." To compound his errors, Owen spent much of 1825 away from New Harmony, traveling on the Atlantic seaboard and, for a few months, in Britain.

Owen's faulty leadership was matched by his lack of discrimination in admitting members. Confident that his system would work with anyone, he did not recruit dedicated Owenites. He took in people who came to him voluntarily, whatever their reasons or beliefs. The best of them were men and women like William Maclure, a prominent geologist and teacher, and his associate, Marie D. Fretageot, an educational reformer. They joined the community in 1826, along with some equally impressive Philadelphia scientists, and they were the heart of its fine educational apparatus. Such people gave New Harmony a substantial intellectual and artistic life. The worst of Owen's other settlers were much less admirable. They were deficient in discipline, willingness to compromise, and the skills of communal life. They were the majority.

In a four-month period in early 1826 New Harmony went through three reorganizations. Owen was pressed to govern more firmly, then to govern more democratically. He was pushed and pulled by his ideas, interests, and constituents. Some members demanded that he be true to his principles, relinquish ownership, and institute a genuine community of property. Others had different proposals. In May 1826 the community adopted Maclure's suggestions and divided New Harmony into three semi-independent communities, defined by their functions—education, agriculture, and manufacturing—and loosely held together by a Board of Union. The chief benefit of the plan was to give New Harmony a month of relative stability and Maclure and his colleagues a freer hand to try out their educational theories. The partition of New Harmony went forward and did not solve any real problems. It may even have had a negative effect by defining the warring factions more precisely and giving them new ways to cripple each other (the agricultural and manufacturing communities, for instance, withheld aid from the school community). In the meantime, New Harmony's economic situation deteriorated, thanks in some measure to the idlers and incompetents it attracted.

The events of 1826 and 1827 did no credit to Owenism or to Owen. The community was splintering out of existence. For his part, Owen persisted in generating confusion and distrust. He also managed to be taken in by a crooked land speculator and to undermine Maclure's Education Society, one of the community's finer achievements. Maclure, a heavy investor in New Harmony, helped bring the sad episode to a close. He made a large payment on behalf of Owen, who was financially embarrassed by that time, called in the loan, took Owen to court, and forced the community into dissolution.

The failure of New Harmony was not the end of Owenite dreams, although it was a severe blow. Other American communities were to be built under Owen's influence: they were far smaller than New Harmony but equally torn by conflict and equally doomed. A total of over twenty Owenite ventures were undertaken, most in the United States, with others in Canada, Wales, Ireland, Scotland, and England. Owenism also contributed personnel and ideas to other kinds of utopian societies. Frederick Evans, the Shaker leader, had been a member of an Owenite settlement at Kendal, Ohio, and Josiah Warren, the anarchistic communitarian, had lived at New Harmony as a young man. But by the late 1820s Owenism itself had a fading hold on the utopian imagination and by 1840 there was a new star on the horizon.

Where the American career of Owenism was bound up with the life of Owen, Fourierism in America had little to do with Fourier. He died in 1837, before his work reached its greatest influence in the United States. He was born in 1772, a year after Owen. Unlike Owen, he was a poor and unhappy businessman, forced by his father to pursue the family trade of cloth merchant. His theories took shape amid the social and political turmoil of the French Revolution, not as a result of factory management as Owen's did. Like Owen, he formulated his program in the provinces, away from his nation's metropolis; but, in contrast to Owen, he never moved in the highest social and intellectual circles (he was so obscure that it took one

loyal disciple two years to locate him). There was an attempt to
form a Fourierist community in France in 1833, but in his native
land Fourier was merely one of a number of interesting social
theorists—and something of a crank at that. Only in America, and
after his death, did Fourier triumph over French competitors like
Henri Saint-Simon.

That was largely the doing of a wealthy young upstate New
Yorker named Albert Brisbane. His conversion came in 1832, when
he was in his early twenties. A friend gave him a book by Fourier
which, Brisbane said, carried him "away into a world of new conceptions." Brisbane repeated those conceptions energetically for
decades as author of *The Social Destiny of Man* (1840), as pro-
moter of Fourierist communities, as a writer for various journals,
and, most effectively, as a contributor to Horace Greeley's widely
read newspaper, the *New York Tribune*. Fortunately, Brisbane did
not advocate all his master's ideas (Fourier was capable of great
absurdity), but he did translate into American terms the French
utopian's awkward vocabulary and intricate system of social relationships.

At the heart of an ideal Fourierist "phalanx" was the "phalanstery," a huge structure to house the community's enterprises and
the 1,500 to 1,800 people ("as varied as possible") Fourier saw as
optimum. With great care, Fourier spelled out the kinds and quantity
of rooms, where each should be located, and what should be reserved for whom. (Children got the mezzanine in order to keep them
"separate from the adolescents, and . . . from all those who are
capable of making love.") Fourier even calculated the minimum
revenue a model phalanx would receive from charging admission to
"curiosity-seekers." The jargon, the fascination with numbers, and
the petty detail were characteristic of Fourier and made him easily
ridiculed.

In addition to providing a design for the phalanstery, Fourier set
up an elaborate method of defining and compensating labor, with
highest wages going for the least pleasant tasks. His systematization
sometimes ran amok and led to such marvelous documents as a
report from a council of New York Fourierist societies in 1844. It
broke Fourier's category of "Industry" into three "classes": Neces-

sity (which, sensibly enough, included baking, washing, and ironing), Usefulness (which, slightly less sensibly, included raising silkworms and teaching), and Attractiveness (which, for some reason, included both landscape painting and poultry keeping).

Fourier's instructions were obsessive and his speculations were daring, but the utopias his disciples built were a bit mundane. They were primarily agricultural, with some light industry, and they did not have a true community of property. Investors put capital into the phalanx and drew interest from its enterprises. That is not to say it was exactly the same as a conventional business corporation. Among their unorthodox beliefs, Fourierists considered labor a form of capital and thought smaller investments of money should receive proportionally greater dividends than larger ones. Phalanxes, moreover, were communal living arrangements as well as economic ventures. Still, they were staid in comparison with Oneida and they often looked like nothing so much as peculiar joint-stock companies.

The economic theories and the spectacular nonsense of Fourierism sometimes obscured its psychological and anthropological assumptions, which were the most striking things it had to offer American communitarian thought. Fourier's great enemy was "civilization." He believed it to be false to human nature and in its place he envisioned a social organization based on "association" and "harmony," key words in the Fourierist vocabulary. Although Fourier resembled Owen in seeking to base his utopianism on a "science" of man, the two were at loggerheads as to what science revealed. Owen pictured human beings as shaped by circumstances while Fourier proposed to make circumstances fit an unchanging human nature. Mankind, Fourier calculated, consisted of twelve passions. Each person had all of them, in varying intensity. It was the particular mix of passions that made up one's personality. Here Fourierists introduced the notion of "attraction," or "attractive industry" in the case of work. Different personality types, they felt, were inherently "attracted" to different sorts of labor. Under the "civilized" way of doing things, people were either misemployed or unemployed and their passions were therefore thwarted. In the phalanx, men and women would gravitate to occupations suited for them. Work would be the pleasure it was meant to be. Like virtually all American communitarians (but more explicitly than most), Fourierists believed the present world had falsely separated humankind's physical and moral selves and that people had to be reconciled with their own true being. (The prevalence of that notion across a wide range of communitarian ideology and in other nineteenth-century systems of thought may say something about the discomfort Americans felt either with their bodies or with antebellum moral and social arrangements.) No brief summary can do justice to the density and obscurity of Fourierism but its promise was clear and ironic. It offered a rigid, almost regimented plan designed to free people to be what nature meant them to be.

Brisbane and his colleagues were tireless propagandists, and effective ones, too, particularly after the literati of Brook Farm joined the cause. American Fourierists wrote, lectured, and held conventions. More impressive, they actually constructed communities, at least twenty-eight of them between 1841 and 1858, with settlements as far afield as Michigan, Wisconsin, Iowa, and (possibly) Texas. These phalanxes, however, were much smaller than Fourier's ideal: the Alphadelphia Phalanx in Michigan claimed "upwards" of thirteen hundred members in 1844, but that estimate is exaggerated and was given before the community even began construction of its central building. The longest-lived phalanx, the North American in Red Bank, New Jersey, had a little over a hundred residents in its best years.

The phalanxes would have disappointed Fourier by their practices as much as by their size. Brisbane, Greeley, and others took liberties with his theories and, just as significant, most phalanx members seem not to have understood Fourier even in simplified, Americanized form. Their mentor's calculations were difficult to comprehend and still more difficult to practice when real people had to confront real crops and animals. "Association" and "harmony," moreover, were elusive ideals for Americans. Phalanx members refused to be passionately attracted to all the things they needed to do to run a community; and the old civilization's corruptions, including greed and religious disputes, refused to vanish.

Yet there were bright spots for the Fourierists. The conversion of Brook Farm was one, but the North American Phalanx was probably the brightest. Begun in 1843, it had the leading Fourierists, Brisbane and Greeley, directly involved in its affairs. It also was close enough to New York City to be a showcase of Fourierism. Blessed with capable managers, the North American was reasonably sound financially. Its nearly seven hundred acres of land produced a variety of crops, many sold outside the community (one source credits the phalanx with being "the first to grow okra or gumbo for the New York market"). In the early 1850s it was looking toward increasing and diversifying its manufactures.

Life at the North American seems to have been reasonably pleasant. The community had its Fourier-inspired buildings: a common dining room and great houses to accommodate families, individuals, and guests. It had its own school, more modest than New Harmony's, but well taught. There was the usual carping about wages, and more serious bickering over how democratically the association should be governed. But members worshipped as they pleased without the religious strife that agitated some Fourierist ventures. Visitors remarked on the apparent joy of residents as they engaged in dancing and other amusements. If it lacked the idyllic reputation of Brook Farm, the North American Phalanx was nonetheless a more genial enterprise than any Shaker community and a more stable one than New Harmony.

It was sold in 1856. The precipitant was a fire, as with Brook Farm. Yet the mill that burned was not vital to the community's livelihood, and Greeley offered to lend money to construct a replacement. Since the phalanx had been paying dividends to stockholders and was economically secure, the vote to abolish it seems to have caught nearly everyone by surprise. The probable explanation is that petty bickering and loss of enthusiasm took their toll: members seem to have gotten tired of the North American and the fire was their excuse to quit.

By the mid-1850s Fourierism was mostly over anyway. It may have been working in New Jersey, but it had failed in too many other places. Fourierists (and Owenites, for that matter) did not have a powerfully unifying creed or a charismatic leader to hold them together through rough periods. In that, they were weaker than the German and Shaker pietistic communities and Oneida.

There is another point of comparison, likewise relating to the staying power of the pietists and Oneida, on the one hand, and the lack of endurance among Owenites and Fourierists, on the other. It has to do with how drastically communal societies altered social relationships. Fourier's assault on "civilization" was sweeping; and Owen, although more restrained, was equally committed to abolishing old modes of thought and ancient ways of doing things. Their communities, however, were not nearly as radical as the pietistic societies, many of which overthrew private property and conventional marriage and one of which, the Shakers, gave much authority to women. It seems the more a community deviated from the American norm, and the more authoritarian it was, the better its chance of survival.

Still, the radicalism of the pietists was a dead end. Their equality was that of saints in Christ; they shared property and did away with families because they felt things of the world were meaningless. Owenism and Fourierism asserted the right of people, here and now, to live happily, cooperatively, and productively. Secular communitarianism was not thoroughly anti-capitalistic or truly communistic, and it was based more on moral impulses than on economic analysis. But, above all, it demanded a just measure of the good things of the earth for every human being. That cast of mind, in its infinite variations, was to outlast particular Owenite and Fourierist utopias and to be more dynamic in the industrial age than pietism ever could be.

Valid as the distinction between religious and secular utopian societies is, the behavior of communitarians ought to be a warning against drawing it too rigidly. There are numerous examples of people who moved back and forth between religious and secular ventures with no trouble—a surprised visitor to the North American Phalanx in 1851 immediately met an ex-Shaker and an ex-resident of Hopedale. One whole community, Brook Farm, went easily from "Christ's Idea of Society" to Fourier's in less than three years.

Although few recognized what it was, a real bond did exist between almost all communities. It was millennialism and perfectionism. Those doctrines were obvious in religious utopias, but they were central to Owenism and Fourierism as well. Robert Owen, irreligious though he was, informed his feuding supporters at New Harmony that his system might "be termed the beginning of the millennium." Nearly twenty years later he was still hoping: in 1855 he issued his *Tracts on the Coming Millennium*. Elizabeth Peabody, promoting Brook Farm, interpreted Fourier as believing "the earth would be cultivated and restored to the state of Paradise." Religious and secular communitarians alike had a faith that humankind could arrive at a state of perfection, and that it could only be achieved collectively and by setting an example for the world to follow, not by politics or revolution.

Converts came to the task with hope and zeal, yet in the secular societies, at least, they wandered off in a matter of months, or a few years at most. Some of that was due to blundering, mismanagement, and personality conflicts, but it also reflected the difficulty of getting Americans to suppress their desires for autonomy, even when they voluntarily became part of a collectivity. Utopianism itself was a reaction against what many perceived as selfish individualism running loose in the land, particularly in political and economic affairs. Communal life was supposed to—and obviously did not—replace the go-getting, self-aggrandizing spirit of the age and create harmonious human relationships.

Paradoxical as it may sound, those were goals of even anarchistic utopians (who were no more successful at reaching them than Owenites or Fourierists were). Josiah Warren, for instance, was so complete an individualist that he once declared "everybody has a perfect right to do everything." He inspired four communities (including an ill-fated settlement named Utopia) in order to free humans to do what they felt like doing. The most notorious venture to follow his theories was Modern Times, in Suffolk County, Long Island, which had nearly a hundred members at its height in the early 1850s and which horrified decent folk by its contempt for marriage and economic orthodoxy. Tolerant as Warren was of deviance, he was also committed to social harmony. He insisted that people would live in peace only if they obeyed conscience rather than external authority. His "sovereignty of the individual," like its apparent opposite, the rigid moral and institutional structures of most communitarians, ended up as an effort to make the lives of men and women consistent with a larger purpose.

Although utopian societies deprived men and women of the family life and autonomy Americans valued, they offered much in return. For disillusioned labor reformers in the 1840s and for others, they were a refuge from the failures of politics and radical agitation. Some people found in them an escape from self-doubt, from anxieties about sex and marriage, or simply from the burdens of having to make choices. Communities promised a stable, morally perfect environment in which a person could find meaning and serve the cause of human uplift. Things did not always work that way, but the prospect was an appealing one in a time of great uncertainty and change.

Communitarians, like antebellum reformers generally, were at too early a stage in the Industrial Revolution to perceive clearly that it was the force transforming the world around them. A number of communal ventures did reject urban and capitalistic society (in that, they resembled the communes of the 1960s). Others nonetheless bore a less hostile relationship to it. Many engaged in business enterprises and some were successful. Very few utopians chose to get away from it all by settling on the frontier, and even the most agricultural-minded ones usually sold crops rather than practice subsistence farming. In that respect their societies, too, were part of the larger market economy, instead of rural paradises, unpolluted by commerce. Many communitarians, moreover, admired the science, technology, and rising standard of living produced by industrialization, despite being appalled at the misery "progress" brought with it. They did not so much oppose economic development as feel humankind had to assert rational control over it, whether through religious principles like Noyes's or the "social science" of Owen or Fourier. Such communitarians were too much products of their times to give up the nineteenth-century middle-class god, Progress, even though other utopians were practicing Christian asceticism or trying to learn how to farm.

It would be simpler if antebellum communitarianism had been all one thing or another. It was not, but in it we do see American reform and radicalism at an exciting and unique moment: moving from religious to secular modes of social thought, trying to harness American individualism in the name of responsibility to mankind, and confronting for the first time (although half consciously and indirectly) the effects of the modern industrial world.

4. Antislavery

In membership, communitarianism and the antislavery movement had little in common. A few abolitionists became involved in Hopedale and similar ventures, yet these were exceptions. As abolitionists saw their duty, it was not to retreat from society, even though they might withdraw from such corrupt institutions as proslavery churches and political parties. They were determined, in the words of a New Hampshire editor, "to stay amid the great community [of the world], destitute of *communion*, as it is, and go for *community-zing* the whole" by breaking down slavery and other barriers separating humans from each other and from their own potential. That was an impulse almost as utopian and far-reaching as any to be found among genuine communitarians—a rarefied vision of brotherhood and a challenge to a system of racial injustice deeply embedded in American life.

On January 1, 1831, William Lloyd Garrison, a young native of Newburyport, Massachusetts, published the first issue of the *Liberator*. During its thirty-five-year run, the Boston newspaper would be abrasive, vituperative, and consistent in its loathing of slavery. It would never have a large circulation nor would Garrison ever represent the whole of abolitionism—the movement was diverse and decentralized. Still, more than any other event, the founding of the *Liberator* marked the beginning of a variety of antislavery that was new in tone, social composition, and doctrine.

Before 1831 opposition to slavery had taken several forms. From the outset blacks made their feelings clear by fleeing bondage, by day-to-day resistance, and by staging occasional insurrections. In the eighteenth century—and especially by the time of the Revolution—increasing numbers of whites were preaching abolition, inspired by religion, Enlightenment humanitarianism, and their own egalitarian rhetoric. Most Northern states ended slavery before 1800. Abolition sentiment, however, was on the wane by then and the institution, if anything, was becoming more strongly entrenched in the lower South, as the newly invented cotton gin and population growth pushed cotton production farther west.

Organized antislavery, although subdued, persisted in the early nineteenth century and differed strikingly from the caustic brand Garrison and his colleagues would promote after 1830. It was concentrated in the upper South, was conciliatory to the master, and had minimal sympathy for blacks. Above all, there was no particular urgency to it. Prior to 1831 most critics of slavery assumed that manumission would be gradual and ought not to cause social or economic dislocation. No organization better typified such an approach than the American Colonization Society, which was founded in 1816. Its mission was to send ex-bondsmen out of the country, preferably to its African outpost, Liberia. The society's supporters included slaveholders, prominent politicians, and distinguished men of the sort who would later shun abolitionism. Their motives were varied and conflicted. Some genuinely hated slavery but believed the races could never coexist without it. Their solution was to get rid of black people. Other colonizationists were proslavery and were merely determined to dispose of the small free black population of the South and to eliminate bondsmen who might become a burden on their owners or society. Without much consistency, idealism, or practicality to recommend it, the Colonization Society nevertheless profited from this ability to satisfy contradictory viewpoints. It sent few black people to Africa but it attracted generally favorable attention, discharged white anxieties about slavery and race, and otherwise did well in the 1820s.

Most post-1830 abolitionists regarded colonization as their great enemy. Their hostility was comprised of a combination of disillusion

—many of them had once believed in it—and tactical necessity. From personal experience they knew how powerful its appeal was and how difficult it would be to get whites to accept a truer, more demanding antislavery position. Yet even allowing for some understandable exaggeration, later abolitionists were right to contrast their crusade with colonization and everything else that had come before. The platform Garrison proclaimed on New Year's Day 1831 *was* different. It would find no favor in the South. It made few concessions to the sensibilities of slaveholders (they were "oppressors," "man-stealers," "despots," and "tyrants"). Although tainted with streaks of racism, post-1830 abolitionists like Garrison dismissed any thoughts of exiling blacks, accepted the idea of civil equality for them, and greeted the slave as "A Man and a Brother" or "A Woman and a Sister," phrases borrowed from British abolitionism. Most important, antislavery after 1831 repudiated what Garrison called the "pernicious doctrine of *gradual* abolition." "Immediate emancipation" became the new battle cry.

The phrase was ambiguous. Abolitionists—even Garrison— seldom insisted that it meant slavery should cease right away. More often, they intended it as a demand for people to decide instantly to renounce slaveholding. Abolitionists admitted that, for the sake of master and slave alike, emancipation might take time to complete. Immediatism, however, tolerated no delay in beginning the process, as earlier, gradualistic approaches had. It was a call to break off an evil practice without hesitation or equivocation, just as sinners, when saved, utterly repudiated sin. The revivalism of the 1820s encouraged abolitionists and most other antebellum crusaders to see reform as something akin to an act of repentance. That approach to problems slighted social, political, and economic factors, and it could be narrow and self-righteous; but it had a passion and moral firmness badly needed when men and women agitated unpopular issues in a society where the instinct to compromise was second nature. Instead of describing a well-worked-out plan, "immediate emancipation" served to jolt people out of their complacency and to infuse abolitionism with a fervor it seldom had before 1831.

Immediatism quickly made converts in New England, New York City and upstate New York, Pennsylvania, and Ohio. The first organization based upon the doctrine was the New-England Anti-Slavery Society (1832). Nearly two years later, in December 1833, delegates from several states gathered in Philadelphia and created the American Anti-Slavery Society. For the next half decade it would play a crucial role in spreading abolitionism throughout the North.

Garrison had been instrumental in founding the American Anti-Slavery Society, but control of it passed to able and dedicated men at its New York headquarters. Chief among them was Lewis Tappan, blessed with ample financial resources and a fine managerial experience gained as a leader of the "benevolent empire" of Protestant charities. He and several energetic co-workers marshaled support for the cause and guided a remarkable outpouring of antislavery activity up to 1837 (when internal disputes and hard times slowed the crusade down temporarily). Affluent members like Tappan himself subsidized the printing and distribution of a wide range of American Anti-Slavery Society publications (at least three quarters of a million pieces of propaganda by 1838). In 1835 the organization flooded the mails with this literature, in an attempt to reach, and presumably persuade, clergy, editors, and other influential people in every state, particularly in the South. Two years later the society began to encourage and coordinate the circulation of antislavery petitions directed at Congress. Abolitionists—especially female ones—were so diligent in collecting signatures that they gathered over 400,000 by 1838.

Among the national organization's most significant enterprises during Tappan's stewardship was the recruitment of agents. These were zealous young men, charged with carrying abolitionism across the American countryside. Like Theodore Dwight Weld, their greatest orator, many were would-be, or former, ministers; several had been brought into the abolitionist fold during highly emotional debates over slavery at Lane Theological Seminary in Ohio in 1834. Whatever their background, the agents sparked controversy and inspired the rapid formation of town, county, and state antislavery groups. By 1838 the American Anti-Slavery Society claimed a membership of a quarter of a million and over 1,300 auxiliaries. Once begun, these local organizations worked in cooperation with the parent society, published newspapers of their own, and waged campaigns of special importance to their areas (including challenges to segregation and racist legislation in the North). Before the 1830s were over, immediatism had passed into the hinterland and the agency system had served its purpose.

Neither its success, nor the bureaucratic expertise of Tappan, nor the blistering rhetoric of Garrison can entirely explain what drew men and women to antislavery. It is easier to understand the motives of the many black people who participated in the movement, sometimes in alliance with whites, sometimes independently. Those from free families often lived in fairly comfortable circumstances and risked retaliation from hostile whites for their public stand; but slavery and prejudice were intolerable insults to their pride in themselves and their race. Other blacks had even more immediate reasons for becoming abolitionists. They were among the thousands of escaped slaves who carved out new, precarious lives for themselves in the North. The most famous of them were Frederick Douglass and two remarkable women, Sojourner Truth and Harriet Tubman (the latter courageously assisted hundreds of runaways fleeing the South). Their firsthand knowledge, and that of their fellow fugitives, made them bitter opponents of slavery and effective propagandists.

More puzzling is the reason why thousands of whites dedicated themselves to immediate emancipation and to achieving justice for black people. As best we can tell, most came from highly moralistic families, influenced by evangelical Protestantism, Quakerism, or Unitarianism. In their own accounts, they made much of the discrepancies between the way the United States was and the religious and political ideals they held. In itself, that described rather than accounted for their objections to slavery. Thousands of equally moralistic Americans, from the same areas and same sorts of families and maintaining the same values, felt no urge to attack the institution. It is difficult to say, with great confidence, what caused such people to ignore slavery while others, very much like them, condemned it.

For those who did become abolitionists, exposure to antislavery agitation often came at a crucial moment in their lives and helped them find direction, meaning, and companionship. To be an abolitionist was to declare allegiance to the principles of brotherhood and equality of opportunity, to suffer for those ideals, and to band together with like-minded individuals. It was to find a moral community in a society that appeared increasingly immoral.

Antislavery also attracted support because it spoke to a complex set of hopes and fears about the future. These were social in origin and they were expressed forcefully in a kind of moral drama present in much abolitionist propaganda. The chief protagonists in it were the master and the slave. The former was lustful and tyrannical; dominion over others, not greed, was what abolitionists usually regarded as his primary motive. The slave, on the other hand, was the epitome of powerlessness: his or her degradation came not primarily from cruelty, but from the loss of the right to exercise choice. Real freedom, abolitionists maintained, meant the absence, as much as possible, of external restraints on one's behavior. Only then could people be morally responsible for their actions and justly rewarded for their labor.

Most of those assumptions were familiar to Americans and permeated other reforms of the day. There was nothing novel about the abolitionist notion that restraint was the mark of a virtuous person, nor were a fear of power and a desire for individual autonomy unique to antislavery. Those attitudes had been current at least since the eighteenth century. Conditions in the 1820s and 1830s, however, gave them special urgency and made it easier for abolitionists to see them reflected in slavery and other evils. By the antebellum period, Americans had become mobile, energetic, and heterogeneous; they capitalized on the opportunities put before them and paid scant attention to anything except personal advantage. Religious and political leaders, according to abolitionists, did little to make the situation better; they were either ineffective or corrupt, or both. Reformers thought it necessary to find some means to make certain that virtue was not trampled in the rush to get ahead. One half of the abolitionist answer was not to trust anyone with too much power, lest he turn it to his advantage at the expense of everyone else. The other half was for people to be sufficiently self-disciplined to do what was right and resist what was wrong without help from ministers or politicians.

Abolitionists aimed that message at all Americans. In their bleak images of the slaveholder, the slave, and the South, they constructed a model of what happened when *any* people did not conquer their worst cravings. The slave states, according to antislavery rhetoric, were characterized by laziness, contempt for honest work, insolvency, violence, licentiousness, irreligion, and disrespect for the family. Tyranny and disorder prevailed. Moral desolation turned the South into a cursed land, upon which God showered few material blessings. It lacked such signs of progress as railroads, factories, public schools, and other benefits of Yankee culture. Abolitionists, however, refused to let Northerners take too much comfort in the contrast between their "civilization" and the "barbarism" of the South. The cardinal sin of Southerners—loss of moral control—appeared in the North in the guise of social turmoil and rampant selfishness; surely the free states would be punished for their transgressions just as severely as the slave ones were, unless repentance came in time. In an unconscious way, abolitionists were using the South as a mirror for their concerns about their own region and about people like themselves.

Although the values behind that view were old, abolitionists were applying them in a manner that would have been unthinkable in the eighteenth century, before economic growth sharpened differences between the sections. Only after slavery vanished in the North, and after factories and cities blossomed there, was it possible to believe that the free states represented a higher level of development than the South. Antislavery men and women, naturally, did not entirely endorse the emerging urban and industrial order of their region—its excesses were what they had in mind when arguing that Northerners were in danger of losing self-control and becoming like Southerners. Yet abolitionists accepted many of the assumptions of Northern capitalism, particularly when they insisted that liberty meant the ability to buy and sell property and labor (although not humans) without hindrance. They used that definition to indict slavery and, to their credit, they worried about the consequences of economic individualism even while they promoted it. They always insisted that entrepreneurship had to conform to Christian morality and they declared that the free market had to be opened to blacks on an equal footing with whites. Far from being uncritical apologists for their section, they demanded that the North live up to its best standards and fulfill its greatest promises.

Race prejudice prevented the majority of Northern whites from acknowledging how thoroughly antislavery expressed many of their own cherished economic and religious beliefs. But there must have been some recognition of the fact: much of the strength of abolitionism was in cities, towns, and rural areas swept by commerce and evangelical Protestantism.

The spread of immediatism in the mid-1830s came in the face of suppression. Defenders of slavery saw abolitionism as a dangerous assault on the status quo and believed it had to be stopped by all possible means. Their response, in retrospect, seems out of proportion to the actual threat—at the time supporters of antislavery were a tiny minority in the North. There were, nonetheless, reasons to be outraged and fearful. Many abolitionists did indeed proclaim radical social doctrines, including the heretical notion that blacks ought to be equal, under the law, with whites. If that idea ever became current, the system of race relations in the South (and in the North, for that matter) would come tumbling down. Moreover, the most terrifying North American slave uprising, Nat Turner's Revolt, occurred just seven months after Garrison began to publish the *Liberator*. Many white Southerners were wrongly convinced that the two events were related and that "agitation" from the North was bound to produce further rebellions. Abolitionists denied the charge and countered by saying that the only way to ensure the safety of Southern whites was for them to free blacks, words which did nothing to calm the defenders of slavery.

White Southerners and their Northern allies were especially adept at using force and the political system to thwart abolitionists in the 1830s. The American Anti-Slavery Society's postal campaign of 1835, for instance, prompted a mob in Charleston, South Carolina, to break into the post office to steal, and later burn, antislavery publications. Instead of deploring this clearly illegal act, public officials in the South, and some in the North, applauded. President Andrew Jackson put his seal of approval on the Charleston riot when he suggested, some months later, that the real problem was with antislavery propaganda and that it ought to be banned from the mails. No such bill ever passed but proslavery forces were soon to be successful in stopping Congress from considering antislavery petitions. In 1836 the House of Representatives resolved that all of them should "be laid upon the table, and that no further action whatever shall be had thereon." Some form of this "gag resolution" remained in effect until December 1844.

Repression was not confined to Congress and the South. Connecticut in the mid-1830s passed legislation to outlaw racially mixed schools and to silence antislavery lecturers. Although politicians in other Northern states were similarly inclined to give the South a helping hand, there was very little they actually could do. Mobs proved to be much more of a danger—from 1834 through 1838 abolitionists were the victims of several major riots. One occurred in Boston in 1835 (the crowd led Garrison through the streets by a rope) and on the same day a similar fracas took place in Utica, New York. In yet another violent episode two years later, Elijah Lovejoy, an antislavery editor, lost his life while defending his press in Alton, Illinois. As abolitionists were fond of noting, substantial citizens— "gentlemen of property and standing"—were prominent in creating most of these disturbances. Such people cared less about the South's "peculiar institution" than about the federal Union and the nation's racial and social hierarchy, both of which they thought the abolitionists were out to destroy.

Although fierce, efforts to stop antislavery agitation probably were more effective in making converts than in slowing down the crusade. Among those joining the movement in the 1830s were people who dated their commitment from revulsion at some piece of anti-abolition mayhem. Abolitionists well appreciated that and made much out of incidents like the slaying of Lovejoy and passage of the "gag resolution." (The American Anti-Slavery Society's great petition campaign, in fact, got under way *after* the first gag resolution passed.) Besides providing opportunities for publicity, repression strengthened the resolve of abolitionists and confirmed, in their minds, two cardinal tenets of their propaganda. The first was a belief that American institutions were dominated by the "slave power" (an alleged conspiracy of slaveholders and their Northern lackeys). The second was an insistence that proslavery men had no respect for the civil liberty of whites. Congress, President Jackson, and mobs seemed to prove that every time they denied white abolitionists their right to free speech and to petition the government.

Abolitionists may have been helped by their enemies, but the results were less beneficial when they began battling each other, as they did with increasing frequency after 1836. The issues were seldom as clearly defined as the warring factions thought they were, and both geographical distance and irascible personalities played a significant part in dividing abolitionists. These disagreements, nonetheless, were severe enough to break the movement into fragments in 1840, a feat no amount of proslavery violence had been able to accomplish.

William Lloyd Garrison was the center around which most internal conflict revolved. He was deeply disturbed by mobs, by the mindlessness of partisan politics, and by the reluctance of well-established ministers to endorse antislavery. There was nothing unusual about Garrison's perception of things: most abolitionists shared his disgust with the level of public morality in the country and with the weak-willed performance of politicians and of many clergymen. But where other abolitionists tried to purge the churches and the government of corruption, the Boston editor sought alternatives. Disillusion and his own spiritual restlessness made him uncommonly susceptible to theological and social notions that upset his straitlaced contemporaries.

Within a short span of time in the mid-1830s Garrison did indeed adopt an impressive number of unconventional positions. He questioned whether Sunday ought to be celebrated as the Sabbath (all days should be holy, he maintained). He denounced both the Protestant denominations and the majority of clergy for "sectarianism"— the sin of putting selfish interests ahead of morality. In addition, Garrison came to believe in a form of Christian anarchism known as nonresistance. It involved repudiating all varieties of force, among which Garrison included laws and governments. As we shall see in the next chapter, nonresistance was subtle beyond simple summary and rooted in evangelical Protestantism. Yet neither its complexity nor its origins made it acceptable to most Americans or to many within the antislavery movement. Along with the rest of Garrison's crusades, it struck the public as silly at best, horrifying at worst.

But there was more. At the very moment that Garrison's multiple heresies were offending many former supporters, he added woman's rights to the controversial causes he favored. Garrison himself had no particular responsibility for raising the issue, which largely grew out of the activities of female abolitionists. By the mid-1830s women had become deeply involved in antislavery agitation, working within separate organizations affiliated with those run by men. That kind of arrangement was common in the antebellum period and suited contemporary notions of propriety. What some antislavery women did, nevertheless, was not so consistent with a Victorian sense of decorum. For instance, they welcomed blacks as equals (thereby stirring white fears of miscegenation), and they left the family circle (supposedly their "sphere") for such unladylike ventures as petitioning the government to end slavery. Women chafed at opposition from the public and at the condescending attitudes of their male comrades. Yet despite the discontent that had been simmering, it took an unforeseen event to elevate the "woman question" into a matter of open contention among abolitionists and further to alienate Garrison from some of his colleagues.

The catalyst was a lecture tour of New England, undertaken in 1837 by two sisters who were valuable and unusual additions to the antislavery crusade, Angelina and Sarah Grimké. Unlike most abolitionists, they were Southerners, members of a prominent South Carolina slaveholding family. Their public appearances drew curiosity seekers. Originally, the Grimkés were to talk only to female audiences—it was generally thought improper for women to address "promiscuous assemblies" (those with both sexes in attendance). Men frustrated the sisters' intentions by sneaking into antislavery gatherings to see them and to hear what they had to say. This outrage to public decency attracted the attention of New England clergy, ever vigilant to spot sin and preserve the social order. A grandiose Pastoral Letter, circulated to the Congregationalist churches, chastised the sisters. It declared that women should not speak in public and should obey men, rather than lecture to them.

Some abolitionists shared the clergy's consternation over the Grimkés' tour, while others, perhaps a majority, had trouble arriving at a consistent view of the matter. They could not entirely repudiate the sisters nor could they endorse the Pastoral Letter, which made extreme claims for ministerial authority; yet they were unwilling to fly in the face of public opinion on issues other than slavery. Garrison, characteristically, was not the least uncertain. He argued that there was nothing immoral about the sisters, or any woman, participating in public life or addressing men. Like many other abolitionists, he was in the process of shaking loose from his old assumptions about feminine roles and beginning to comprehend, in quite sweeping terms, the injustices done to women.

Taken along with his other enthusiasms, Garrison's support of the Grimkés convinced many abolitionists that he was either abandoning antislavery or taking it straight to ruin by associating it with strange crusades and by assaulting the sensibilities of decent folk. Garrison responded that expediency should never prevent a person from speaking out against evil and, moreover, that his views on questions other than slavery were his own, not an essential part of the crusade for abolition. He advocated an "open platform" where all who believed in immediate emancipation were welcome, no matter what their differences were on other social or theological questions. That point was lost on anti-abolitionists, who saw Garrison as representative of the cause and who cited him to show that the movement consisted of dangerous crackpots. Some of his colleagues felt they had to put distance between themselves and him simply to refute such charges and to gain respectability and credibility. Garrison, meanwhile, subtly closed the "open platform" and frittered away support by using harsh language to describe allies who disagreed with him. By 1838 he had repelled many admirers while retaining an intensely loyal cluster of followers, concentrated in New England and labeled "Garrisonians." They were diverse in religion, had a high proportion of women, were flamboyant in their tactics, and were extreme on social issues.

Abolitionist opponents of Garrison were not of one mind, nor did they ever form a coherent group. They included a great number of evangelical Protestants who were put off by Garrison's heterodoxy and who believed that the clergy and other influential men, if approached tactfully, would provide greater support for the movement (a notion many of them lost with time). Some, like Lewis Tappan, were quite traditional regarding the role of women, while others, like Theodore Dwight Weld—who married Angelina Grimké—took a woman's rights position but felt it should not be proclaimed openly, lest it detract from abolitionism.

Divisive as Garrison and the "woman question" were, the most serious dispute among abolitionists came over politics. From the beginning antislavery had been non-partisan, as well as non-sectarian. Abolitionists did, however, expect to have political influence by acting as a pressure group, by changing public opinion, and by extracting pledges from major-party candidates for office. In the late 1830s a number of abolitionists in New York and Ohio, led by such men as James G. Birney, Myron Holley, and Henry B. Stanton, became dissatisfied with those tactics. They recognized that abolitionists were being taken in by wily politicians who found promises easier to make than to keep. Politicking, moreover, seemed a good way to focus abolitionist energies and to give publicity to the cause. Since many abolitionists regarded the Whigs and Democrats as hopelessly corrupt and chained to Southern votes, the logical conclusion was to form a separate antislavery political organization, with its own electioneering apparatus and candidates. After months of talk, the Liberty Party emerged in time to run Birney for the presidency in 1840.

Garrisonians opposed the move on practical and philosophical grounds. Politics, they felt, demanded unacceptable moral compromises as the price of success. They further argued that an antislavery party would do poorly in elections (they were right) and that it would actually diminish the influence of abolitionist votes since the major parties would no longer bother to compete for them in close elections. Even if they had swallowed those objections, many Garrisonians would not have joined the Liberty Party under any circumstances. As Christian anarchists, they believed the proper course of action was *not* to vote or to have anything else to do with human governments, which they regarded as inherently sinful. Yet Garrison and his followers did not entirely reject political means—for others.

Garrison frequently said that he expected antislavery to be manifested at the ballot box. He added that it would only get there if abolitionists kept their moral purity (which meant staying clear of party politics) and if they persuaded public opinion of the evils of slavery. What Garrison failed to see was that the Liberty Party did not necessarily have to make moral compromises or to win elections in order to have a purpose: in a highly political nation, electioneering and losing can serve as a valuable form of propaganda.

Well before the Liberty Party materialized, cracks in antislavery unity became too obvious to ignore. The worst of the early breaches appeared in Garrison's home territory. In 1838 his critics organized an alternative organization to the Massachusetts Anti-Slavery Society (which he dominated). In the meantime, politically minded abolitionists like Henry B. Stanton and James G. Birney pressed for resolutions defining the voting obligations of antislavery men. Although Garrisonians suggested compromise declarations, Birney and his allies stuck to a formula calculated to purge the movement of nonresistants and of abolitionists who wanted to stay within the Whig or the Democratic Party. The "woman question" also remained a source of irritation. It nearly broke up the American Anti-Slavery Society in 1839, when female delegates were admitted for the first time on equal terms with men.

The following year the American Anti-Slavery Society did indeed split under the accumulated weight of all the disputes. With the election of a woman, Abby Kelley, to serve on a previously all-male committee, a substantial minority of delegates walked out of the annual meeting. Some of the seceders left to work primarily within the Liberty Party; others joined Lewis Tappan in a new, largely ineffective venture, the American and Foreign Anti-Slavery Society.

The schism might have been averted. When the positions taken by Garrison and his critics appeared in various state and local organizations they often did not cause any comparable disruption. Abolitionists in places remote from the battles in Boston and New York commonly regarded the feuding as silly and refused to take sides. The antagonists, and historians, nevertheless persisted in blaming the division of 1840 on drastic and irreconcilable differences in world-views between the factions. Supposedly, it was Garrison, the radical, opposed by moderates who accepted Protestant orthodoxy and the legitimacy of American institutions. That interpretation, however, fails to acknowledge that Garrison's "radicalism" grew out of the values of the day (it stemmed from Protestant perfectionism and millennialism) and that he was capable of altering it with circumstances—in spite of his pacifism and anarchism, for example, he accepted the Civil War and the Republican Party as means of achieving reform goals. His abolitionist opponents, furthermore, were not always so "moderate" as they seemed to Garrison. They, too, made drastic criticisms of the political system and of American religion (James G. Birney called it the "bulwark" of slavery). Non-Garrisonians also had visions of a society morally transformed and they endorsed causes in addition to antislavery, although usually in more temperate fashion than the Boston editor. Indeed, all factions recognized that the basic principles of abolitionism—control of one's self and one's labor, personal moral responsibility, human brotherhood, and so on—applied to a great many situations beyond the institution of slavery. Still, whatever underlying agreement there was among abolitionists, their personality conflicts and disagreements over tactics made a parting of the ways difficult to prevent by 1840.

The schism seemed a major tragedy to Garrison, who blamed it on "traitors" and insisted that it was a blow to the cause of antislavery. The results were less dramatic than he made them out to be. Neither the American Anti-Slavery Society nor the American and Foreign Anti-Slavery Society was especially effective in coordinating abolitionist efforts after 1840; yet the movement may no longer have needed firm central direction. The American Anti-Slavery Society seems to have been past its prime before the division occurred. The Panic of 1837 dried up funds for major undertakings of the sort it mounted earlier. More important, the functions of the national society were already being passed down to the auxiliaries—probably a healthy thing since local control permitted maximum participation in decision making and allowed abolitionists to modify tactics to suit circumstances in their areas.

Whether for better or worse, the fate of the American Anti-Slavery Society paralleled that of other reform organizations in the antebellum decades. National voluntary societies were a relatively new and exciting development, a product of early-nineteenth-century improvements in communication and transportation. Virtually every antebellum movement generated its own central organization, although some, like phrenology, did so belatedly. Virtually every such organization fell apart within a short span of years. National reform institutions—national institutions of any sort—were hard to maintain in a country as diverse and with such a tradition of localism as the United States. Yet few crusades seem to have suffered irreparable damage from lack of central direction (the exception may have been labor reform, which needed to be able to control wages and working conditions over a broad area). More remarkable than the failure of organizations like the American Anti-Slavery Society is the fact that antebellum Americans were able to build them in the first place.

After 1840 Garrisonians continued to rely on "moral suasion," believing that slavery would end when Americans were convinced of its sinfulness. But they did shift tactics, most notably when they endorsed "disunionism," the idea that the free states ought to secede from the Southern ones. First promoted by Garrison in 1842 and officially proclaimed by the American Anti-Slavery Society in 1844, disunionism had several things to recommend it. It shocked public opinion, got publicity, and provoked defenders of slavery into behaving foolishly. It also fit well with the "ultraist" desire, prevalent among antebellum reformers, to be cut off from anything impure.

Disunionism, finally, expressed a principle abolitionists had long been trying to establish—that slavery was the responsibility of all Americans, not just Southerners. To a degree, abolitionists *had* to make that argument or find some other line of work since they had no audience among whites in the South. But they sincerely believed that slavery depended upon Northern military might, available to put down slave insurrections, and upon Northern economic assistance. Remove these, Garrisonians argued, and the institution must fall. In its own fashion, disunionism was both a politically sophisticated tactic and an affirmation of American nationhood—a curious thing coming from the branch of abolitionism which seemed most non-political and most sectional. (The real irony was that the South, not the North, made disunionism a reality in 1860, and in the name of preserving slavery.)

After 1840 non-Garrisonians worked to free slaves in their own fashion, with little sympathy for disunionism. Lewis Tappan corresponded with foreign abolitionists, financed propaganda, and mounted religious and legal campaigns to help blacks. Liberty men continued electioneering, with minimal success, until 1848, when the thrust of political antislavery was drastically redirected.

Even earlier, there were stresses and strains apparent within the Liberty Party. The lines of conflict crisscrossed in complicated ways and, as usual, personality conflicts figured in. Some members were dissatisfied with Birney, the presidential candidate in 1840 and 1844 —he spent much of his first campaign for office in London and was given to casting aspersions upon the morality of the electorate, neither of which did much to stir enthusiasm. Matters of more substance also divided Liberty men. There were debates over whether to stay with the one issue of slavery or to add others in an effort to apply abolitionist ideals to all social problems and thus to become a party with a broad platform. There was disagreement over the constitutionality of slavery and over Congress's power to touch the institution. And there were those who wanted to keep to the purest possible antislavery position and those who were willing to make concessions in order to attract moderate, even racist, voters.

These quarrels continued among abolitionists into the 1850s, but by the late 1840s events had upset the calculations of Liberty men and Garrisonians alike. At first the trouble had to do with Texas. In the 1830s American settlers there declared independence from Mexico and set up their own republic, sparking controversy over whether Texas ought to join the Union. To bring it into the United States meant adding slave-state representation in Congress and shifting the delicate balance there. Not to bring Texas in implied a censure of slavery and denied political and economic advantages to the South. Texas was eventually annexed in 1845, although through a devious procedure which reinforced the abolitionist suspicion that Southerners secretly controlled the federal government.

The worst was yet to come. Shortly after annexation, the United States and Mexico went to war over a disputed boundary. Although the war was not glorious, the United States won. The total amount of real estate acquired from Mexico (counting Texas) came to over a million square miles, including what is now the state of California.

The war disturbed many Northerners who cared nothing for black people and who were not especially hostile to the South. So long as slavery stayed where it was, they could tolerate it and comfort themselves by believing it would die a natural death. They were not prepared to see it expand and they were uneasy about the acquisition of fresh soil for the South's "peculiar institution." In 1846 David Wilmot, a Pennsylvania congressman, spoke for them. A piece of legislation he sponsored—the Wilmot Proviso—demanded that slavery be prohibited in territories taken from Mexico as a result of the war. The upshot was sharp sectional conflict in Congress (where the South defeated the Proviso in the Senate) and, through a long chain of circumstances, the emergence of a new force in American politics. In 1848 an odd coalition—disaffected Democrats, Liberty men, and a few stray politicians looking for a home—formed the Free Soil Party. Its candidate was ex-President Martin Van Buren, once an obnoxious figure to abolitionists. Its platform advocated the non-extension of slavery, the position of the Wilmot Proviso.

The Free Soil Party posed an intellectual problem for all abolitionists and a tactical one for Liberty men. It was far from being truly antislavery: it did not demand immediate emancipation, nor did it propose to touch slavery where it already existed. It depended, as the Colonization Society did, on an alliance of ardent racists and genuine racial egalitarians. To the former, it promised that Northern whites could preserve western land for themselves and keep blacks out. To the latter, it offered the possibility of a broadly based coalition capable of checking the power of slaveholders in government. Perhaps because of its ideological adaptability, the Free Soil Party met with far greater success than the Liberty Party. It drew 10 percent of the presidential vote in 1848, a respectable showing for a hastily assembled organization, and it elected candidates to state and national offices.

Quick to point out the Party's moral lapses and personally unable to endorse it, Garrisonians were cheered nonetheless. They interpreted Free Soil gains as encouraging signs that the Northern public was slowly moving toward abolitionism and that the South would

soon be at bay. Many Liberty men agreed and a few prominent
ones such as Salmon P. Chase of Ohio were among the party's
founders and most diligent supporters. James G. Birney and some
other key Liberty men, however, saw Free Soil as a betrayal of the
cause and had nothing to do with it. They persisted in waging hope-
less, but morally pure, campaigns of their own in the 1850s, running
as self-styled "radical political abolitionists." Free Soil further frag-
mented the abolitionists at the very time public controversy over
slavery was reaching its peak.

The question of the territories remained unresolved throughout
1849, only to be "settled" in the Compromise of 1850, which created new tensions while trying to soothe old ones. The terms of the
Compromise cost the South a bit of political leverage. Until then the
number of states—hence the number of U.S. senators—had been
evenly balanced between slave and free. The admission of California
in 1850 as a free state changed that. In return for accepting its new
minority status in the Senate, the South received concessions. The
most significant of these was a Fugitive Slave Act to assist masters in
retrieving their runaway property, some of whom were providing
Northern audiences with eyewitness testimony about the South. The
law was not the first of its kind, but it was offensive because, contrary to the principles of Anglo-American justice, it stacked the deck
against the accused and because it gave Northerners direct responsibility for helping to retake bondsmen. As almost no other piece of
legislation could have done, the Act gave credence to the abolitionist
argument that slavery rested on a total disrespect for civil liberties
and that it could not survive without the support of Northerners,
who were now called upon to do the slaveholder's dirty work for
him.

The Act probably captured more headlines than fugitives. It led to
well-publicized episodes of civil disobedience—blacks and whites
fought slave catchers, rescued fugitives from courtrooms and jails,
and broke the law in the name of a higher law. Abolitionists made
the most of these incidents and wrote movingly of the runaways and
their quest for freedom. Beyond that, the Act inspired the single
most effective piece of antislavery propaganda, *Uncle Tom's Cabin*,
published in 1852 by Harriet Beecher Stowe, who was more of a

colonizationist than an abolitionist. With its vivid cast of characters, the novel was wildly popular in the North and was quickly transformed into countless stage productions (leading one abolitionist to note wryly that the theater became antislavery before many churches did).

It is in the nature of compromises to outrage people at the extremes, to please no one fully, and yet to work, at least for a while. Despite the furor over the Fugitive Slave Act, the Compromise of 1850 undercut abolitionism by settling the fate of slavery in the territories, seemingly in favor of freedom. The Free Soil Party did poorly in the election of 1852.

The relative calm was easily shattered. In 1854 a Democratic senator from Illinois, Stephen A. Douglas, introduced legislation to organize territory west of Iowa and Missouri. In order to secure Southern support for the Kansas-Nebraska Act (as it was known), he wrote in the principle that settlers ought to be able to decide for themselves whether the newly formed territories would be slave or free. He graced this notion with a glittering phrase, "popular sovereignty." The problem, so far as Northerners were concerned, was that this changed the rules of the game. According to the Missouri Compromise of 1819–20, slavery had been prohibited from much of the area. Now, with passage of the Act, slavery might gain a foothold there.

Dismay over this brought together ex-Free Soilers, a few old Liberty men, a smattering of disaffected Democrats, and many onetime antislavery Whigs, who created the Republican Party. Like its predecessor, the Free Soil Party, it stood for the non-extension of slavery while professing not to want to harm the institution in the Southern states. Even so, the party's rhetoric was bound to make white Southerners edgy. In addition to criticizing slavery, Republicans (again like Free Soilers) envisioned a nation consisting of independent, prosperous white property holders. That image implied a criticism of the Southern way of life and was powerfully appealing to Northern voters. In a short time the Republicans made remarkable gains and threatened to win the presidency and control Congress without having any support in the South.

These events of the mid- and late-1850s partially vindicated abolitionists, and then passed them by. As Garrison and others predicted, slavery had become something the major parties could not ignore: it broke up the Whigs, divided the Democrats, and produced the Republicans. Southern aggressiveness and political maneuvering also made it appear that abolitionists had been right in their charge that there was a sinister conspiracy in the government, hell-bent on promoting the interests of slavery. The actions of Southerners and their Northern supporters, furthermore, lent weight to the abolitionist argument that the institution was a national evil. The Fugitive Slave Act, of course, did that, as did a Supreme Court decision in the case of Dred Scott. (It appeared to write slavery and racial discrimination into the Constitution.) Yet even while Northerners slipped closer to abolitionist views, older members of the antislavery vanguard had little to do with guiding public affairs. Initiative and leadership belonged to people like Charles Sumner and Henry Wilson (senators from Massachusetts), Salmon P. Chase, and others. Many of these men were ex-Whigs, some former Free Soilers; all were antislavery politicians and Republican stalwarts. Few came out of the original abolitionist organizations.

That was not especially disturbing to the older abolitionists. None expected popularity and most had always assumed their greatest effect would come from persuading others. Many, including Garrison, were pleasantly surprised to find a politician as righteous as Sumner winning office and they had cordial feelings for such men (even while being critical of their public stands and suspicious of their involvement in partisan activities). For abolitionists the unsettling thing about Republican victories was their partial nature. Northern voters were indeed beginning to elect moderately abolitionist candidates. They were also beginning to see slavery as a threat to the republic and to the civil liberties of whites. They were not, however, convinced of the utter sinfulness of slavery, ready to demand its immediate extinction in the South, and prepared to accept black people as fellow citizens. Clearly there was a great deal left to do before the abolitionist message got through to the white public in its entirety.

Yet the time for propaganda seemed to be passing: violence, not moral suasion, was the order of the day in the late 1850s. Vicious guerrilla warfare raged in Kansas between free- and slave-state settlers, each exercising "popular sovereignty" with firearms rather than honest ballots. Violence even invaded the chambers of the United States Senate. A speech made by Sumner in 1856 maligned slavery, administration policy toward Kansas, and, almost incidentally, a fellow senator from South Carolina. The senator's kinsman Preston Brooks (himself a representative from South Carolina) approached Sumner, then seated at his desk, and used a cane to administer a savage beating, presumably vindicating the honor of Brooks's relative and his region. Feelings about slavery were running so high that each man became a hero to many. Sumner was glorified as a martyr to Southern brutality; Brooks, whose cane broke over Sumner's skull, received a fine collection of replacements from well-wishers.

The bloodiest and most ominous episode of the late 1850s was the work of John Brown, a strange old man and a veteran of anti-slavery battles in Kansas. In October 1859 he and a small band of black and white followers attacked the Federal Arsenal at Harpers Ferry, Virginia. Most of his men were killed or captured. Brown survived, only to be tried and executed soon after. In the minds of Southerners the raid raised the nightmarish prospect of future slave revolts in which Northern whites might similarly assist blacks in the carnage. Northerners, abolitionists among them, had a harder time interpreting the meaning of Brown's actions. Insurrection was abhorrent to them; yet Brown had taken up weapons in order to strike down evil—a noble gesture, many thought. A failure in most things in his life, Brown helped his reputation in the North by dying well: he accepted his fate with eloquence and dignity. He was an avenging angel. Admiration for the old man appeared even among pacifists like Garrison and Transcendentalist intellectuals like Henry David Thoreau, who had not previously committed himself unreservedly to antislavery.

From the beginning abolitionists had advocated peaceful means to end slavery; but they also predicted it would die violently if emancipation did not come quickly. Kansas, the beating of Sumner, and Brown's raid appeared to justify their darkest fears. Some of them began to wonder, in the bleak days of the 1850s, whether America's sins might not be so horrible that they would have to be washed away in blood.

They were. On December 20, 1860, South Carolina responded to the election of Abraham Lincoln, the Republican presidential candidate, by declaring that the Union between it and the other states was "dissolved." Four months later the Civil War began. As usual, abolitionists were divided. Consistent with their pacifism (and with Garrisonian nonresistance), many believed the Southern states should be allowed—even encouraged—to secede. Others endorsed the use of force to prevent them from going. Abolitionists were far more agreed upon the moral inadequacy of Lincoln's position, which was that the North was fighting only to preserve the Union, not to meddle with Southern institutions. Opposition to the war, however, faded as the Emancipation Proclamation (to take effect in 1863) and the course of events made it impossible to deny that the conflict was over slavery after all. In 1864 Garrison, for thirty years a nonvoter and nonresistant, cast a ballot for Lincoln.

The war did end slavery. Many abolitionists, pleased with the North's victory, were aging and ready for retirement. A weary Garrison published the last issue of the *Liberator* and left the American Anti-Slavery Society in 1865. The organization continued another five years until the Fifteenth Amendment to the Constitution promised to guarantee civil liberties for blacks. Yet even in 1870 there was much left undone: racism lived on, although slavery did not.

A few abolitionists did recognize that only the first battle had been won and continued throughout the rest of the nineteenth century to press for equal justice. They, however, were not intellectually prepared to agitate for the freedman with the same passion and thoroughness they had brought to the cause of the slave. In common with most antebellum reformers, abolitionists tended to believe that both evil and success were problems of the human spirit, not matters of economics and social structure. Blacks, they felt, needed opportunity, not help. With freedom, ex-slaves could fend for themselves. Those who were virtuous would succeed; those who were not would fail. Although some former abolitionists recognized the weaknesses in that line of reasoning, it was a common one and it tragically underestimated the economic, psychological, and social damage slavery inflicted on both sections and both races.

It is difficult to gauge precisely the importance of the antislavery crusade. Unlike temperance and school reformers, abolitionists were not directly responsible for any great amount of legislation, nor did the original band of abolitionists ever wield much influence in government, although such antislavery politicians as Charles Sumner eventually did. Propaganda campaigns, nevertheless, have an effect. Reformers often find that they remain personally unpopular while voters and leaders come, in time, to accept much of what they have to say. Certainly antislavery images and language passed into common usage and into the rhetoric of elected officials. When that happened, it was because abolitionists phrased things in a manner making sense out of events and speaking to general concerns of the day. In the best example, antislavery talk about a conspiracy of slaveholders gained currency by playing to American fears of arbitrary power and by seeming to describe the actual behavior of Southerners. The importance of antislavery (or any antebellum reform) came through a similar ability to help the public perceive situations, or institutions like slavery, in a new, emotionally charged way. The pity is that abolitionists could not communicate their entire vision: slavery was ended, but largely as a boon to whites. The higher goals of racial harmony and of a society ruled by God's law remained elusive.

5. Women and War

Virtually all the major figures of antebellum reform participated in several causes besides the one they were primarily engaged in. These additional commitments usually fell into predictable patterns. Secular communitarians, for instance, often were interested in health or labor reform; prison reformers tended to be concerned with such related issues as construction of almshouses, insane asylums, and schools. Among abolitionists the secondary reforms frequently had to do with health and morality—temperance, anti-licentiousness campaigns, and so on. But the causes most closely linked to anti-slavery were the woman's rights and peace movements. The connection was not entirely a matter of numbers: probably more abolitionists were active in temperance than in either of the other crusades, both of which were relatively small. The common bond was a set of assumptions about human beings and human society.

"The investigation of the rights of the slave," Angelina Grimké wrote, "has led me to a better understanding of my own." What Miss Grimké had come to realize was that power and domination were sexual as well as racial. In the antebellum period she and thousands of other reformers—male and female—created the first feminist movement in the United States. From a late-twentieth-century perspective, their demands for increased opportunities and legal protection seem a reasonable, even modest, reaction against discrimination. Only the most hardened present-day male chauvinists would not accept much of what they sought. Yet the fact that there were legitimate grievances does not entirely explain why protest began in the 1830s and 1840s. Many injustices were centuries old and had never been met with more than isolated attacks such as Mary Wollstonecraft's *A Vindication of the Rights of Women,* published in England in 1792. The real roots of nineteenth-century feminism lie not simply in inequities between the sexes but also in material and cultural changes affecting the way women saw themselves.

From time immemorial there had been a sexual division of labor, with woman's duties marked off from man's. That was not especially invidious so long as each member of the household contributed in an obvious manner to the well-being of all—clearly the case in a world of farms, small shops, and cottage industries, where young and old, male and female, each had a role. Economic development after 1800 changed that by widening the range of careers available and by altering the chances for individuals to rise or sink on the social scale. The best of the new opportunities, of course, were reserved for males and required spending long hours away from the rest of the family. The home increasingly became a female domain, cut off from business and public affairs. It might fully occupy a woman's day with the details of management, but if she were middle class she no longer worked in ways society recognized as work. Low-paid Irish servants, fewer children, and improved school systems reduced some traditional duties of homemaking; store-bought bread, clothing, and candles took away others. Given the cost of child raising and of maintaining a suitable home, the advantage belonged to males who controlled their domestic urges and waited until they could afford marriage and children. Such calculations show up explicitly in advice literature and implicitly in demography: the birth and fertility rates declined steadily from 1800 through the antebellum period and beyond. Where in earlier times children and wives had been producers of goods and income, in the nineteenth century and among the middle classes they almost seemed to be luxuries.

Antebellum images of masculinity and femininity both reflected these social changes and helped shape them. Men, according to most writers, were naturally strong in body and mind, aggressive, and sexual. Women were innately weak, passive, emotional, religious, and chaste. These were complementary virtues and vices—men supported women; women provided the sensitivity men lacked. Although such stereotypes were not necessarily true, they reassured each sex that it belonged where it was. Woman was too fair a flower to survive in business or politics, where man's cunning and intellect were prime virtues; in the home she was protected, her goodness blossomed, and she refined man's coarseness.

From a twentieth-century view, those notions imply a belief in female inferiority. That was not how most antebellum commentators saw it. Their respect for emotion and intuition—the result of nineteenth-century romanticism—led them to think of these views of women in highly positive terms. Some writers went so far as to suggest that feminine traits were morally superior to masculine ones and that females had a great social role to play, despite being banned from politics and the professions: through their influence over men and children they controlled the destiny of humankind. Although a woman "may never herself step beyond the threshold," a clergyman gushed, "she may yet send forth from her humble dwelling, a power that will be felt round the globe. She may at least save some souls that are dear to her from disgrace and punishment, present some precious jewels to shine brightly in the Saviour's crown."

That sort of rhetoric—recently labeled the "cult of domesticity" —may have described some lives, but it was sheer nonsense for others. To poor women (who often worked outside the home), it represented, at best, a standard to which they might aspire; at worst, it was a measure of their failure. Middle-class women also had problems matching the ideal to their reality, particularly when faced with heavy demands on their time, financial insecurity, or demonic children. Men, furthermore, refused to live up to their part of the bargain. They drank, frittered away money, philandered, or generally behaved like scoundrels—with perfect impunity since their wives had neither legal rights nor economic independence to defend themselves from their protectors. Even many women with tranquil marriages, or no husbands, had cause to be dissatisfied with the role allotted them. They found it stifling.

Some females, however, discovered that the common assumptions about them could justify activities other than being a housewife. Reform was one of these. If woman's influence was so beneficial, why should it be kept at home? Why not bring to the outside world all those feminine virtues necessary to counteract masculine vices? The first and most frequent answers to those questions were timid. Women, a majority in many church congregations, participated actively in early-nineteenth-century religious and charitable enterprises. By the 1830s they were involved in more secular causes: health reform, temperance, antislavery, and campaigns to redeem prostitutes and curb licentiousness. A radical few were interested in communitarian ventures and had started talking about rearranging relations between the sexes. In the late 1820s a daring Scotswoman named Frances Wright lectured audiences of men and women (bad enough in itself) on her heretical ideas about education, religion, economics, and marriage. (So scandalous was her thought and behavior that "Fanny Wrightism" became a pejorative term, liberally applied to the Grimké sisters and later woman's rights advocates.) Most of the first generation of female reformers posed no direct challenge to the status quo. If anything, they reinforced feminine stereotypes by displaying the moral impulses everyone expected of them, by doing little that was unladylike, and by deferring to masculine leadership, particularly of the clergy.

Antislavery changed that. At the outset it received an intensely hostile reception, largely because it generated anxieties about race relations and social stability. Quite probably the Grimké sisters would have been treated gently by clergy in 1837 had they been lecturing to "promiscuous assemblies" on the conversion of heathen in foreign lands or on a similarly safe subject. Instead, they were talking about slavery and, to make it worse, about licentiousness in the South. Consequently, the assault on them was harsh, as it occasionally had been on other antislavery women (literally so in the case of the Boston Female Anti-Slavery Society, a target of mob violence in 1835). Resistance forced the Grimkés and their supporters to examine their own beliefs and to become aware of the social restrictions placed upon women.

In fact, critics provoked the sisters into writing what became classics of American feminism. Sarah responded at first with a direct rebuke to her clerical opponents and then, in 1838, with a less defensive and more sweeping work, *Letters on the Condition of Women and the Equality of the Sexes.* Angelina's main contribution came in a series of *Letters to Catharine E. Beecher,* also published in 1838. The sisters defended woman's "moral and intellectual capacities" and attacked "subordination to man." In forceful language, the pamphlets insisted that both sexes had the "same rights" and "same duties."

This egalitarianism was anathema to conservatives, but it similarly disturbed people like Catharine Beecher, whose position was more complex. Herself a pioneer in female education, Beecher—in common with many feminists—accepted the idea that there were inherent moral differences between the sexes and that woman was the better of the two. Her view, however, was that feminine power should be exercised in the family. (Angelina suggested that "the Presidential chair of the United States" might be a more appropriate aspiration.) In truth, the Grimkés sometimes likewise assumed that woman's character was different from, and superior to, man's. Yet in the exciting days of the late 1830s each sister issued ringing declarations of equality and rejections of domesticity.

Abolitionists could have repudiated the Grimkés, and some did; but many joined in with their own assertions of female rights. An influential minority in the antislavery crusade were Quakers (the Grimkés among them), whose religious practices predisposed them to accept women speaking in public. Still, there is a better explanation for the transition from abolitionism to feminism in the late 1830s: women could identify with blacks more intensely than they could with the objects of other reforms. In working for the slave, furthermore, they could comprehend their personal situation more clearly. "The comparison between women and the colored race is striking," declared Lydia Maria Child, herself a female abolitionist. "Both are characterized by affection more than intellect; both have a strong development of the religious sentiment; both are excessively adhesive in their attachments; both . . . have a tendency to submission; and hence, both have been kept in subjection by physical force, and considered rather in the light of property, than as individuals."

Seldom have so many racial and sexual stereotypes been compressed in so small a space, or used for such a radical purpose. Child's message was not that women belonged in the home and blacks on the plantation, the deduction antifeminists and racists would have drawn from her analysis. Instead, she went on to argue that women and blacks were morally sensitive, innately good human beings who were degraded by the authority white males exerted over them. Both were victims of man's lust; both lacked economic independence; neither had a role in public affairs. The solution was to end man's tyranny and to allow weaker (but morally true) people to act as responsible individuals—a conclusion which seems sounder than the line of reasoning producing it. Certainly abolitionists like Mrs. Child accepted notions about gender and race most twentieth-century Americans find offensive, yet the effect was for middle-class women suddenly to be able to see slavery as a metaphor for their own plight.

Although abolitionists divided in 1840 partly over the "woman question" (both sexes were on both sides), hundreds took the step from antislavery to feminism with ease. The leading lights of the post-Civil War woman's suffrage movement—Elizabeth Cady Stanton, Lucy Stone, and Susan B. Anthony—began their careers in the antebellum period and had abolitionist backgrounds. Early feminist gatherings were comprised of antislavery crusaders (usually Garrisonians and including such prominent black abolitionists as Frederick Douglass and Sojourner Truth). Even the Liberty Party made a bow toward sexual equality by admitting women to some of its meetings in the West.

It would be 1869 before there was a separate national organization to coordinate feminist activities—at which point there were two of them, thanks to a division in the ranks. As early as 1840, however, there had been talk of creating a formal institutional structure to advance the cause. In that year Elizabeth Cady Stanton was in London with her abolitionist husband, a delegate to a World's Anti-Slavery Convention. Female representatives from America were excluded after an acrimonious debate. Stanton's indignation at the insult coincided with her discovery of those whom she later called (probably incorrectly) "the first women I had ever met who believed in the equality of the sexes." Among them was an American Quaker and abolitionist, Lucretia Mott. The two became close friends and, according to Stanton, "resolved to hold a convention as soon as we returned home, and form a society to advocate the rights of women." For eight years nothing came of their idea. Stanton traveled in Europe briefly, then settled in for a period of motherhood and intellectual stimulation in Boston. By 1848 her circumstances had changed. The family moved to upstate New York, where life was hard and drab for her. She realized, as she had not before, "the impossibility of woman's best development" under the usual order of things. A visit with Mott, then passing through the area, led to a call in a local paper for a meeting at Seneca Falls on July 19 and 20. That left five days to get ready for the first woman's rights convention.

Working in haste, Stanton, Mott, and three friends still managed to produce documents which presented the antebellum feminist case effectively and comprehensively. For the opening, they prepared a Declaration of Sentiments modeled upon the Declaration of Independence. It began with the premise that "all men and women are created equal" and substituted "man" for King George as the tyrant. This was both clever and a hint of how woman's rights might best be argued in the future. Although most antebellum reformers reminded Americans of the natural rights ideology of the Revolution, feminists were deeply committed to it. Religious rhetoric, the mainstay of so many pre-Civil War crusades, was often ineffective for them, particularly since the clergy were fond of retaliating with biblical quotations, especially Paul's pithier calls for female subordination. In any event, Stanton, Mott, and their collaborators submitted "to a candid world" a bill of indictment against male domination, just as their forefathers had done against the British seventy-two years earlier. The chief points in it would be repeated for decades without great modification, as would the suggested remedies.

Stanton and her collaborators accused man of endeavoring, "in every way that he could, to destroy her [woman's] confidence in her own powers, to lessen her self-respect, and to make her willing to lead a dependent and abject life." They specifically objected to the lack of educational and professional opportunities for women as well as to laws depriving wives of control over property and awarding

custody of children to fathers in cases of divorce. The convention
initially considered eleven resolutions asserting sexual equality, advocating a single moral standard for males and females, and urging
women not simply to stay at home but to "move in the enlarged
sphere which her great Creator has assigned her." In the final hours,
Lucretia Mott offered an additional resolution calling for "the over-
throw of the monopoly of the pulpit, and for the securing to woman
of an equal participation with men in the various trades, professions,
and commerce." The most controversial proposal approved at Seneca Falls—and the only one not to pass unanimously—was Stanton's. It insisted that women fight to gain "their sacred right to the
elective franchise."

The vote may have seemed too much to ask for in 1848 but
within three years a Massachusetts feminist convention labeled it
"the corner-stone of this enterprise." It would continue to be from
the Civil War until woman suffrage became a reality in 1920. Emphasis on the franchise posed a slight problem for the Garrisonian
abolitionists so prominent in the woman's rights movement. Many of
them did not believe *anyone* should vote. But even they could up-
hold the proposition that the chance to do so should not be confined
to one sex. Rightly or wrongly, feminists became convinced as early
as the 1850s that obtaining the ballot was the crucial objective and
that once achieved it would permit women to protect their own
interests. The demand for the vote gave force and coherence to
nineteenth-century feminism, although it stressed a limited goal at
the expense of agitating against basic social and economic injustices.

Seneca Falls inspired the formation of local woman's rights
groups and it was followed by numerous other meetings. Among the
more noteworthy were two in 1850: a gathering at Salem, Ohio
(unique for prohibiting men from speaking or voting), and the first
"national" convention, held at Worcester, Massachusetts, under
Garrisonian auspices. Such events kept the movement alive in the
1850s, as did feminist publications (including journals like the *Una*,
run by Paulina Wright Davis in Rhode Island in the mid-1850s).
Yet through the Civil War feminism remained closely tied to antislavery, as often promoted by abolitionist lecturers and newspapers
as by people or periodicals exclusively devoted to woman's rights.

The union between the two causes had both negative and positive effects. On the debit side, it closed Southern ears to feminism (anything connected to antislavery was suspect) and it complicated matters after the war, especially when the Fourteenth and Fifteenth amendments were under consideration. These granted voting rights to blacks, but used the word "male" in defining suffrage and citizenship, making it likely that there would have to be another constitutional amendment, rather than simple legislative action, for women to obtain the ballot. Feminists were divided between their loyalty to ex-slaves and their self-interest—the result was a deep rift in the movement in the late 1860s, as some leaders supported the amendments and others did not. The old bond between abolitionism and woman's rights, nonetheless, had been valuable. It had provided feminism with articulate supporters and with an established forum in such antislavery journals as the *Liberator*. Most important, it had given both crusades the kind of emotional power that comes only when personal grievances resonate with a larger social situation.

It would be wrong to think that antebellum feminism was nothing more than an adjunct to abolitionism. Like their antislavery sisters —although slower and more cautiously—women in most crusades grew in perception of their own grievances as they helped others and battled male sins. Female reformers of all sorts often began by staying within the bounds society and culture set for them, only to challenge these restrictions as time went on. From being meek, discreet, and deferential to males, they changed to the point where, by the end of the antebellum period, they took charge of their own organizations, lectured to mixed audiences just as Frances Wright and the Grimkés had done, waged political campaigns, and left their domestic "sphere" in favor of public life. What such women found in reform was one of the small number of careers open to them. Although it initially did not upset conventional ideas of femininity, it gave ever-expanding opportunities for talented women.

It would, moreover, be a mistake to imagine that the only activity of significance for antebellum women came from reformers. Margaret Fuller, a Transcendentalist whose commitment was more to art than to social causes, produced an influential feminist statement,

Woman in the Nineteenth Century, published in 1845. For that matter, there were many middle-class non-feminists doing things of long-range significance for women. Catharine Beecher and other female educators, for instance, had little sympathy for woman's rights, yet they founded antebellum schools which gave girls confidence in their mental abilities and presented them with intellectual skills that were difficult to confine to the home. In still other fields changes were taking place more or less independently of feminist pressure. Legislation increasing the property rights of wives owed something to female lobbying, but it had been proposed by male lawmakers before the Seneca Falls convention. (In fact, Elizabeth Cady Stanton listed public discussions of these bills as an "immediate cause" of female awareness of political inequality.) Contraception—which eventually benefited women by reducing the burdens of childbearing—was practiced by people whose motives were not especially ideological. (Many feminists opposed it as an encouragement to male lust: their preferred form of birth control was continence.)

While these developments were taking place primarily among the middle classes, working women (largely ignored by feminists) were making demands of their own. As early as 1824 female factory hands participated in a strike in Rhode Island. Their most intensive protests, however, came in Lowell, Massachusetts. The town itself was a marvel of the American Industrial Revolution. It had not existed in 1820; by 1840 it had thirty-two mills and a labor force of eight thousand, the great majority of it female. These were mostly women in their twenties, native-born farm girls, away from family life for a few years of hard work and marginal economic independence. In 1834 they mounted a strike to block a proposed cut in wages. They struck again in 1836. To justify this unfeminine conduct the mill girls, like woman's rights advocates, fell back on natural rights and the rhetoric of the American Revolution. Calling themselves "daughters of freemen," they declared their resistance to the arbitrary actions of factory owners to be in the "spirit of our Patriotic Ancestors, who preferred privation to bondage." They lost both times.

Failure in 1834 and 1836 did not stop collective action at Lowell or elsewhere. There were more strikes among New England women operatives and in the 1840s there appeared important, if short-lived, Female Labor Reform Associations, the result, in good measure, of the organizing skill of Sarah Bagley, a former factory hand at Lowell. These groups channeled most energy away from strikes and into petition campaigns, often in cooperation with men and designed to bring about the ten-hour workday. To some extent, such activities were peculiar to New England (where industrialization and feminine self-confidence were most advanced) and they were related to a general labor reform movement. Yet the efforts of mill operatives marked a growing assertiveness among females who were neither part of the "cult of domesticity" nor within the mainstream of antebellum reform.

Quite obviously, developments affecting women were so diverse that no antebellum organization could have comprehended or guided them all. It is no wonder that woman's rights had the least developed institutional structure of the important pre-Civil War crusades—by 1860 it was still more a movement in potential than in form. Yet there was a good beginning. In books, pamphlets, and resolutions at Seneca Falls and elsewhere, feminists had begun to define problems and to articulate widely held grievances. They were clear and to the point in advocating such things as educational and economic opportunities, political power, legal protection, control over childbearing and intercourse, and greater autonomy. Moreover, by trying to change the world, female reformers (like their poorer cousins at Lowell) were making a place in it for women, subtly edging themselves, and men, away from the idea that feminine influence should only hold sway in the home.

Although critical of man's behavior, feminists were not arguing for a female universe. They wanted a society in which the sexes would have both independence and interdependence. In their ideal, women would be able to chart their own destinies, yet supposedly male and female characteristics—intellect and emotion, ambition and sympathy, aggression and passivity—would remain and would balance each other harmoniously. In proclaiming that, feminists simultaneously accepted many of the stereotypes of the "cult of domesticity" and fashioned them into an image of human unity transcending gender, just as abolitionists and pacifists hoped to transcend race and national boundaries.

One of the most cherished antebellum paintings commemorated William Penn's eighteenth-century treaty with the Indians. It illustrated its theme of peace by showing animals (both gentle and savage) coexisting harmoniously with small children in the American wilderness. The artist, Edward Hicks, did approximately a hundred versions of this scene, the best known of them entitled "Peaceable Kingdom." As an image of America, it is deeply moving, all the more so for being out of touch with reality. Hicks was turning out "Peaceable Kingdoms" in the 1830s, a period of great mob violence and of extreme cruelty to Indians. He continued through the late 1840s, during the war with Mexico. The strength in Hicks's art was in the ideal behind it. His sect, the Quakers, had been pacifistic since its seventeenth-century beginnings. In the eighteenth century non-Quakers, touched by religion or Enlightenment humanitarianism, also repudiated war as inconsistent with Christianity or reason, or both. One of the major figures of the Revolutionary era even suggested that the new nation ought to have a Peace Office to counterbalance (and eventually replace) its military departments.

The suggestion was ignored and the peace movement in America did not actually begin until a generation later, in 1815. That year, not coincidentally, marked the end of the War of 1812, an ignominious conflict staunchly opposed in New England. It had done a great deal to make pacifism attractive. Well before then, however, war had been a burden on the mind of a devout New York Presbyterian layman, David Low Dodge. A well-to-do merchant, Dodge first committed his ideas to print in 1808, marshaling an abundance of biblical quotations to demonstrate the evils of violence. In 1815 he published a more penetrating essay, *War Inconsistent with the Religion of Jesus Christ*, and helped found the New York Peace Society, probably the first of its kind in the world. Almost simultaneously, Noah Worcester, a Unitarian minister and a veteran of the Revolutionary army, was preaching on peace (as were many New England clergy) and offering to the public his *Solemn Review of the Custom of War* (1814). On December 28, 1815, he and several friends created the Massachusetts Peace Society.

At the outset there were disagreements. Dodge rejected all violent means and declared governments to be under "Satan's dominion" for using them (he came close to the nonresistant position which would seem extreme when William Lloyd Garrison adopted it two decades later). Apparently Dodge recognized that his ideas were a bit too elevated to suit the majority of pacifists. The New York Peace Society restricted leadership to people who shared his beliefs, but opened membership to those who considered force to be permissible under some circumstances. The latter held what Dodge called "lax doctrines"—precisely the sort preached by the Massachusetts Peace Society.

Its leader, Worcester, believed pacifism would gain followers gradually and he was willing to take half measures in order to encourage its growth. He did not insist upon Dodge's absolutist proposition that war was inherently evil, nor did he demand that everyone follow the Quakers and refuse military service, although he admired those who did. For him, armed conflict between nations was the primary evil and it was to be eliminated through arbitration and reason. In private, Worcester may have been almost as radical as Dodge, but his public expressions of moderation and his "expediency" annoyed the New Yorker. The two men—and all antebellum pacifists—could agree that war was un-Christian and economically wasteful. Beyond that, serious disputes were brewing over tactics, over the moral duty of individuals, and over how far to go in doing away with coercion.

By the early 1820s there were over a dozen local peace societies. These were concentrated in the Northeast and attracted respectable men—politicians, merchants, judges, professors, and preachers. The greatest proportion of support came from Presbyterians, Congregationalists, and Unitarians (the denominations most committed to reform), with surprisingly little help from Quakers. These early pacifist organizations quickly established close contact with their overseas counterparts—a London Peace Society had begun in 1815, quite independently of the American ones founded the same year. (All antebellum reforms had international contacts, but they were most developed among pacifists.)

For the first decade, the American side lacked dynamic leadership. Worcester and Dodge, both capable men, made their major contributions through their publications. Neither was able to fashion a unified movement. That became the task of William Ladd, a prosperous Maine farmer and former sea captain. Already middle-aged when he became a pacifist in the early 1820s, Ladd dedicated the remainder of his life to the cause. Not overly theoretical, he would nonetheless write perhaps the most significant pamphlet of the antebellum peace movement, his *Essay on a Congress of Nations* (1840). Ladd suggested the formation of world organizations to resolve conflicts through moral means and put forth a plan very much like an agreement which emerged sixty years later from the Hague Conference of 1899. In its day, the *Essay* touched off a fruitful debate on arbitrarion of international disputes.

Ladd's significance in the 1820s, however, came from his ability to bind peace groups together. His energy, persistence, and personality were crucial in preparing the way for the creation of a national organization in 1828, the American Peace Society. It was tiny— about three hundred members at the start—and it never expanded much beyond New England; but it was useful in coordinating pacifist activities and it provided a pulpit for Ladd, who was its secretary and the editor of its journal, the *Harbinger of Peace*.

Privately, Ladd seems to have grown closer to Dodge's absolute pacifism as time went on, yet he resembled Noah Worcester in his conciliatory public posture. In the *Harbinger of Peace* he remained neutral on the controversial question of whether defensive wars might be justified and his platform was so broad that the American Peace Society had military men on its rolls. Ladd's tolerant policy worked for nearly a decade. Under his direction, the number of peace societies increased to around fifty and notable converts joined the fold, one of them being Thomas Grimké, a distinguished South Carolina lawyer and brother of Angelina and Sarah.

For all his good humor and hard work, Ladd could not forever smooth over conflicts between pacifists. In 1838 the American Peace Society split, just as the American Anti-Slavery Society would two years later (with some of the same people involved). The problems in both instances were sociological, temperamental, and intellectual. As the peace movement grew, it began to attract middle-class reformers who were less distinguished and more impassioned than the founders of the New York and Massachusetts Peace Societies. Such men were impatient with moderation and inclined to be unequivocally against whatever evil they were fighting, whether it was slavery, ill health, sensuality, ignorance, alcohol, or war. Some of them held to an extreme variety of pacifism—nonresistance, or Christian anarchism—and in their eyes even Dodge had not gone far enough in opposing force. Their ranks included William Lloyd Garrison, who would argue the position vigorously and abrasively.

At its most elementary, nonresistance was based on a syllogism: force is sinful; governments use force; therefore, governments are sinful. Straightforward as that was, critics were appalled. They insisted that humankind would always be liable to do evil deeds, and thus would always need laws, courts, police, prisons, and other restraints. In responding, nonresistants argued that governments, by relying on coercion to achieve their goals, set the lowest possible moral standard and gave a legitimacy to force as a means of settling disputes. Hard though it was for others to accept, nonresistants thought the best defense was no defense and that the most orderly society was one in which there was no effort to compel people to be orderly. That logic rested on evangelical Protestant millennialism and perfectionism. Nonresistants literally believed men and women could cease sinning and become sanctified while on earth. When they did, the Kingdom of God would begin and supplant present-day political arrangements. Humankind had the ability to bring this millennium of peace about; people just had to resolve to give up violence and other evil practices toward one another. Rather than encouraging chaos (which is what critics charged them with doing), nonresistants had as their goal the ultimate in harmonious social relationships: all humanity knit together in love and sympathy, behaving decently because the most exacting law of all—God's—lived in their hearts.

Millennialism, perfectionism, and yearning for the Kingdom of God were not the exclusive beliefs of nonresistants. Such ideas ran throughout antebellum reform and since 1815 older pacifists like Dodge had been preaching doctrines similar to those announced by Garrison. Furthermore, both the old American fear of power and the Jeffersonian bias against strong political authority predisposed many conservative Americans toward an extreme individualism that verged on anarchism. What made the younger nonresistants seem so radical in the 1830s was their strident tone and the degree to which they repudiated the state. Dodge had refused to vote or hold office, but he and others of his persuasion believed some measure of government to be necessary. Later nonresistants, in theory, were more consistent. They totally rejected human governments.

In practice, things were not so clear-cut. There were obligations to the state even the most dedicated anarchist could not avoid. (Ideology has never gotten anyone out of paying taxes.) Nonresistant doctrine, moreover, meant different things to different people. For some, including Garrison, it was as much a metaphor as a program. The nonresistant Kingdom of God served them as an ideal against which to measure the imperfections of the status quo; it was a model of what the world should be and a counter-image of what it actually was. Others went further and regarded Christian anarchism as a plan of action. They felt their beliefs required them to separate from morally corrupt and coercive things, whether they were a religious denomination, society as a whole, or marriage. In many such cases nonresistance simply merged with "come-outerism," or withdrawal from supposedly impure churches (an impulse not confined to anarchists); but it also inspired more thoroughgoing responses, such as the construction of utopian communities based on pacifist principles—Adin Ballou's Hopedale being the most conventional and successful.

Wherever it may have taken individuals, Christian anarchism led the peace movement directly into a schism. After months of criticizing the American Peace Society for accepting men who were not complete pacifists, Garrison and his followers called a convention in Boston in September 1838. Ladd and other moderates from the national organization were present, although many quickly fled, realizing they were a minority and dismayed at the participation of women in the gathering (yet another bit of Garrisonian unorthodoxy). Ladd—much respected by Garrison—stayed, but his influence was negligible. Nonresistants were in charge and they soon adopted a Declaration of Sentiments, largely written by Garrison. Those who accepted it pledged themselves to deny the validity of social distinctions based on race, nationality, or gender. They refused allegiance to human governments and recognized Jesus as "our only ruler and lawgiver." They were against any violence or retaliation, whether it took the form of war, personal self-defense, or prisons. To promote their views, they created the New England Non-Resistance Society. Only a few of them had qualms about what they had done. Believers in human unity and individual autonomy, they had divided the peace movement and created yet another organization, although an anarchist one.

For several years after the schism all branches of the peace movement, in common with other antebellum crusades, suffered the financial aftereffects of the Panic of 1837. In the 1840s, however, there was a strong upsurge of pacifist sentiment brought about by the annexation of Texas and the prospect (soon realized) of war with Mexico. The bullying behavior of the United States, as well as the complex issues involved, suddenly made it respectable to oppose warlike government actions. Pacifists of all sorts mobilized to stir public outrage and, without success, tried to prevent armed conflict.

Rather than present a united front and capitalize on the newfound popularity of their position, peace advocates quarreled once more. The center of controversy this time was the Reverend George C. Beckwith, successor to Ladd (who died in 1842) as secretary of the American Peace Society. Beckwith was opposed to international ware and he believed the society should not drive away potential members by taking a position against other conflicts. He and his followers wished to dilute a controversial article in the organization's constitution, which condemned all wars as un-Christian. Although he controlled the society, his machinations alienated the large number of absolute pacifists. At first they tried to displace him. When they failed, they seceded in 1847. There were then three major groups of peace advocates, not counting religious sects like the Quakers: Beckwith's faction of the American Peace Society, which believed some kinds of conflicts might be moral; the Garrisonians of the New England Non-Resistance Society; and, somewhere in between, people who wished to do away with war but who were willing to tolerate governments.

If the last group had a leader, it was Elihu Burritt, the heart and soul of American pacifism from the mid-1840s to his death in 1879. While in England in 1846 Burritt founded the League of Universal Brotherhood, which soon absorbed the energies of many who abandoned the American Peace Society over Beckwith's policies. By 1850 more than 50,000 people in Britain and America signed its pledge not to participate in anything related to war. Throughout the 1840s and 1850s Burritt also engineered propaganda campaigns and mass meetings for the purpose of easing international tensions. In addition, he traveled ceaselessly and put together societies to accomplish various goals, ranging from aiding emigrants to codifying international law. All those things he did in the United States and in Europe, in more or less equal measure.

Burritt himself was as interesting and impressive as his accomplishments. His nickname—"the learned blacksmith"—marked him as the exotic he was. Except for a few people prominent in laboring men's organizations, he was, among leading reformers, almost alone in having worked with his hands. Most of the others came from the middle classes. Burritt's erudition, the second remarkable thing about him, was largely self-acquired and principally represented an interest in languages (he had knowledge of several dozen). In common with many pacifists, he believed improved transportation and communication among the world's peoples would foster human unity. His linguistic studies and his travels were a personal witness to that faith, as was his long crusade to have the transatlantic postal rate dropped from twenty-five cents to a penny.

Burritt's internationalism and his background as a workingman gave a different flavor to his propaganda. He recited the familiar litany about the un-Christian nature of man-killing and about the economic destructiveness of international conflicts. But more than his peers, he spoke of the burden war put upon the laboring classes. Perhaps because of that, his League of Universal Brotherhood appears to have drawn support from poorer folk than those usually reached by other pacifist organizations. By 1850 Burritt was urging workingmen to take collective action for peace and in 1867 he wished for the day when they "will form one vast Trades Union, and make a universal and simultaneous *strike* against the whole war system."

The rhetoric was radical and Burritt had the firsthand knowledge of European socialisms to have made it even more so. He did not. His perspective was that of a devout Christian and a skilled craftsman—a petty entrepreneur as much as a worker. He neither thoroughly understood the factory system nor deeply questioned capitalism (in that respect he resembled the nonresistants, whose anarchism rarely threatened private ownership of property). Burritt's economic analysis of war had more passion than depth and he remained respectful of governments and of the men who ran them. During his last decade he devoted much of his failing strength to international arbitration, an eminently distinguished cause by that time, and to religion. Statesmen listened to him courteously, prestigious institutions such as Yale honored him, and war-making continued.

Despite Burritt's hard work, pacifism waned in the 1850s. It had never made headway in the South and had, from 1830 on, been closely tied to abolitionism. Whatever else peace advocates disagreed on, they uniformly considered slavery an unjust use of force, in the same category as war. Southern actions after 1848 made it increasingly difficult for them to believe slaveholders would accept peaceful overtures. Many pacifists also began to wonder if it was fair to ask slaves to turn the other cheek after all the wrongs inflicted upon them. Even Christian anarchists reconsidered their objections to coercion. Garrison and Henry C. Wright, leaders of the nonresistants, began to emphasize the difference between their ideal, in which force had no place, and the corrupt reality of American society, where it was a fact of life. That distinction allowed Garrison and Wright to condemn coercion in the abstract and still—judging by the standards of a violent society—to root for the best side to win, no matter what weapons it used. Slavery simply was so disturbing to most pacifists that, if given the choice, they cared more for its abolition than for accomplishing it without bloodshed.

By 1860 few were as firm in their principles as they had been in the 1830s. A year or two later, after the Civil War had begun, it was a rare peace man or woman who was not cheering the Union Army on. The American Peace Society did its part by declaring in 1861 that the war was not a war, but rather a rebellion; therefore, by its reasoning, the Lincoln administration was entirely correct in trying to crush the Confederacy. (That stand did not increase respect for the society.) Slightly earlier, Garrison admitted to a friend that his "sympathies and wishes are with the government, because it is entirely in the right, and acting strictly in self-defence and for self-preservation." He added, not completely convincingly, "This I can say, without any compromise of my peace-principles." He regarded the war as God's just judgment upon a nation that had lived by the sword and he could not conceal his pleasure that slavery was dying, although by the wrong means.

A minority of pacifists kept the faith. Burritt had hoped, in the late 1850s, to avert war by convincing the North and the South to accept a plan under which masters would be paid as their slaves were freed. Bitter at the unwillingness of all sides to consider his scheme, he remained certain to the end that the Civil War was both wrong and unnecessary. Only Adin Ballou and a handful of other colleagues agreed.

Burritt's isolation was not completely surprising. In some respects he was an unusual figure among antebellum reformers. His dream of brotherhood and his desires for a society based on choice, not coercion, were commonplace. But he was atypical because of his artisan-class origins and, especially, for the tenacity with which he clung to his ideal. Despite their absolutist and uncompromising rhetoric in the 1830s and 1840s, many of his fellow reformers showed a great capacity for choosing lesser evils in the 1850s and 1860s.

There was a common conviction in antislavery, feminism, and pacifism (especially in nonresistance). All expressed a belief that the world should be ruled by God's law, not force, and that people could act morally of their own free will. This was both a millennial dream and a response to a vexing question in Jacksonian America. How could men and women be made to behave properly in a mobile, heterogeneous society where church and state had little hold? The answer, for abolitionists, pacifists, woman's rights advocates, and some other reformers, was to do away with external restraints and to trust moral people with freedom.

Different answers were possible, however, and there was always a tension, sometimes within individual reformers, sometimes between them. On the one side were voluntarism and anarchistic impulses of the sort appearing in nonresistance and, to a lesser degree, in antislavery and woman's rights. On the other side, reformers wanted to be certain that people would not sin, even if it took coercion, that ungodly instrument, to deliver them from evil.

6. Strong Drink

Historians, with some exceptions, treat abolitionists with a respect they seldom received in their own times. The temperance* movement, by contrast, has dropped into disrepute. It has suffered from its crabby, joy-denying nature, which runs counter to the latter-day American sensibility, and whatever popular goodwill it once had, it lost after Prohibition in the 1920s. Its image is fixed forever in a famous photograph of Carry Nation, steely-eyed, grimly holding the hatchet with which she smashed late-nineteenth-century saloons.

Yet the crusade against alcohol was extremely significant, both for its practical consequences and for its effect on reform tactics. In the 1850s, when slavery overshadowed every other issue on the national scene, the temperance crusade became a major force in state and local politics and achieved remarkable, if temporary, legislative triumphs. In terms of longevity and membership alone, the crusade against alcohol far surpassed abolitionism. It has continued to the present day and, in the antebellum years at least, attracted the largest, most diverse collection of supporters of any reform. They ranged from shy, pious churchwomen to militant feminists, from

---

* I am using "temperance" in the conventional, but misleading way. It is a catchall term—the lowest common denominator for the crusade against alcohol. Some people believed in temperate use of alcohol, others were for total abstinence, and some were for prohibiting its manufacture and sale. For the sake of convenience, I—and most historians—lump them all together under the label "temperance."

freethinkers to fundamentalists, from the high and mighty to the lowly and degraded. It was one of the few things that William Lloyd Garrison, the abolitionist, and Robert Barnwell Rhett, a Southerner and a defender of slavery, could agree upon.

William Cobbett, an Englishman who closely observed drinking habits in the United States and Britain, lamented in 1819 that "Americans preserve their gravity and quietness and good-humour even in their drink." He believed "it were far better for them to be as noisy and quarrelsome as the English drunkards; for then the odiousness of the vice would be more visible, and the vice itself might become less frequent." He may or may not have been correct in his comparison, but he was on to something true. Drunkenness is partly what people make it. Even in such closely related societies as America and England, human beings differ in how they act when drunk, in what groups commonly get intoxicated, and in where, when, and why they do it. Equally important, cultures, classes, and generations vary in how they define drunkenness and in what moral judgments they pass upon it.

At the time Cobbett was writing, alcohol was a perfectly acceptable part of life in the United States. "You cannot go into hardly any man's house," he lamented, "without being asked to drink wine, or spirits, even *in the morning*." Men put down beer or harder beverages to fortify themselves for work, to be sociable, or out of habit. Rum was a staple of New England trade and farmers in the West converted their grain to whiskey, a less bulky commodity to transport to market and a convenient medium of barter in a currency-poor region. There are stories of frontier clergymen being paid with jugs of the local product and even New England ministers, the most priggish in the land, were not opposed to taking a drop or two. Alcohol was everywhere; whether it was used for commerce or conviviality, few people were much disturbed by it. That, however, was beginning to change. Before Cobbett put his critical words to paper, some Americans had come to think of drinking as a new, extremely serious problem.

There had been scattered protests against alcohol in the late eighteenth century, most of them coming from within religious groups such as the Quakers and, especially, the Methodists, who after 1780 were often among the more strident opponents of hard liquor. But the most distinguished and persistent early temperance advocate was neither a clergyman nor a Methodist. He was a physician, Dr. Benjamin Rush, signer of the Declaration of Independence and a major figure in the histories of medicine and reform alike. In 1784 he published *An Inquiry into the Effects of Spirituous Liquors on the Human Body and Mind.* Rush accepted the notion that beer, cider, and wine were good for health and well-being, but he put his prestige behind the argument that distilled beverages led straight to physical, mental, and moral destruction. Rush's *Inquiry* was widely distributed (by himself and others) and it continued to be quoted, reprinted, and plagiarized into the middle of the nineteenth century. Rush did generate sentiment against liquor, both by his writings and through personal appeals to influential people; but the process of forming anti-alcohoLorganizations was slow.

The first seems to have come in Saratoga County, New York, in 1808, when a doctor and a clergyman persuaded over forty of their neighbors to create the Temperance Society of Moreau and Northumberland. Members obliged themselves to forswear use of wine and distilled spirits, "except by advice of a physician, or in case of actual disease." That loophole may have been an act of deference toward the doctor, but it was consistent with Rush's teachings and with temperance activity for the next generation. Up to the late 1820s most reformers would oppose hard liquor while believing that beer and, usually, wine had medicinal value. Some would not even go that far, merely criticizing intoxication, not temperate drinking. The leading lights of one local society reportedly were so relaxed about things that they met in a tavern and drank a toast to their own moderation.

The Moreau and Northumberland society quickly inspired an imitator in nearby Greenfield, New York, but for half a decade little organizational work was done. The cause was carried largely by church groups and individuals, some of them destined to become important later: a young clergyman named Lyman Beecher began to speak out against liquor, and by 1812 the General Assembly of the Presbyterian Church had gone on record against drunkenness, appointing a committee to see what could be done about it. There were similar rumblings from Congregationalists and Methodists.

Finally, in 1813, the year of Rush's death and three decades after his *Inquiry*, two promising organizations were begun with the idea of helping to stamp out intoxication. They were the Massachusetts Society for the Suppression of Intemperance and the Connecticut Society for the Reformation of Morals. Their founders were distinguished clergy and laymen, most of them Federalists. Neither organization bound its members to do much more than agree to lead godly lives, and both engaged only in mild and dignified activities. Cautious though their approach was, it led to the creation of auxiliaries in Massachusetts and Connecticut and it encouraged people elsewhere to form similar groups. For temperance to grow, however, it would have to loosen its association with New England Federalism, already a political dinosaur, shed some of its elitism, and generally become more passionate in seeking a constituency.

Those conditions began to be met in the mid-1820s. Federalism did its part by dying out. Lyman Beecher helped supply the other ingredients, even though he shared many of the narrow prejudices of the other early leaders of temperance. (He hated Unitarianism and described Jefferson's followers as "Sabbath-breakers, rum-sellers, tippling folk, infidels, and ruff-scruff generally.") Whatever support his views cost the movement among political and theological liberals, he made up for with his ability to stir evangelical Protestants. In the fall of 1825 Beecher preached six thunderous sermons on temperance; these were published the following year and had a tremendous influence, both at the time and over the decades.

What Beecher said was not entirely novel, but he said it well and gave a badly needed sharpness to the debate. Moderate drinking, approved by some temperance writers, was anathema to Beecher. According to him, to take any amount was to be intemperate, whether or not it resulted in drunkenness. Having cut away any happy middle ground, Beecher went on to envision a glorious day when there would come "banishment of ardent spirits from the list of lawful articles of commerce"—an omen of the political turn temperance would take in the next generation. Beecher's goal in 1825, nonetheless, was more immediate. He demanded a new, vigorous attack on alcohol to be carried across the land by voluntary associations.

There were, as Beecher knew, many temperance societies at the time he gave his sermons. What he had in mind was increasing the number of them and fashioning a national organization to provide central direction, sponsor publications and speakers, and supervise creation of auxiliaries. Something of an answer to Beecher's call came in February 1826 in the form of the American Society for the Promotion of Temperance (or American Temperance Society). Those who joined it repudiated moderation in favor of abstinence from hard liquor—Beecher's position.

Beecher himself was not present to sign the constitution of the American Temperance Society, but of the sixteen who did, several were confederates of his in various Protestant religious and charitable enterprises. This close connection with the evangelical "benevolent empire" helped the society greatly. Its first secretary, Reverend Justin Edwards, adopted techniques made familiar by the American Bible Society and related organizations. He and the executive committee, moreover, were able to draw upon the churches and laymen who backed other Protestant crusades. The benefits of annexing temperance to the benevolent empire were apparent in the statistics. By 1834 there were estimates that 5,000 state and local societies were promoting the cause, that millions of pieces of propaganda were in circulation, and that a million members had taken some sort of pledge to avoid alcohol.

Even allowing for exaggeration, the figures are impressive. They also are deceptive. Many local groups originated independently of the national society and a majority of them stayed unaffiliated with it. The American Temperance Society acted as a valuable clearinghouse for information, but it could not provide firm direction for the movement. Supporters of the cause in different places continued to interpret their obligations differently and to keep their vows with greater or lesser faithfulness.

In part to bring about a degree of uniformity, the society's executive committee called for a convention to convene in Philadelphia in 1833. The gathering was attended by delegates from throughout the country and they put together a more genuinely national organization, the United States Temperance Union (American Temperance Union after 1836). Its first president was a wealthy New Yorker, Stephen Van Rensselaer, whose popularity at the meeting was undoubtedly increased by his willingness to pay for publication of 100,000 copies of the proceedings. Like Van Rensselaer, the officers of the Union and of its state auxiliaries were men with money and prestige, many of them successful in business and (a few) in politics.

By the mid-1830s prospects looked bright. There was still opposition, even within the churches, but much of the weaponry of evangelical Protestantism was in the service of the cause. Temperance had many of the high and mighty behind it and the message seemed to be filtering down to honest workingmen, groups of whom began taking the pledge—like conservatives, they had begun to see drinking as a cause of poverty. There was a national organization, many newspapers, no shortage of pamphlets, and an abundance of grass-roots enthusiasm.

Arguments in favor of temperance had likewise come to maturity. Several lines of attack had developed by the 1830s and, although the supporting evidence and the emphasis would shift, these would last throughout the century with only slight alterations. One sort of appeal was personal and frightening. "The Holy Spirit," according to a circular, "will not visit, much less dwell with him who is under the polluting, debasing effects of intoxicating drink." Intemperance, in short, led to hell. In a more secular vein, temperance writers pictured alcohol as a form of tyranny, resembling slavery in depriving people of their ability to act as morally responsible creatures. Giving in to it meant destruction of one's autonomy.

If damnation and loss of self-control were not terrifying enough, there were other themes in temperance propaganda. Facts and figures demonstrated that alcohol produced insanity, poverty, and crime. It devastated families, thus causing suffering, robbing society of a crucial institution, and sending innocent women and children out into the cruel world. Get rid of liquor and everyone would gain, from the ex-drunkard to the hard-working taxpayer. As a flourish, temperance writers and orators could always play upon a powerful blend of patriotism and fear. They conjured visions of rum-soaked debtors using their votes to take charge of the country (a credible view, given the realities of Jacksonian electioneering). Reverend Herman Humphrey warned in 1828 that "if the emblems of liberty are ever to be torn from our banner—if her statues are to be hurled from their pedestals—if the car of a despot is to be driven over our suppliant bodies, it will be by aid of strong drink."

Like much temperance rhetoric, those words now sound exaggerated to the point of absurdity. But they were uttered seriously and in the spirit of reform. Temperance advocates (including Abraham Lincoln in the 1840s) claimed that drunkenness was a worse national evil than slavery and that doing away with alcohol would uplift America, Americans, and the world. Although they were often among the more conservative antebellum reformers on social matters, anti-alcohol crusaders were not blue-nosed reactionaries, as twentieth-century critics made them seem. They had a sense of progress and of the nation's potential. As they saw it, prosperity, godliness, and political freedom were to be the fruits of sobriety. Poverty, damnation, and tyranny were the consequences of intemperance.

Between 1835 and 1840 the temperance movement became a victim of its logic, which led to ever more extreme assaults on alcohol. Beecher and the American Temperance Society worked to destroy the notion that moderate drinking was tolerable. They were not entirely successful, although the pledge after 1825 usually did involve agreeing to abstain from "ardent spirits." By implication that exempted wine and beer. Yet the sin was supposed to be in the alcohol, not in distilling, and one could get as drunk on beer as on whiskey. By 1836 a large faction, which included Beecher and Justin Edwards, pressed the American Temperance Union to adopt a "teetotal" pledge, binding signers to abstain from any alcohol. That view prevailed, but it cost the Union some auxiliaries and it continued to meet resistance from people who believed that wine and beer were healthful and useful in weaning tipplers from harder drink. The teetotal position had in its favor the moral purity, or "ultraism," many antebellum reformers insisted upon; yet it raised further problems. What about communion wine? Was it sinful? Some people thought so. That proposition caused dismay among evangelicals, who found their reading of the Bible pitted against the consistency of their reform principles.

Not that teetotalism exhausted the ability of temperance people to quarrel. Like abolitionists, they disagreed among themselves on the role of women in the movement. Unlike abolitionists they usually resolved their differences by not pressing the issue: some societies separated the sexes, others included them both. More divisive was the question whether temperance meant going beyond simply trying to convert individuals. In his sermons of 1825 Beecher had raised the possibility of using legislation to stop the making and selling of liquor. The matter was openly debated in the Philadelphia convention of 1833 and it would continue to be for years afterward.

Battles over such questions alienated temperance advocates from each other and split organizations. The most socially prominent leaders had begun to drift away in reaction against teetotalism, and there was a general decline in membership by 1836. The movement was in the doldrums by the time the financial panic of 1837 cut further into its resources. Within three years temperance would be suddenly revived, but changed. The new inspiration did not come from New England or the saintly folk of evangelical reform.

The setting was Chase's Tavern in Baltimore and the unlikely heroes of the piece were six friends, later to describe themselves as ex-drunkards. Their story was the stuff of which legends are made. They met on the night of April 2, 1840, with anything but sobriety on their minds. Tavern humor being what it was, they delegated a "committee" to attend a nearby temperance lecture, presumably so they might know their enemy. The committee report, duly delivered, was unexpectedly persuasive. The six swore off intoxicants and decided to form an organization, called the Washington Temperance Society in honor of the first President (a drinker but a virtuous man nonetheless). By Christmas there were a thousand Washingtonians in Baltimore and before a year had passed the society established a beachhead in New York City. At the end of three years supporters were claiming—with more enthusiasm than accuracy—pledges from 600,000 intemperate men, 100,000 of them formerly habitual drunkards.

Existing temperance organizations first greeted the Washingtonians as allies, but tensions soon appeared and were based on more than just competition for members. Several things separated the new phase of the movement, begun at Chase's Tavern, from the old one. The first anti-alcohol societies had been dominated by clergy and by wealthy evangelical laymen. The Washingtonians did have help from ministers, and many of their methods were derived from revivalism, but their leaders were neither clergy nor men of social prominence. Of their two greatest lecturers, one had been a hatter and the other a bookbinder and minstrel. Such men were distinctly uninterested in theological niceties; occasionally they were even hostile to the formal trappings of religion, much to the disgust of American Temperance Union officials.

An equally crucial difference between Washingtonians and their predecessors had to do with the people they tried to reach. Older temperance societies had not been eager to deal with drunkards. The Massachusetts Society for the Suppression of Intemperance was candid about its position. "The design of this institution," it admitted in 1814, "is . . . not so much to wrest the fatal cup from those who are already brutalized and ruined, as to keep sober those who are sober." In contrast, the Washington Society had as its chief goal getting tipplers to pledge total abstinence. Not every member was an ex-alcoholic, but many were, and almost all were workingmen or from the bottom ranks of society.

Besides opening membership and leadership to drunks and men of low status, the Washingtonians also helped increase participation by women and children. Some women had been involved in earlier temperance activity, and in 1836 Reverend Thomas Hunt began organizing Sunday-school youth into a Cold Water Army. These efforts were almost tepid compared to those of the Washingtonians. They placed special emphasis on alcohol as a destroyer of families and exhorted females and juveniles to lend the cause a hand, lest they be left helpless by a drunkard. The invitation may have been maudlin, but the response was stirring.

Temperance would never be the same after the Washingtonians. Up to 1840 anti-alcohol crusaders had used a fair number of devices, ranging from the usual sermons and pamphlets to such institutions as temperance hotels for the sober-minded traveler. Leaders of organizations like the American Temperance Union, nevertheless, had primarily worked through religious groups, engaged in fairly rational discourse, corresponded with like-minded people elsewhere in the United States and Britain, and held meetings which, despite sharp debates, were reasonably staid. The Washingtonians adopted many of the same instruments of reform—they also gave lectures, published newspapers, and had conventions. There the resemblance ended. Like their clientele, the Washingtonians' behavior and tactics were not genteel.

Using wit, pathos, and the language of common folk, their orators moved audiences to tears, laughter, and signing the pledge. More unusual, they gave accounts of their own careers as drunkards and demanded similar confessions from those who attended their gatherings, an emotionally charged practice older temperance reformers found vulgar. The Washingtonians also sponsored picnics, parades, and fairs, techniques they learned from political parties and, probably, from abolitionists. They put together grand spectacles like a giant day-long parade in Boston in 1844, which was addressed by the governor of the state, a temperance man. It was an easy step to move from that sort of public festivity to popular entertainment, a transformation best represented in the work of Timothy Shay Arthur. Already a believer in temperance by 1840, Arthur was inspired by the Washingtonians to begin writing fiction for the cause. He was not the first or the last to do so, but his output was formidable and easily translated into stage productions. His enduring reputation rests upon the anti-alcohol equivalent of *Uncle Tom's Cabin*, *Ten Nights in a Bar-Room* (1853), a novel, a widely produced melodrama, and, for a time in the mid-twentieth century, a staple of drama groups aiming at quaintness. In the 1840s, however, it was the final indignity to the stuffier older leaders when temperance became theater.

The Washingtonian movement was long past its prime when Joe Morgan, the fictitious hero of *Ten Nights*, took the pledge. The Washingtonians could not control their auxiliaries—the typical fate of national organizations in the antebellum period. Growth was as haphazard as it was swift and there was not enough central direction to sustain local societies. Despite their flair for parades and picnics, the Washingtonians had trouble figuring out what to do once the pledge was taken, the confession made, and the first enthusiasm gone. People lost interest or went into newer, more exciting organizations. The Washingtonians also suffered from putting too much faith in men who were better at swearing off alcohol than at staying off. One lecturer was lost for nearly a week in New York City, only to be found sobering up in a bawdy house. Such episodes, combined with institutional weakness, personality conflicts, and disagreements over issues, led to the quick decline of the Washingtonians. Within a few years most of their organizations were dead.

Their influence lingered. The American Temperance Union and other, older organizations took on some of the Washingtonians' fervor, although they found the public confession and the use of popular entertainment hard to swallow. Thanks to the Washingtonians, the drunkard continued to get more attention than he had in the past and efforts were made to broaden the movement still further, even to extend it to Catholics, the largest single group relatively unaffected. So long as evangelicals dominated temperance there had been no real chance for cooperation with what anti-liquor elements existed among Catholics. The Washingtonians, on the other hand, were not especially concerned about religion and in their public festivities they embraced organizations like the St. Mary's Mutual Benevolent Total Abstinence Society, a Catholic participant in the Boston parade of 1844. The most ardent recruiting of Catholics would come later, in a lecture tour by Father Theobald Mathew, an Irish priest, in 1849; but the Washingtonians had helped prepare the way by separating temperance from Protestant sectarianism.

The Washingtonians were valuable to the cause in their failure as well as for their innovations. Several societies begun after 1840 sought to remedy weaknesses obvious in the Washingtonian movement. The majority were similarly non-sectarian, committed to total abstinence, and aimed at common people, but they had the sturdy institutional structure the Washingtonians lacked. The Sons of Temperance, begun in 1843, was the most important of these organizations, although there were others of consequence. With an elaborate hierarchy and centralized control, the Sons recruited a quarter of a million dues-paying brethren by 1850. They exercised discipline over those who took their pledge, adopted the air of a secret fraternal order, and offered important forms of mutual assistance—all things that secured the loyalty of members to a degree unapproached by the Washingtonians.

The magnetism of secular groups like the Washingtonians and the Sons does not mean that religious campaigns against alcohol ended in the 1840s. The evangelical tradition persisted in the American Temperance Union, in churches, and in later organizations like the Woman's Christian Temperance Union (1874). They, too, learned from the Washingtonians, particularly from their tactics, some of which, like the public confession, fit well with the modes of revivalism popular among lower-middle-class folk. Even use of the performing arts, begun in the Washingtonian phase of the movement, had its impact on later evangelical temperance crusaders. At the century's end Carry Nation's assaults on Kansas saloons were as theatrical as anything written by Timothy Shay Arthur. (She, along with her bar-smashing hatchet, ended her days as sideshow attractions at county fairs.)

There was one important new tactic in the 1840s that the Washingtonians neither initiated nor accepted with enthusiasm. It was political action. When reformers divided over whether or not to press for temperance legislation, the Washingtonians were often among those most opposed. In that, they were uncharacteristically backward.

Lyman Beecher, in 1825, had spoken of banning the sale of distilled spirits and there were other early indications that political involvement might be on the horizon. In 1833 a group of lawmakers and public officials formed the Congressional Temperance Society. Their avowed purpose was not to legislate alcohol out of existence but rather to provide a sterling moral example, something politicians rarely did. Yet the very existence of the society was a sign that an influential anti-alcohol faction might possibly be put together in Congress. The first president of the society, moreover, had already used his political position as Secretary of War to accomplish a temperance objective, that of removing liquor from the Army's rations. In 1833 the political issue also surfaced within the convention that created the American Temperance Union. A controversial resolution was introduced by Gerrit Smith, an abolitionist later involved in the Liberty Party. It declared that "the traffic in ardent spirits" was *"morally wrong"* and that "the inhabitants of cities, towns, and other local communities, should be permitted by law to prohibit the said traffic within their respective jurisdictions." This was a direct statement of the prohibitionist position that would come to characterize the movement by the end of the nineteenth century. The resolution passed.

In the 1830s and 1840s, however, many temperance people had their doubts about prohibition. Some feared casting aspersions on liquor dealers, a few of whom they thought to be pious, if misguided. There was also a feeling, common to many reformers, that politics was degraded and disgusting to moral men. It seemed as if electioneering required appealing to base instincts and putting expediency above virtue. Political action, furthermore, went against the evangelical belief that true goodness could only flow from a converted heart. People had to *want* to behave properly, and that came from enlightenment, not force. It took soul-searching, and a bit of evasion, for many temperance advocates to accept legislation as a legitimate means of reform.

Still, the prohibitionists had arguments in their favor. The liquor trade was licensed by the government and people were under no obligation to let their government license sin. Besides, most reformers agreed that if the public was godly, decent laws would follow as a matter of course. Prohibitionists felt that the process could be speeded up if temperance men engaged in political action (which would serve as a form of propaganda) and if alcohol, which corrupted many voters, were gotten out of the picture. A final argument —although few cared to put it so bluntly—was that prohibition promised to be successful.

Beginning in the 1830s temperance voters agreed not to cast ballots for heavy drinkers, breaking the chains of party loyalty if need be. They also sought, and sometimes got, local-option legislation, which gave communities the power to stop the traffic in liquor within their jurisdictions. The first statewide victory for temperance forces came in 1838, with a Massachusetts law banning the sale of distilled spirits in amounts of less than fifteen gallons, an act which removed hard beverages from taverns and kept them away from poor people, who could not afford such a quantity. The statute inspired civil disobedience from "rum-sellers" and much agitation for and against, during which many temperance people who had opposed political action fell into line behind the law. It was repealed in 1840 and Massachusetts prohibitionists shifted their attention to the towns, persuading about a hundred of them to go dry by 1845. In 1839 Mississippi passed a law like Massachusetts', although more modest. It forbade the sale of less than a gallon of liquor. After intensive lobbying on both sides, New York voters presented prohibitionists with a massive victory in 1846 and a defeat the following year. The Supreme Court gave the movement a boost in 1846 by deciding in favor of the right of states to deny licenses to sell distilled spirits. Reformers were not always so lucky—a disastrous political campaign set the cause in Georgia back for almost a generation—but temperance battles at the ballot box and in the courts were becoming fierce by the mid-1840s. And by that time Maine had begun to lead the nation.

Much of what happened in Maine was due to two circumstances. The first was a strong antislavery movement. Abolitionists joined the fray and their organizational and propaganda skills were a significant addition to temperance firepower in Maine. Prohibitionists had a second advantage in Neal Dow, a wealthy merchant and an ex-Quaker. Born in 1804, he had been converted to temperance in 1827 after exposure to Beecher and to Justin Edwards of the old American Temperance Society. By the early 1830s Dow was a total-abstinence man and before the decade was out he had taken his principles into politics, in part because he found them there already.

At about the time Massachusetts was experimenting with its fifteen-gallon law, Maine's legislature considered, then tabled, similar restrictive legislation. Meanwhile, Dow began to try to move public opinion in Portland, his home town. He and a coalition of groups, the Washingtonians among them, won in 1842, when the Portland electorate voted by an almost two-to-one margin to stop the sale of alcohol in the city. The ban was evaded and temperance men, led by Dow, agitated for statewide, and presumably more effective, legislation. In 1846 they got almost what they wanted—a law forbidding the sale of intoxicating beverages in less than twenty-eight-gallon lots. Enforcement, however, was the responsibility of town selectmen, who often looked the other way at infractions. Partly to remedy the situation, Dow ran for mayor of Portland; in 1851 he won. His office magnified his influence and within a few months Dow and his supporters had prodded the legislature into passing the so-called Maine Law of 1851. It prohibited the sale and manufacture of intoxicating beverages within the state.

Dow went on to have a long career in public life, although little of it in office. He was a tireless campaigner for prohibition in other states, as well as in Maine; he was a nativist, an abolitionist, a Republican, and, in the Civil War, the colonel of a regiment as sober as he could make it. His handiwork, the Maine Law, had as much impact as he did. After its passage the American Temperance Union swung around to endorse prohibition. Within four years, thirteen states had their own versions of it and there were narrow defeats in others. By 1855 all of New England was dry, as was New York and large parts of the Midwest. Those triumphs were swift and encouraging to prohibitionists, but temperance had achieved quieter, perhaps more impressive, objectives well before Maine saw the light. Per capita consumption of alcohol declined sharply between 1830 and 1850; and large parts of several states were dry before 1851, the result of local-option laws. Statewide prohibition legislation in the 1850s, moreover, was usually not well enough drafted (or defended) to survive court challenges. By the Civil War, Maine Laws had virtually disappeared outside New England, gone but—as it turned out—not forgotten.

Temperance politicking in the 1840s and 1850s, whether it was for prohibition or something else, had a testy but reciprocal relationship with the electioneering style of the day. On the one hand, temperance was a protest against the demagoguery of Jacksonian office seekers. It reeked with contempt for the besotted rabble and those (usually Democrats) who got their votes by praising "the people," attacking the "aristocracy," and ignoring moral issues. On the other hand, temperance campaigners learned lessons from such politicians and ended up teaching them a few. Rather than just reviling the masses for not electing their betters—the self-destructive course of the Federalists in the early 1800s—anti-alcohol men worked hard to get enough votes to make a majority. They perfected their own brand of demagoguery, with lurid propaganda against drink and against "conspiracies" on the part of "rum-sellers." Realizing the effectiveness of public spectacles, they followed the Washingtonians in imitating the parades and picnics of conventional party politics. They held such things as cold-water Fourth of July celebrations to keep their supporters happy and away from the standard patriotic gatherings, with their deadly combination of oratory and alcohol. The considerable political successes of temperance in the 1850s demonstrated that appealing to moral prejudices could be as effective as democratic bombast had been for the Jacksonians.

From the antebellum period on, temperance was to play a great role in American politics. In numerous local elections throughout the nineteenth and early twentieth centuries alcohol mattered more than all the national issues of the day. At times it fractured parties; at other times it formed a sharp division between them, as when wet Democrats ran against dry Republicans. In most instances temperance mingled with religion and ethnicity, and it easily fused with other political crusades—with antimasonry, nativism, antislavery, the Republican Party, and even woman's rights. Yet the crusade against alcohol had a vitality of its own, separate from the fortunes of any party or any other cause, which is partly why it stayed alive so long in American politics.

In itself the hardiness of temperance is remarkable, but the most important thing for the history of reform is that it became political at all. More than antislavery, it convinced reformers not to rely exclusively upon moral suasion. The fifteen-gallon and Maine laws were proof that vices might be legislated away more easily than sinners could be converted.

Besides venturing into politics, temperance made its way across the Mason-Dixon line. Although strongest in the usual havens for reform—New England, New York, and the Midwest—it was among the least sectional of the antebellum crusades. That is not accurately reflected in statistics from the 1830s, which underestimate the appeal of the cause in the South. Many Southerners were disgusted by the antislavery activities of American Temperance Union leaders like Arthur Tappan and Gerrit Smith; they often pursued an independent course or else responded more enthusiastically to the organizations created in the 1840s, particularly the Washingtonians and the Sons of Temperance. In rural as well as urban areas throughout the South, temperance organizations of one sort or another popped up, inspired by a local clergyman, a traveling lecturer, or a few neighborhood enthusiasts.

Temperance also made considerable headway in the West. In 1861 a woman in Eugene, Oregon, assured an absent friend that the local society "is prospering finely since you left. Nearly all the drunkards in town have joined." (She added, however, that "most of them are now about as temperate as before they signed the pledge.") Even California, in the rowdiest period in its history, had a strong anti-alcohol movement. A visitor to San Francisco in 1853 could avoid the city's fleshpots by staying at Hillman's Temperance House, with sixty rooms for lodgers and able to serve two hundred teetotaling diners. At the same time, the Sons of Temperance claimed thirty chapters in the state, including an Oriental Division. In part because of politicking by the Sons, California had a vote on a "Maine Law" of its own in 1855. Although opinion ran against it by about a five-to-four margin, the gold-mining districts turned out narrowly in favor of the measure. That is impressive because of the rough-and-ready reputation of the Mother Lode country and because women, often the mainstay of temperance agitation, were outnumbered by men ten or twelve to one in the area. Thanks to the Sons, the Methodists, and a desire for law, order, and respectability, over 11,000 men in the mining counties went on record in favor of banishing alcoholic beverages.

The most intriguing question is what made temperance so attractive to such a diverse collection of people—men and women, Northerners, Southerners, and Westerners, urban and rural, rich and poor? The easy answer (and there is much to it) is that America had a drinking problem. Reliable figures are difficult to come by, but it seems as if per capita consumption of alcohol was higher around 1810 than in the supposedly hard-drinking 1970s. One authority aptly describes the estimates for the early nineteenth century as "staggering." (By 1850 the use of alcohol declined to a rate perhaps lower than present-day consumption, testimony to the effectiveness of reform.) Yet temperance was more than a response to rampant intoxication. The real rise in drunkenness must have gone back into the last half of the eighteenth century, when Americans improved their ability to make rum and whiskey. That was more than a generation before the first anti-alcohol society was formed. Much the same thing happened in England, where gin put its stamp upon the working classes long before temperance organizations materialized.

It took social and cultural pressures, combined with that prior increase in intoxication, to make some Americans see alcohol as a problem and temperance as a solution. For the gentlemen and clergy who were prominent in the 1820s and 1830s, the reform was a badge of their own superior virtue and of their disapproval of the antics of poor people, set loose from traditional moral controls by economic and religious changes. If temperance took hold among the masses it would reduce the nastiness of life in the burgeoning cities, elevate the tone of politics, and help preserve the old moral order, which seemed to be rapidly vanishing. If temperance did not take hold, sobriety would be a measure of the social distance between decent folk and others. Changes in the nature of work, moreover, made it desirable that the labor force have the discipline to stay in factories for long hours rather than pursue the traditional course of artisans, who had enjoyed greater independence, conviviality, and tippling. Those calculations swayed some early temperance advocates, as did a genuine hope for human progress, but the majority of men and women who entered the movement in the late 1830s and 1840s were neither wealthy nor distinguished and they clearly had different expectations.

Men with a taste for liquor had the most straightforward reasons for joining, particularly after 1840, when the Washingtonians began to seek them out. Temperance provided self-discipline, moral support, and a way of gaining control over a destructive impulse. Yet ex-drunkards never were a majority in the movement and certainly there were few of them among the thousands of women attracted to the crusade. More likely, temperance provided them with unique opportunities. It was far less threatening to the social order than antislavery, woman's rights, and most other antebellum reforms. If anything, it promised to defend the status quo against the forces of dissipation. Even though it attracted militant feminists, its respectability made it equally acceptable to timid or conservative women who feared or rejected radical agitation but who nevertheless wanted a place for themselves in public life. Temperance could also be a way to reproach males. Anti-alcohol propaganda, like the sentimental fiction American females read and wrote, consisted of a catalogue of awful sufferings men inflicted upon their loved ones. It was almost always the father (or son, or brother) who brought grief to his wife (or mother, or sister) and his innocent children. If he was redeemed, it was often through the agency of a woman (or child, or both) whose natural goodness exorcised the demon rum. These melodramas had a ring of truth—American men were capable of swinish behavior—but such stories also sound like acts of revenge by women against the male world that glorified them, confined them to the home, and failed to live by its own preachings.

That simply makes more curious the matter of what drove thousands of reasonably sober men to sign the pledge after 1840. The evidence is fragmentary, but it gives some hints in their ages, which appear to have clustered in the early twenties, and in their occupations. Many belonged on the fringes of respectability, working in the lesser professions (including teaching), as petty entrepreneurs, or as artisans in skilled trades such as carpentry. These were men making their way in the world (upward, they hoped). An image of propriety could be very important in increasing their prospects. If that were not a consideration, self-control, which temperance required, was a valuable virtue for people whose success in an expanding economy depended on thrift and hard work. As we shall see, there were other crusades—notably health reform—offering much the same thing to youth wandering through the opportunities and temptations of antebellum America.

There were still more reasons for joining temperance societies. Beginning in the late 1830s, they provided important services. The Sons of Temperance were especially strong in that respect, having as one of their primary objectives "mutual assistance in cases of sickness." In fact, they offered life, as well as health, insurance, and the San Francisco branch, perhaps others, acted as an employment agency, posting the names of members who needed work. Those were no mean advantages in days when the government did nothing to help the ill, destitute, and unemployed.

Temperance societies—particularly ones begun after 1840—also provided opportunities for sociability. The Sons of Temperance, with their rituals and regalia, satisfied the same impulses that sent American males into lodges like the Odd Fellows and countless similar voluntary organizations in antebellum America. Throughout the year there were various excuses for getting together—picnics, fairs, and Fourth of July celebrations. These were fine places to enjoy companionship and for decent women and men to court. (A North Carolinian described a neighborhood zealot as "a young widower" who "wanted a wife—and he spoke to show how well he could speak rather than for any immediate practical effect in advertising the cause of temperance.") Besides saving drunkards, the movement redeemed the uncertainty and loneliness of life in antebellum America, and only when it did that could it become a genuine substitute for the solace of alcohol. Like sports and popular stage shows, temperance societies became nineteenth-century alternatives to the camaraderie of the old tavern.

Despite the social and practical advantages of belonging to anti-alcohol organizations, interest waxed and waned. Members acquired families and ceased to participate actively; brethren fell from grace, some to be forgiven, to fall again. But at the core of the movement were dedicated people and they carried it through the years. They were a diverse lot: reformers who saw conquest of alcohol as an important part of some broader program; religious men and women who felt abstinence was a divine command; and those who knew from personal experience the evils of strong drink.

One of the impressive facts about temperance agitation is its survival into the twentieth century. (Of course, alcoholism remains a problem—but then so was poverty an antebellum problem, and it still is today, and yet it never had continuous, well-organized opposition.) Prohibition organizations persist and candidates run for office under their banner, without the chance of winning they had in the nineteenth century. The movement has triumphed over defeat, internal conflict, ridicule, and utter disaster. The secret of temperance's durability is probably its combination of clear focus and infinite adaptability. It has a definite demonology: alcohol and those who consume, sell, and produce it. Battling them, however, can satisfy any number of impulses. It can be a religious imperative or a solution to personal difficulties. It can be elitist or vulgar, dignified or boisterous, private or sociable. It can be a gesture of dismay at the modern world, as it was for some of the early leaders and as it often is today; or it can reflect the bourgeois virtues of discipline and self-control the modern world has called forth, as it did for middle-class and working people in the 1840s.

There is another important aspect to temperance besides its endurance. It directed attention to the physical being. In that it foreshadowed several other, less conventional reforms, and became part of a large, important process in American social thought.

7. The Body and Beyond

The human body has always been a problem for Christians. They have been torn between glorifying it as God's handiwork and mistrusting it for getting in the way of spiritual life. At first glance, it seems that most antebellum reformers held the latter view. While their contemporary Walt Whitman praised "the body electric" in memorable poetry, they were busy depicting mankind's physical state at its most disgusting. Temperance propagandists described the excesses of the flesh with disapproval, as did anti-prostitution crusaders and others.

Despite a streak of prudishness, antebellum reformers seldom rejected the body in favor of the spirit. The point to temperance propaganda, after all, was not that humankind's physical nature ought to be despised but rather that men and women had to control it in order to be virtuous. In similar fashion, most antebellum reformers blurred the old distinction between body and soul and made each dependent on the other. Only on the periphery of reform or in such sentimental works as *Uncle Tom's Cabin* was there much trace of the romantic notion that so long as the spirit is free it makes no difference whether the individual is in chains. More often, reformers assumed that a person could not behave in a morally responsible fashion unless his or her body was unfettered and uncorrupted.

That assumption marked a half step away from the religious traditions that shaped antebellum reform and toward the biological and

145

materialistic modes of thought that dominated late-nineteenth-century social criticism. This was a transition from theological per-fectionism, like that preached by Charles G. Finney in the 1820s, to physical perfectionism, a belief that salvation was to be found in improvement of the body or of the species. By the early twentieth century the latter view took many forms, including scientific racism. In the antebellum years, however, the most intriguing signs of that progression were not obviously racist or religious: they were in health reform, phrenology, and spiritualism.

Although different in many respects, the three—which I will label "body reforms" for want of any better term—had some things in common. Each appealed to a great variety of people, many of whom were not reformers and had no interest beyond better health, getting ahead in the world, or contacting a dead loved one. Yet each—for a few people—became a genuine reform movement, with a vision of how humanity might be perfected and with organizations, lecturers, and publications to carry the message. Perhaps more important, each attracted a considerable number of men and women who were centrally involved in such crusades as communitarianism, anti-slavery, woman's rights, and temperance. For them and for the larger world of antebellum reform, the three gave a new vocabulary for expressing concerns that ran through most other causes of the day. The primary significance of the "body reforms," in fact, lies in the part they played in translating reform rhetoric from evangelical Protestant to "scientific" and secular language.

Each of the "body reforms" was possible because in the early nineteenth century there were none of the academic and professional groups we have today to tell us what is respectable and what is not. In the 1820s, 1830s, and 1840s, for instance, it was easy for a poor New England farmer named Samuel Thompson to acquire a con-siderable following for his belief that illness was the result of "clog-ging the system." (He unclogged it with botanical preparations, especially *Lobelia inflata*, an emetic.) The American Medical Asso-ciation was not formed until 1847 and much time would pass before it was powerful enough, and state requirements strict enough, to drive laymen like Thompson from the field. The situation was the same in all branches of science and in other professions as well. Every man, so it seemed, could be his own doctor, lawyer, or political oracle.

By present-day standards the results were appalling. Quackery flourished and the worst of fools and knaves announced they had unraveled the secrets of the universe. In truth, the situation was not so bad. Physicians trained in medical schools—and, for that matter, trained lawyers—often proved as destructive of health and happiness as their amateur competitors were. Fads like the Graham diet at times actually cured people of real illnesses without doing additional damage to them, a rare thing in early-nineteenth-century medicine and not always the case today. Besides, there was a certain consistency to the antebellum period. Any nation that gave a hearing to the Graham system, phrenology, and spiritualism clearly applied its democratic principles to matters of the intellect as well as to politics.

The most famous health reformer of the antebellum period had a career shortened by illnesses. Sylvester Graham was the son of an elderly Connecticut clergyman who died when Sylvester was two years old. Poverty and a physical collapse prevented Sylvester from being ordained as a Presbyterian minister until the relatively advanced age of thirty-two. In 1830 he became a lecturer for the Pennsylvania Society for Discouraging the Use of Ardent Spirits. He was then thirty-six and had yet to give any sign of distinction. Indeed, his time in the limelight would be brief. By 1832 he discovered the cause that would make him something more than an obscure clergyman and temperance lecturer, but five years later he went into semi-retirement, emerging and then retiring again in the 1840s, for physical as well as psychological reasons. Yet, as fate would have it, he achieved a fame that eluded contemporaries who surpassed him in stamina and intellect. He had a cracker named after him.

Cholera gave Graham his opportunity for notoriety. In the spring of 1832 Americans uneasily awaited its arrival from Europe, where an epidemic had been raging since the previous year. By that time Graham had ended his connection with the Pennsylvania Society, moved to New York, and broadened his horizons. He had come to believe that alcohol was not the only substance damaging to the body, and he had begun to lecture on diet and hygiene in general. In March he announced a series of talks on cholera, promptly attracting considerable attention and plunging himself into controversy. Cholera had never before appeared in the United States and authorities were not of one mind on how to prevent or cure it. Although physicians agreed with Graham that drunkards and unclean people were most susceptible, some doctors urged Americans to eat hearty, stimulating food to build up their systems to withstand the ravages of the disease. Graham dissented. He saw irritation of the stomach as the primary cause of all illness. A person who ate properly, he claimed, should not get sick. Eating properly, however, meant a bland, plain diet of fruits, vegetables, and coarsely ground grain—no meat, spices, alcohol, coffee, or tea. The initial stage of cholera gave some credibility to Graham's idea that overstimulation or irritation of the stomach produced the disease. The sufferer first went through a period of vomiting and diarrhea, which Graham saw as the stomach's convulsive attempt to cleanse itself. Whatever the merits of Graham's system, he gained an audience, thanks to his self-promotion and to his enemies, who attacked his views in the press, thus passing them along to a public whose resistance to new medical ideas was low.

It is not clear how Graham happened to develop his theories. He did his best to confuse the issue by insisting that they were completely his own. When accused of lifting them from European medical writers he proudly declared that "it is nearly twenty years since I have read any work on intellectual and moral philosophy." Ignorance may have been his best defense, but his ideas did seem to owe something to French physiological theory, also to the work of Dr. Benjamin Rush. Some of Graham's remarks on diet and sex, moreover, sound suspiciously like folk wisdom dressed up as science. Be that as it may, Graham deserves considerable credit for elaborating and promoting concepts that were not entirely original.

Despite his emphasis on the stomach, Graham advised the public to pay attention to all aspects of hygiene, not just food. A consistent Grahamite would bathe (something Americans tended to avoid), exercise, wear loose-fitting clothing, and live in a well-ventilated house. Graham also warned against such bad habits as "indolence"; these, too, he felt could damage one's health.

And then there was sex. In 1834 Graham published his lectures on *Chastity*. It would be easy to dismiss the book as nothing more than nineteenth-century prudery, a view for which Graham provided much evidence. Although he was harshest in denouncing masturbation, he was vitriolic about sexual "excess" of any sort. He described "venereal indulgence" as sweeping over the body "with the violence of a tornado" (even among married couples). Rather than regard that as a good thing, he warned: "too frequently repeated [it] cannot fail to produce the most terrible effects." These included insanity, debility, and death. Fierce as his words were, Graham was not the only nineteenth-century American to have dire things to say about sexuality. A restrictive attitude toward intercourse and a genuine fear of masturbation emerged, at least in print, in the antebellum period. *Chastity* was just one among many similar books, and not the most repressive of them. But unlike many of the others, it was part of a general scheme of hygiene. Graham's advice to any man "troubled by concupiscence" was virtually a summary of his whole regimen. Such a person should be "more abstemious, and less stimulating and heating in his diet, and take more active exercise in the open air, and use the cold bath under proper circumstances."

Deep psychological forces may have caused Graham to link sexual indulgence and eating habits as the greatest menaces to health, but he felt the two had something very obvious in common. Both came from "weaknesses" within human beings. Graham recast original sin into biological terms: it was raging and destructive bodily appetites, which the sanctified person had to resist. The road to heaven was paved with restraint in food and sex; those who yielded to temptation were doomed. Salvation was freedom from illness and infirmity; the hellfire Graham preached for lechers and gluttons was dissolution of their bodies. The Kingdom of God depended upon abstemiousness. According to the Grahamite American Physiological Society, "the millennium can never reasonably be expected to arrive, until those laws which God has implanted in the physical nature of man are, equally with his moral laws, universally known and obeyed."

That was a curiously physical theology for a former clergyman to have developed. Although not openly in conflict with Protestantism, the message was slightly subversive. It depended upon science and physiology rather than the Bible. The millennium and the perfection it promised did not require divine revelation, church attendance, or a conversion experience. All one had to do was follow rational laws of health, easily understood by common people, without help from clergy or physicians.

Whatever Graham's program cost a person in sensual pleasures, it repaid in autonomy. Mastery of the diet meant mastery of one's self and one's destiny. Like evangelical Protestantism, temperance, and many other antebellum reforms, the Graham regimen instilled discipline and a willingness to forgo gratification in its followers, virtues that lead to survival, even success, in industrial and commercial societies. Self-controlled people who do not fritter away time or energy are not always pleasant, but they are fine employees and businessmen. They also are not likely to be overwhelmed by the confusion of city life or by religious and political turmoil—they have no compelling need to look beyond themselves for moral guidance, a considerable comfort in a day when other sources of moral authority seemed unreliable. Even in the hustle and bustle of New York City a Grahamite could prosper, be virtuous, and preserve many Protestant and rural patterns (including plain living).

The regimen may have been a psychological help for Grahamites coping with a society in flux, but it had another advantage as well. Very likely, it *was* healthy. Even though nineteenth-century Americans did not have the perils of additives and of junk food, they ate as badly as we do, and possibly worse. Wealthy and middle-class people gorged themselves on course after course of rich dishes. Poor people ate food that was ill preserved, ill prepared, and not always nutritionally sound. Graham's diet was extreme, but an improvement. Similarly, he was right to urge exercise and to attack Americans for their reluctance to let fresh air into their houses, trains, and public buildings. Bathing also proved to be a good idea, once people got used to it.

Concern for the well-being of the public appeared in many different places in antebellum America, ranging from advice books for homemakers to medical publications like a *Journal of Health*, begun in 1829 by prominent doctors in Philadelphia and possibly an influence upon Graham. Someone with Graham's magnetism and a more conciliatory personality might have tied this widespread sentiment into a unified movement. As it was, health reform remained amorphous and Graham's role was primarily that of inspiration and occasional nuisance.

There was, however, no shortage of institutions and publications to spread the gospel. Much of the activity was in Boston. In 1837 Grahamites in that city formed the American Physiological Society. It had a membership of over two hundred before a year was out, and it quickly began publication of the *Graham Journal of Health and Longevity*. In 1838, Bostonians were instrumental in calling the first Health Convention, which drew a mixed crew of reformers—including many abolitionists—from New England and New York. Yet at that very moment Boston began to lose some of its preeminence and the movement itself faltered temporarily after the financial panic of 1837. The second Health Convention, held in New York in 1839, was a success in terms of numbers attending, but it ran up debts that had to be paid by a wealthy Bostonian. There would not be a third one. Also in 1839 the *Graham Journal* ceased publication and the New England branch of health reform suffered its cruelest blow. The American Physiological Society sought, and failed, to receive incorporation from the Massachusetts General Court. Grahamites were used to public ridicule, but they were stung by the General Court's rejection. One politician did not help matters by declaring "people might eat bricks, bran, or saw-dust, or anything they chose, but that subject was entirely beneath the notice of the legislature."

Fortunately for the cause, it did not depend on the Massachusetts legislature. Grahamism, along with the other "body reforms" and temperance, was national in scope. Although strongest in Boston and New York City, it had converts throughout New England and across the country. The *Graham Journal*, for instance, had an agent in Crawfordsville, Georgia, and the second Health Convention had delegates from as far away as the West Indies. Through the years, publications and local societies, many of them for women, kept health reform alive. In small towns and large cities Grahamites set up stores and boardinghouses run on correct principles—these apparently acted as gathering points for crusaders of all sorts who happened to be in the neighborhood. By 1840 Grahamism had a major bastion in the West. Oberlin College, sympathetic to every antebellum reform, invited the former editor of the *Graham Journal*, David Cambell, to run the student commons. Many of Graham's teachings had been put into practice well before Cambell and his wife arrived, but his appointment marked Oberlin's full, although brief, commitment to health reform. (Cambell resigned in 1841, after protests from parents, students, faculty, and townspeople, some of whom described the food as "inadequate to the demands of the human system as at present developed.") Despite setbacks, health reform endured, increased its audience, and went through schisms and transmutations after 1840.

Graham's part in this larger movement was small. During much of the greatest excitement in Boston he stayed in western Massachusetts, away from the center of things. When he did reappear, he often proved to be a divisive, rather than unifying, force. As the movement widened, he narrowed. Although he had always advocated a general plan of hygiene, he came to place more emphasis on diet than many other health reformers thought was wise. That side of Graham was obvious in his *Treatise on Bread and Bread-Making* (1837), with its glorification of bygone days when mothers supposedly did all the family baking and used only coarse, wholesome flour. Some of that may have been nostalgia for an imagined past (Graham's mother probably was mentally unbalanced and had difficulty caring for him, her youngest child). It definitely was a criticism of the way in which industrialization moved production of items like bread out of the household and into commercial enterprises. Whatever it represented, the *Treatise* neither endeared him to bakers nor restored him to the forefront of health reform. Even his return to the speaking circuit and his ambitious *Lectures on the Science of Human Life*, both in 1839, left him a leader more in name than in fact.

It was another native of Connecticut, Dr. William Andrus Alcott, who reached the broad constituency Graham felt he deserved. Four years younger than Graham, Alcott became a schoolteacher at the ripe age of eighteen. A serious illness inspired him to study medicine, which he did in the mid-1820s, receiving his training at Yale. For the next several years his life took twists and turns, in part because he was still dogged by illness. In 1831 he came to Boston to edit an educational journal and a periodical for children; by then he was thirty-three and his career as a writer was under way. Before it was over he had published scores of books and hundreds of shorter pieces on almost every aspect of moral and healthful living.

Although sometimes at odds with Graham, Alcott was a devoted health reformer and first president of the American Physiological Society. Alcott stressed a vegetarian diet, with no tea, coffee, alcohol, or spices, but his interests were more catholic than Graham's and he was not so committed to bran bread as the cornerstone of health. He dispensed advice to young men, to young women, to mothers, to anyone who would listen, on such subjects as gymnastics, proper reading matter, manners, friendship, ventilation, sex, diet, education, and much more. The book-buying public was eager to be told how to live and behave (probably because families and churches were no longer conveying that information satisfactorily). Alcott sensed the market and spoke to it in languge that was neither theological nor overly technical. On the one hand, his message appeared less intense than Graham's because it was more genial and diffuse; on the other hand, it may have been more effective precisely because it did touch on so many things. A person could only achieve his or her full potential, Alcott was saying, by attending to all the details of life.

In spite of Alcott's success, health reform in the 1840s and 1850s went the way of most antebellum crusades. Rather than coalescing as it gained a hearing, it subdivided. Some members remained staunch Grahamites, with bran bread as their bible; others followed Alcott's broader path. Still others dwelt upon some particular aspect of health and hygiene. Exercise, especially, had zealous promoters. (Since the 1820s Americans had been influenced by German gymnastic practices and by European educational theories linking physical and mental development.) But it was hydropathy more than anything else that marked a new departure for some health reformers after 1840.

Originating in Europe, hydropathy was a system of cleansing the body—and presumably curing it—by bathing and filling it with water in every imaginable manner. Like the Graham diet, the water cure proved to be the bane of regular medical men and singularly attractive to all kinds of reformers, including numerous abolitionists. Also like the Graham diet, it may have done some good. (It is no accident that it appealed to women: in addition to escaping from their husbands while at hydropathic resorts, they may have gotten relief from otherwise untreatable urogenital infections.)

Probably no one better symbolized the transition from Graham-ism to hydropathy than Mary Gove Nichols. In 1838 she ran a Graham boardinghouse in Boston and lectured to female audiences on physiology and related subjects. In the remaining forty-six years of her life she would write fiction, be divorced, have an affair, be drawn to communitarianism, advocate free love, advocate chastity, participate in séances, become a Catholic, and claim the power to heal. In the midst of that pilgrimage she was exposed to hydropathic theories; after studying at establishments in Vermont and New York in 1845, she became a water-cure evangelist.

Mary Gove Nichols never entirely lost her early health-reform principles: what is significant is the way she, and others like her, subordinated and reshaped them. Hydropathy and the Graham diet were quite compatible (they often went together) but the water cure clearly became the overriding concern of Nichols and many of her later colleagues. To put it cynically, the Graham regimen had offered fewer entrepreneurial opportunities. Other than writing and lecturing there was little one could do to make a career out of extending its principles. To be sure, there had been many Graham boarding-houses, but those were small operations, unable to promise the dramatic results or charge the higher rates of water-cure resorts. Hydropathy, however, required building and operating fair-sized establishments, with facilities for patients and for students of the art. By 1862 seventy of them dotted the landscape from coast to coast, springing up in such out-of-the-way places as rural Oregon and Sacramento, California—wherever there was clean water and a clientele searching for good health or a respite from family respon-sibilities.

Besides marking a new stage in health reform, water cures signaled the beginning of a quest for legitimacy. Mary's second husband, Thomas Nichols, went back in 1850 to complete conventional medical studies. Until their conversion to Catholicism in 1857 the Nicholses worked strenuously to make water-cure training more formal and respectable. They founded the American Hydropathic Institute in 1851, in which they offered a full scientific, medical, and physiological curriculum. Similar efforts continued well after the Civil War, most notably in New York by Dr. Russell Trall, whose Hygeio-Therapeutic College was incorporated in 1857 and was to be the hydropathic counterpart of conventional medical schools. The professional ambitions of the Nicholses and Trall were ironic in a movement originating with Sylvester Graham, who believed that people were healthiest when they avoided irritating foods and medical men.

Regular physicians won the war. Their organization, the American Medical Association, eventually achieved its monopoly at the expense of hydropathy (which declined in the 1870s) and other now-discredited panaceas, of which there were hundreds. But many of the ideas of health reform gained wide acceptance, even among Graham's archenemies in the medical profession. Doctors who scorned Graham's "quackery" often gave advice on some matters very much like his: they, too, generally urged a moderate diet, cleanliness, sexual restraint, exercise, and avoidance of stimulants. They refused to go to his extremes or to accept the exaggerated claims reformers made for preventing and curing diseases; but on the principles of health and on underlying moral values, regular physicians and Grahamites were in greater agreement than their mutual hostility made it seem.

Health reform had an effect in many places and its constituency was broad, comprising such crusaders as communitarians and abolitionists, some affluent people, and many young men and young women who had more hope than social position. Exercise and fresh air became especially respectable and popular, even in social circles where bran bread was not—there is testimony to that in the multitude of parks and gymnasia built in antebellum America. Through William Andrus Alcott, health reform also seems to have had an impact on the development of school systems. Alcott promoted the idea that students should work in a hygienic environment, have periods of recreation, and be taught the elements of good health. These recommendations filtered into Horace Mann's landmark *Reports* to the Massachusetts Board of Education and, in 1850, physiology and hygiene became a required course of study in Massachusetts' schools, as Alcott had hoped. Health reform also had a role in shaping some nineteenth-century religious sects (they recombined its physical perfectionism with the older theological variety). In the case of the Seventh Day Adventists, the connection was very direct. The denomination's founder, Ellen White, was a Grahamite and a believer in hydropathy; and a prominent layman, John Harvey Kellogg, ran a huge health-care establishment at Battle Creek, Michigan, where he put into practice many of the old physiological doctrines. Still other aspects of American life were touched by health reform, but the point is beyond doubt: although bran bread failed to become a staple of the national diet, traces of Grahamism survive in what we are taught, how we live, and in how some of us worship.

"For more than forty years," an exasperated phrenologist wrote in 1882, "we have been trying to convince the world, that in examination of the head we do not look for 'bumps.' " Even at that late date he was rankled by critics who pictured phrenologists as nothing more than charlatans who felt the skulls of ignorant men and women. Phrenology was something more, although not the grand science of the age, as defenders claimed. Like health reform, it was an assertion that biological "laws" could be used to uplift humankind. It was also a system of psychology, a form of career and marital counseling, and the nineteenth-century equivalent of educational testing.

Although it may have seemed like groping for bumps, serious phrenology involved charting the shape of a person's cranium. Rather than assume that the mind is a single entity, phrenologists divided it into thirty-seven "faculties." These corresponded to personality traits: an individual could have too much, too little, or just the right amount of each. Take, for example:

AMATIVENESS—the faculty of physical love lends attractiveness to the opposite sex, and a desire to unite in wedlock and enjoy their company. *Excess:* Tendency to licentiousness. *Deficiency:* Indifference to the other sex.

Every one of the thirty-seven was represented in an "organ," or position on the head, the size of which indicated the strength or weakness of the faculty. (Amativeness was located at the base of the skull, between the ears.) To this point, phrenology was a science: that is, a legitimate attempt, given the state of knowledge in the nineteenth century, to understand how the mind functioned.

It also would seem as if phrenology were a variety of biological determinism—after all, there is not much a person can do about the shape of his or her head. The perfectionist impulse in antebellum America, however, was not to be stopped by logic. In defiance of intellectual consistency, phrenologists argued that men and women could indeed take immediate steps to remedy defects. Obviously, they could take advantage of their assets and compensate for their liabilities; but, more surprising, phrenologists went on to insist that substandard "organs" could be improved by exercise, diet, education, new surroundings, or other means. Rather than assert that people were prisoners of bone structure, phrenologists assured them that they could be better than their skulls indicated. The goal of the science was to show individuals "what they *are*, and what they *can* be, as well as how to make themselves what they should become." Orson Fowler reduced that to a cheery cliché: "Self Made or Never Made."

The founder of phrenology might well have blanched, had he lived to hear Fowler's words. He was a more cautious man, a German physician named Franz Joseph Gall, born in 1758. From his days as a medical student, Gall had begun to note connections between facial types, configurations of the skull, and personal characteristics. Over the years he made thousands of meticulous observations—his was the first, best, and nearly the last detailed empirical research done by a phrenologist. By 1802 Gall set off to spread his findings across most of Europe, accompanied by his pupil, Johann Spurzheim. They eventually settled in Paris, where Gall acquired a distinguished clientele and, in collaboration with Spurzheim, wrote large medical treatises on the nervous system and the brain. It was Spurzheim who cast their work in popular form, coined the word "phrenology," and claimed that it was a means of perfecting human-kind, all somewhat to Gall's disapproval.

Beyond a handful who had heard Gall's lectures in Paris, few Americans knew of phrenology until the 1820s. In 1822, however, a group consisting largely of prominent Philadelphia doctors created the Central Phrenological Society, evidence of rising awareness in the medical profession. Two years later, Dr. Charles Caldwell published the first phrenological book authored by an American. By the end of the decade works by Spurzheim and especially by George Combe, a Scottish lawyer, were gaining a broad audience. But Spurzheim's trip to America in 1832 did more than any other event to bring the subject before the people. He charmed and impressed his hosts in New England, lectured, performed a public dissection of a brain, observed criminals and inmates of asylums, and generally behaved like the medical celebrity he was. Unfortunately, his organ of vitativeness ("love of life; a desire to exist") was not strong enough to carry him through. He died in Boston after little more than two months in the United States. Even in death he served his science. A Harvard professor conducted a public autopsy of Spurz-heim, coupling it with a phrenological lecture. (Spurzheim's brain was preserved as a specimen. He would have wanted it that way.)

Phrenology continued to generate excitement throughout the 1830s. Combe had already done a great deal to advance the cause in the United States through his influential *The Constitution of Man* (1828), described many years after by an American phrenologist as "not surpassed in scope and value by any work in any language." His own eighteen-month tour of North America, begun in 1838, was a social success—he met Presidents, past and future, befriended writers, bankers, medical men, and reformers. The visit was espe-cially opportune for phrenology. Combe was able to draw attention to the subject while treating it in a manner dignified enough to sustain his scientific credentials.

The impressive performances of Spurzheim and Combe gave phrenology much credibility among ladies and gentlemen of intellect and standing. Horace Mann brought its principles to bear on educational practices and treatment of the insane. (He was so much an enthusiast that he named a child after Combe.) Phrenology also claimed a convert in Henry Ward Beecher, Lyman's son and after midcentury the best-known clergyman in America. While a student at Amherst in 1833, Beecher took on the task of attacking phrenology in a debate. After studying it, he changed sides. The list of prominent supporters went on and on, and the very terminology of the "science" crept into the public discourse of the day. Good fiction and bad, essays, sermons, and political oratory contained references to its "faculties," "organs," and—yes—bumps.

Lecturers carried phrenology across the land, to rural folk as well as urban, to poor as well as rich, Southerners and Westerners as well as Northerners. Practitioners of varying honesty dispensed quick character analysis along the highways and byways of the nation. (Beware of the man who "has great development between and back of the ears and is short in front . . . he is not intelligent, but very passionate, selfish, base, and animal in his instincts.") Professionals made handsome careers out of helping individuals find occupations and spouses by means of its principles. Publications proclaimed the glory of phrenology, told people how to apply it, and offered further assistance for a fee.

In the midst of this activity, local phrenological societies formed, some of them with libraries, plaster casts, and real skulls available for study. These organizations often drew members of the local elite and a few of them had considerable staying power. Many, nonetheless, met the fate of the Phrenological Society of Cincinnati, as described by an English traveler. Founded by "between twenty and thirty of the most erudite citizens," the society's "first meeting dissolved with every appearance of energetic perseverance in scientific research." One half the original number showed up for the second meeting "and they enacted rules and laws, and passed resolutions, sufficient, it was said, to have filled three folios." A third meeting was set, at which time subscriptions to the society were to be paid. Only the treasurer came.

Reluctant though Americans might be to pay membership dues, they had given phrenology a fair hearing by 1840. But those who endorsed it soon divided into two camps. Some people regarded phrenology as a serious science, to be investigated with care and precision. These men and women, quite intellectually responsible, had no means of setting professional standards since phrenologists did not bother to hold a national convention or create a national organization—the American Phrenological Society—until 1849. By that time a second, much larger group predominated. It consisted of "practical" phrenologists, less interested in research than in giving character readings and in trying to solve immediate problems of human unhappiness. The split in the ranks eroded the discipline's scientific respectability but increased its constituency in the 1840s and 1850s, as phrenologists fanned out into the hinterland, un-hampered by a code of ethics.

Of all the practical phrenologists, none was more practical than the Fowler brothers. Orson was an Amherst classmate of Henry Ward Beecher and he combined the passion of an evangelist with some very secular abilities. Abandoning thoughts of becoming a clergyman, Orson and his brother Lorenzo became missionaries for phrenology in the 1830s. It was primarily their ambition and en-trepreneurial skill that set them apart from the hundreds of men and women also taking to the field to promote the new fad.

In common with other touring phrenologists, the Fowlers were as much showmen as reformers or scientists. They lectured to an audi-ence and, simultaneously, engaged in a battle of wits with it, inviting it to debate and test the accuracy of phrenology. More than one practical joker, hoping for a misanalysis, took the challenge and presented an unsuspecting phrenologist with the village scoundrel, who appeared to be harmless. Phrenologists reported their triumphs in these cases; literature and local lore recorded their failures. But where the majority of their competitors eked out a living on the road, the Fowlers were able to set up headquarters in New York City in 1835. There they constructed an enterprise of considerable vitality, run by themselves and assorted relatives.

The keystone of the operation was a publishing house, Fowlers and Wells, which began the *American Phrenological Journal* in 1837 and ground out countless books on phrenology. The company also printed works on temperance and health reform (there were many in those crusades who endorsed phrenology): it took over the *Water-Cure Journal* in 1848 and kept Sylvester Graham's *Science of Human Life* and *Chastity* on its lists at least into the 1880s. Not content with that, Fowlers and Wells acted as an agency for phrenological lecturers, ran a museum of cranial curiosities in New York, with branches in Boston and Philadelphia, and sold various artifacts—among them, plaster casts of famous heads, a model of the brain, and real human and animal skulls. At one time the company boasted of being the largest mail-order business in New York. The Fowlers were among those Americans who deserve a place in the annals of capitalism as well as of reform.

Despite their managerial talents, Fowlers and Wells and their colleagues would not have been successful if they had not spoken to real concerns of nineteenth-century Americans. There are clues to phrenology's appeal in the fact that much of it was advice to people seeking the right mate, employee, or employer. The rapid pace of change in the antebellum decades made that valuable information to have. In a period of fluidity and high geographic mobility, it was difficult to know whom to trust and phrenology provided answers. It let businessmen size up potential workers and clients, and permitted men and women to calculate, presumably rationally, their prospects for future happiness together. Before phrenology, an enthusiast declared, "the wisest of men had no means of deciding, with anything like certainty, the talents or character of a stranger."

In the same fashion it assisted individuals trying to choose from among the new opportunities opening up in the wake of economic development. The *American Phrenological Journal* received ample thanks from young men who had been unsure of a course to pursue, only to be set straight after phrenological analysis. The marvel was that phrenology allowed Americans to make crucial predictions about themselves and others with nothing more than an easily acquired knowledge of basic principles—available by mail from Fowlers and Wells, if need be.

Unlike most antebellum pseudo-sciences, phrenology lived to a ripe old age. The publishing house of Fowlers and Wells lasted into the twentieth century; the *American Phrenological Journal* did not disappear until 1911. But a combination of internal weaknesses and external events sent phrenology into a decline decades earlier. Few "discoveries" were made after the 1840s: virtually all practitioners shunned research in favor of pronouncing the same principles over and over. Phrenology simply did not—perhaps could not—grow as a science. Meanwhile, more dynamic disciplines (and fads) overshadowed it. By the end of the century serious scholars ignored Gall and Spurzheim and looked to William James, G. Stanley Hall, and other gifted psychologists for more exciting discussions of the human mind. Since the principles of phrenology were fixed and easy to understand, the general public likewise found more reliable sources of information or became bored. Lack of innovation by relatively responsible operators like the Fowlers left a small but profitable field open for rascals who traveled the countryside and who discredited the whole enterprise by mixing phrenology up with fortune-telling, magic, and raw greed.

Although it ended as little more than a sideshow attraction, phrenology was both a reform movement and the beginning of a retreat from the reformist belief in human perfectibility. That curious position is clearest when phrenology is set alongside the so-called American School of anthropology, current in the 1840s and 1850s. The "school" consisted mainly of several scientific treatises dealing with racial differences, which the authors measured partially in terms of the average cranial capacity of each "racial" group. Since people assumed that humans with the largest heads were smartest, the implications of these measurements were considerable. The American School "discovered" that in its samples whites were superior and that other groups trailed behind. This was a strong and early variety of scientific racism, somewhat shunned at the time because it conflicted with the biblical version of creation (writers of the American School argued that the races did not stem from Adam and Eve but had separate origins). On the surface it seems as if phrenology had much in common with the American School, an impression borne out by the latter's seminal work, Dr. Samuel George Morton's *Crania Americana* (1839). This book is devoted to painstaking cranial measurements and descriptions of racial "characteristics," but Morton did permit George Combe to add a chapter on phrenology. Yet that, and a mutual interest in skulls, was not enough to make the two men comfortable allies. Morton was wary of phrenology and ignored opportunities to try to "prove" its virtues. Combe, for his part, was not entirely satisfied with the work or with Morton's attitude toward him.

The differences between the American School and phrenology were more serious than even Morton and Combe may have sensed. The American School sought to prove that the character of human beings was fixed for eternity: white people were white people, others were others, and there was nothing to do except recognize the truth. That line of reasoning cut against phrenologists' doctrines and practices. Their role, as they saw it, was to help individuals understand their nature in order to make them better, not to keep them in their place.

Despite its hopefulness about the improvability of humankind, phrenology did have a part in preparing the public to accept later-nineteenth-century biological determinism. There was an ominous undercurrent to phrenological advice such as that Nelson Sizer gave to a potential suicide. "[Y]our *organism*," Sizer counseled, "*not* your *fate*, is at fault." Sizer meant, of course, that the person's problems were rooted in his or her physical being but that they could be solved. Yet phrenologists, like health reformers, were sailing into uncharted waters when they pictured morality and virtue as being dependent on the body. Once that assumption was made, optimism about mankind became fragile. After 1860, Charles Darwin, evolutionary theory, and the failure of reform itself would make it easy to decide that (contrary to phrenology) biology is destiny after all, and thus beyond the efforts of do-gooders to change. In the antebellum years, however, phrenologists and Grahamites had no way of anticipating how biological thought could be turned against them and against any scheme of social uplift. True enough, they believed that the body set limits on human potential. But they were reformers precisely because they believed those limits could be transcended.

In a different, but equally significant, manner spiritualism also dealt with issues of body, soul, and human progress. These concerns, nonetheless, seldom troubled the two girls who began the antebellum craze of "spirit-rapping." They were Kate and Margaret Fox, aged twelve and fifteen, daughters of a poor farming family who lived about thirty miles east of Rochester, New York. In the winter and spring of 1848 strange knocking noises began to keep everyone in the house awake at night. The girls got the sounds to respond to their words and, by means of a code, to signal answers to questions. After a time, neighbors gathered to hear the revelations. The knocks, the girls claimed, came from the spirit of a peddler, murdered in the house and buried beneath it years before the Foxes moved in. A hasty excavation of the cellar revealed no bones (although stories have it that some were found later).

Failure to find a skeleton in the family basement did not stop the Foxes. The sisters were believed and they were also challenged: they were praised and they were denounced. Some right-minded citizens avoided them and there was an attempt at exorcism. Despite that, the knocking persisted wherever they went. An older sister, Leah, took one, then both of the girls, to Rochester, where they gave effective demonstrations of "spirit-rapping." Soon Leah and an early disciple, Eliab W. Capron, were promoting Kate and Margaret skillfully, at first locally, in the "burned-over district," then in New York City, and eventually elsewhere in the United States and England. Belief in spirits was ancient, but this was something different and exciting: a whole system of communication between living and dead, available for public observation.

In 1888 Margaret and Kate, both of whom had bouts of alcoholism, confessed that the noises came from a cracking sound they made with the joints of their big toes. It had all begun as a prank. Margaret later went back on that explanation and declared that she and Kate were not frauds. Whatever the truth may have been, in 1849 and 1850 the girls were putting forth revelation after revelation from the great beyond. Soon word came of similar happenings in other places. The dead suddenly became communicative, speaking out in séances and public gatherings, rapping and banging, bumping furniture, or merely holding private conversations with mediums. As with every antebellum crusade, spiritualism took strongest hold in the Northeast and Ohio—New York led the way in mediums (seventy-one to Massachusetts' fifty-five in 1859) and probably in numbers of believers. But within a few years spiritualist periodicals spread the cause across the land (there were sixty-seven of them by 1857) ; and, in any event, there was no shortage of seers willing to bring the spirit world to the cities and small towns of America.

Spiritualism crossed class lines as easily as geographic boundaries. Reformers, as was usual with any new idea, were fascinated. So were men and women who were ignorant, credulous, and poor. Yet well-educated and distinguished people also became spiritualists. A prominent New York jurist was a founder of the Society for the Diffusion of Spiritual Knowledge in 1854, and among the other early promoters was a former territorial governor of Wisconsin and United States senator (from New York, of course). In both the New World and the Old, and in the nineteenth century as well as the twentieth, no one social group has had a monopoly on hearing voices and rappings from other worlds.

As it grew in popularity and inspired controversy, spiritualism (like temperance and phrenology) became a form of popular entertainment. Spiritualists baited their opponents, submitted to examination by "experts," and generally encouraged audiences to test them. In that respect they, in common with phrenologists, were not so different from P. T. Barnum, the showman, who dared the antebellum public to determine if his exhibits were marvels of nature or hoaxes. There were, of course, those who scoffed at spiritualists, and even a few acts of mob violence against them. But the worst that usually could be demonstrated was that the rappings *might* have been produced fraudulently, not that they were.

The most vehement attackers of spiritualism were ministers, whose case against it was theological rather than empirical. Orthodox clergy were appalled at the high number of unchurched men and women, religious liberals, and—later—sexual radicals drawn to the movement. Such people were bound to preach dangerous doctrines. Sometimes they did. On the rare occasions spiritualists talked about God, they described him or her as an amorphous entity, pervading all existence and not intervening in human affairs. (Spiritualist theology collapsed God, nature, and humankind into a harmonious unity, and yet insisted that people kept distinct personalities after death: an example of American individualism conquering metaphysics.) In the phrase of one leading spiritualist, God was the

"Supernal Soul of Nature"—a far cry from the omnipotent being of Calvinism and surely one of the most cumbersome labels ever given a deity. Some spiritualists described Christ as no more than an extraordinarily capable medium, declared that hell did not exist, and dismissed Protestant doctrines of predestination, atonement, and salvation. Sin, in the words of Andrew Jackson Davis, was "an atavism, merely." Rather than be unorthodox and leave it at that, a few spiritualists were aggressively hostile to organized religion. Davis spoke of going to church as a matter of putting innocent young minds "in the pen, with those domestic animals known as *cat*-echism and *dog*-matism." The "contact," he concluded, "is contaminating to the last degree."

Conventional ministers found that rhetoric galling and they fought back. But they were not entirely correct to believe that spiritualism was antithetical to Christianity. Antireligious spiritualists were balanced by many ministers and laity who believed Christianity and spiritualism reinforced each other. Even where spiritualists were unorthodox, their heresies were not unique in antebellum America. Well before the Fox sisters heard (or produced) rapping sounds, some Americans had accepted the teachings of Emanuel Swedenborg, an eighteenth-century Scandinavian mystic who likewise conversed with spirits. (For a variety of reasons, however, Swedenborgians usually disavowed spiritualism.) Universalists had previously abolished hell; Transcendentalists had formed a conception of God similar to that of spiritualists; and members of several sects had pretty much done away with the concept of sin.

It is, nonetheless, futile to argue whether spiritualism and Protestantism were enemies. For some people they were, for others they were not. Americans, furthermore, had an ability to keep what they believed at a séance separate from what they believed in church on Sunday. They did not exert themselves to find inconsistencies. Thousands of men and women came to spiritualism for reasons they could keep totally distinct from their theology. For some, it was a chance to see a show and, in addition, to try to figure out life and death. For others, it offered comfort. Many and touching are the stories of conversations people had with departed parents, spouses, and children.

Since spiritualism frequently was a private experience, gone into for intensely personal motives, it was difficult to form institutions to propagate the faith. People preferred lectures and séances to rules, regulations, and meetings. Local and state societies appeared and disappeared. Conventions, summer camps, and spiritualistic Sunday schools came and went. Communitarian societies were founded on spiritualistic principles, and they, too, vanished quickly. Like the phrenologists, spiritualists were late in creating a national association and they had trouble keeping it going once they had it—the National Association of Spiritualists lasted only from 1863 to 1869. This institutional weakness, as well as the large element of entertainment and fraud involved in spirit-rapping, make it hard to think of spiritualism as an antebellum reform movement. (For that matter, it was not entirely antebellum: it continued to branch out and flower with strange growths, many of the most interesting of them coming after 1860.)

It was primarily through the efforts of Andrew Jackson Davis that spiritualism did become a genuine reform movement in the pre-Civil War period, although an odd and limited one. Davis, like the Fox sisters, began his contacts with the spirits in rural New York, where, as a boy, he had experiences with "animal magnetism," or hypnotism. Instead of rappings, he heard voices and carried on conversations with dead people, including Emanuel Swedenborg. By 1847 the "Poughkeepsie Seer," age twenty-one, was in New York City, explaining the origins of the universe, suggesting how society might be improved, and, in a trance, dictating his discoveries. The title he chose for his book was no more modest than its nearly eight-hundred-page length: *The Principles of Nature, Her Divine Revelation, and a Voice to Mankind.* The reviews were mixed. A few took it for what it claimed to be. Others dismissed it as nonsense and had the ill grace to accuse Davis of plagiarizing the work of his long-deceased spirit friend, Swedenborg. All this was happening in the months before the Fox family began to lose sleep over noises in the night.

Davis claimed that Kate and Margaret Fox demonstrated the validity of his work, but in reality he and the sisters moved in different circles. The girls had little interest in ideas or in changing the world. Davis, on the contrary, believed that higher spheres were trying to help humans transform this one—and he did his part to assist them. He endorsed virtually every contemporary reform, including antislavery, temperance, and woman's rights. He and his followers, furthermore, took action of their own to hasten the dawn of the new day. They created "Harmonial Brotherhoods" to discuss and implement his teachings; and in 1863 Davis organized the Children's Progressive Lyceum, a spiritualist alternative to Sunday schools which had, by 1871, branches in seventeen states and in Britain. Also in 1863 he began the Moral Police Fraternity, an attempt to use spiritualist principles to solve problems of crime and poverty in New York City. (It did not succeed.) Davis' commitment to reform remained strong after the Civil War and was a factor when in 1878 he broke with the mainstream of spiritualism, which he saw flowing off into magic and superstition.

Over the years Davis spun out his thoughts (and other people's) in a comprehensive "Harmonial Philosophy." Its intellectual origins were not extraterrestrial: a smattering of mesmerism; a big helping of Swedenborg; maybe a dash of Fourier; and surely a pinch of folklore. Added to that were his belief in science and natural law, and concepts he got from the reformers he associated with. Probably not even Davis was aware of all the influences that went into Harmonial Philosophy.

It is perhaps as well to let the roots of Davis' theories remain tangled and obscure. What mattered was the message. On one level, it was positive and surprisingly unmystical. Davis did not counsel readers to lie back, listen to spirits, and trust to intuition. He urged them to think, to study, to receive wisdom from all sources, and to act. Spiritualism was not supernatural, in Davis' mind, but another kind of knowledge to be used for the benefit of mankind, as science and technology were.

On another level, Davis was attacking some specific enemies. He was opposed to religious sectarianism, the clergy, conflict between North and South, "the confusion among the political parties now *so* numerous," and unfair accumulation of property. That list is strikingly close to ones most other antebellum reformers would have made. He, and they, were against the disruptive and divisive forces then at work in the United States. He (and, again, they) wanted to expand freedom and erase political, religious, and many social distinctions. He wanted to preserve morality and make *"our country the best place in the world* for the industrious." He wanted perfect human beings and the millennium.

A job that big definitely required some help from the spirit world. Still, the good society Davis described in *The Harmonial Man* (1853) was not especially unearthly. The "Harmonial Republic" rested on "ORGANIC LIBERTY, which brings to every man his natural Rights and attractive Industry!" It was to be protected by *"Free speech . . . Free schools for the masses . . . Freedom of the press . . . Free churches and honest teachers . . .* And Nature's own religion." The government's role in such a society would be severely limited, although it would "permit no monopolizing of the land by the few, to the injury of the many," and it should make certain that "Industry is Happiness." Most of those points would have brought nods of agreement from reformers and a substantial number of non-reformers. When the spirits gave such advice they were telling Americans to live up to their own ideals.

Davis was a major figure, with a large following, but he did have a tendency to wander. For instance, after devoting twenty-four pages of *The Harmonial Man* to "the Harmonial Republic," he used most of the remaining hundred and five pages to develop a plan to produce rainfall electrically and to discourse on the merits of facial hair. For all his "Brotherhoods" and other groups, he was not—it almost goes without saying—entirely successful in turning spiritualism away from séances and into a vital reform movement.

In spite of Davis' efforts, much of spiritualism's significance for reform came indirectly, through its influence on men and women involved in other crusades. The Reverend John Pierpont defended it as staunchly as he did phrenology and antislavery while William Lloyd Garrison received an important communication on abolitionist tactics through a medium in contact with a departed ex-colleague. Robert Dale Owen, son of Robert Owen and a reformer in his own right, was so impressed with spiritualism that in 1859 he published a 528-page defense of it. Hundreds of antebellum reformers, although not so verbose, were just as taken by it as he was.

They found several things appealing about it, many of them identical to aspects of Grahamism and phrenology. All three causes provided support for the notion that the nineteenth century was a special moment in history—each was a sign of progress in understanding mankind and the universe. Reformers also discovered in spiritualism their long-time message that human beings had the power to transform themselves and, moreover, that they had an obligation to do so. Since people remained for eternity as they were in life, Owen concluded that spiritualism proved "We are architects of our own destiny: we inflict our punishments; we select our own rewards." More than a generation before, the same faith sent Americans into communitarian societies (including his father's) and into the antislavery and temperance movements.

Spiritualism also made its mark by erasing the old Christian line between body and soul. "Matter is the foundation of Mind," Davis declared. "Mind is the spiritualization of Matter." There, once again, was the belief that no distinction exists between humankind's moral and physical selves, a familiar enough notion in health reform and phrenology, but evident in temperance, antislavery, and communitarianism as well.

Spiritualism similarly played a variation on another common theme in antebellum reform: a desire to create a world of harmony and order. In most reforms that meant eliminating the source of disorder, whether it was slavery, bad diet, alcohol, or the social system. Spiritualism's answer was to assert (or "prove") that the world *was* harmonious. Despite chaos and uncertainty in the present, existence was a continuum, not bounded by the human body, space, or time.

On a more mundane level, spiritualism attracted reformers because it provided solace. Seldom, if ever, did a spirit do anything except encourage a reformer or suggest new directions. One young man claimed to be guided in his activities by Thomas Jefferson, whose social views had been modified by death. (The ex-President's postmortem opinions of slavery were nearly those of a Garrisonian abolitionist.) The same man later received advice on building a communitarian society from the spirits—Martin Luther was especially helpful. His heavenly collaborators may also have endorsed some sexual experimentation.

Clearly there was an unconscious element of self-serving in such contact with the dead, as well as much self-delusion. But reformers were searching for justification. They mistrusted older moral authorities—clergymen and politicians—yet they also wanted moral certainty: they were not ready to concede that any person's conscience might be as good as any other's. Unless one wanted to base everything on traditional religion (and some reformers did), the only way out was to find a new dispensation. Physiological laws and voices from the spirit world were non-theological revelations and served as well as any others to reinforce the reformer's sense of what was right and wrong.

The issues between the "body reforms" and American Protestantism were never clearly joined. Grahamites, phrenologists, and spiritualists often denied any conflict between their crusades and Christianity. Clergy spoke on both sides of each cause. In a sense that was appropriate, for the three movements each rephrased Protestant moralism, millennialism, and perfectionism in "scientific" and physical terms. The Kingdom of God became good health, understanding one's self and one's fellow humans, and communicating with the rest of the universe.

Yet that represented a significant change. Communitarianism, antislavery, and temperance, as well as the "body reforms" moved away from formal religion and away from arguments based on the Bible (Sylvester Graham, a former minister, seldom referred to it). Each of these was part of a much larger nineteenth-century search for new, secular modes of understanding the world, rooted in an analysis of "human nature" and "science" (even many spiritualists were fascinated by electricity and likened their contact with the dead to the recently invented telegraph). The Graham diet, phrenology, and spiritualism scarcely seem rational by twentieth-century standards, but—like much of antebellum reform—they were often rationalistic and egalitarian. By following definite rules, every man and every woman had the opportunity to achieve health and happiness; individuals even had the ability to reach past the fact of death. When reform made those promises it was both staking out its claim on this world and poaching on religion's territory.

There were difficulties—and unrealistic expectations—when reformers expressed their solutions in personal and physical terms. It was misleading to think that perfection was little more than an individual matter, to be gained through an understanding of the relation between body and soul. Most of the problems in nineteenth-century America were urban, economic, and collective.

8. Dangerous Classes
and Working Classes

Much of twentieth-century reform has aimed at doing things for the victims of urban and industrial life, whether through settlement houses, consumer-protection legislation, welfare, or some other means. There was little sentiment for anything like that in antebellum America. Most commonly, reformers either wanted to stop a sinful practice, like slaveholding or drinking, or else help people help themselves without "charity" or "interference" from the government. There was a bright confidence that individuals could accomplish almost anything on their own if they really wanted to, including overcoming alcoholism, ill health, and (with phrenology) the deficiencies of one's own brain. If a person could do all that, surely he or she could conquer poverty. The notion was naïve and, in any event, it was not universal. Some antebellum reformers did assist unfortunate and suffering Americans; still others tried to improve the lot of working people. They were never so numerous or nationally organized as temperance advocates or abolitionists, but their endeavors show antebellum reform confronting (as directly as it ever did) the new industrial order.

The chief problem of urban areas was poverty and neither it, nor treatment of it, began in the nineteenth century. Boston in 1664 opened a public almshouse to care for the indigent. Other cities slowly followed suit. Well into the nineteenth century, governments did little else for unfortunates except put them in asylums or in jails.

Beginning in the late eighteenth century, private charity—spurred by the humanitarian doctrines of the day and by Christian piety—began to assume a significant role in providing necessary services for the needy. Within a few decades Americans had formed a variety of voluntary agencies to help their destitute and deserving fellow citizens (always drawing a distinction between the worthy and unworthy poor, the latter being idlers or criminals, who got nothing but contempt). By the end of the first quarter of the nineteenth century, according to one historian, over a hundred relief organizations had appeared in New York City alone, many of them short-lived and designed to meet particular crises. Americans generally assumed, however, that poverty was part of the social order and could never be eradicated, that neither the state nor individuals had an obligation to alleviate it, and that poor people were usually the cause of their own troubles. Those attitudes did not vanish after 1815, but they softened somewhat and mingled with newer ones, particularly when evangelical Protestantism entered the picture.

As early as 1810, local Bible, tract, and missionary societies were making efforts to reach heathen in the cities as well as those in the West and in foreign lands. These organizations established urban missions and assigned particular neighborhoods to volunteers, who then called upon residents, distributing literature to them and inquiring about their spiritual state. Whatever else these visitations did, they exposed middle-class and wealthy Americans to the realities of squalor and vice. Many responded with efforts to treat worldly as well as spiritual problems. Among the enterprises arising out of this missionary zeal was, for instance, the Society for the Prevention of Pauperism in the City of New York. Founded in 1817, its prime movers had ties to the evangelical "benevolent empire" (even the Episcopalian and two Quakers among its active leaders had been involved with such organizations as the American Bible Society). The society investigated both economic and moral aspects of slum life, suggested changes in city-run institutions, and opened savings banks to encourage thrift. It also sent out home visitors, corresponded with similar groups in other cities, and gathered statistics (some of the best antebellum urban data came from such organizations). One of its schemes involved selling firewood cheaply to poor families.

Contact with slum dwellers may have inspired well-to-do Protestants to create more organizations, but it did not necessarily lead them to feel great empathy for their clients. If anything, the contact may have confirmed charity workers in their dismal expectations about poor people. (In 1821 women running a mission in a black district thought it a major triumph "that the torch of an incendiary has not been applied" to their building.) Through the early 1820s, people involved in urban charitable societies remained conservative and cautious—appropriately enough, given the wealth some possessed. They tended to see moral failings as the root cause of squalor and to insist that religion, temperance, and thrift were the cures (although savings banks and firewood helped). They did not wish to upset relations between classes and few of them expected to end poverty. If poor people could be made pious and comfortable, the thought was, they would be less dangerous to themselves and to social stability.

By 1830 several things made poverty appear in a slightly different light to Protestants. After 1819 there had been much pressure on states to stop imprisoning people for debt, a practice that prevented them from paying their obligations and brought misery upon their families. Even Jacksonian Democrats, disdainful of moral crusades like temperance, could defend debtors, some of whom were well-off speculators and almost all of whom voted. The cause was beginning to prevail in the 1820s and agitation for it increased general awareness of the plight of honest poor people. At the same time, poverty in the cities appeared to be getting worse, largely the result of great population growth in the 1820s and the arrival of hordes of immigrants, many of them destitute. In New York, Boston, Philadelphia, and other urban areas the extremes of wealth and deprivation were obvious and offensive in a land as supposedly democratic and bountiful as the United States. Observers feared for the fate of the nation unless something were done to make the masses virtuous, contented, and American.

Charles G. Finney's brand of revivalism directed this growing perception of poverty into a new, activist campaign to bring Protestant benevolence into the slums. Finney himself came to New York City in 1829 at the urging of—and with financial assistance from—

Arthur Tappan and Anson Phelps, merchants heavily involved in tract distribution. He inspired them and all other reform-minded urban Protestants to renew their efforts to reach the unregenerate. Even among non-evangelical sects there was a sharp rise in city missionary activities after Finney's arrival on the scene. The home visitors of the 1830s never lost their sense of social distance from the people they met, but they were deeply touched by the misery they saw. Unlike their predecessors of the 1810s and 1820s, they had come to the task feeling that poverty and sin might be eradicated. Millennialism and perfectionism had prepared them to believe that all the nation might be converted; prosperity in the 1820s had made them think opportunities were limitless. Yet in the slums they found depravity and degradation more stubborn and crushing than they imagined. They began dispensing larger amounts of material support to the poor and degraded in the 1830s.

Optimism faded quickly. Some urban ventures turned out to make more enemies than converts. The New-York Magdalen Society, for instance, was the center of a controversy within a year of its founding in the 1830s. It hired an enthusiastic young agent, Reverend John McDowall, to help it save prostitutes from lives of penury and sin (and to save young men from them). His first report scandalized New Yorkers with its claim that there were "not less than TEN THOUSAND" prostitutes in the city, not to mention kept women and ruined servant girls. The outcry against McDowall's accusations was so embarrassing that the society disbanded. (A group of pious women, including Mrs. Finney, continued its work for many years, in a new guise and with greater discretion.)

Public hostility, however, was less of a challenge to millennial expectations than was poverty itself. After a few years of contact with the slums, missionary workers grew depressingly aware of the extent of destitution and vice. They lost their confidence that they could eradicate it or the patterns of life it produced. As they became less hopeful, they fell back into their old habit of chiding poor people for being the authors of their own misery through intemperance and licentiousness. The Panic of 1837 simply made matters worse. Prompted by their own financial difficulties and by rising fears of disorder from the lower classes, many middle-class people withdrew from programs to aid the needy. The ranks of paupers swelled at the very moment sympathy and aid for them disappeared.

Although the Protestant attack on poverty stalled in the late 1830s, simply for it to have existed was an achievement, given two slightly contradictory attitudes held by many evangelicals. Coming primarily from agricultural areas, they could be as anti-urban as any Jeffersonian Democrat and they thought of cities as moral cesspools to be avoided by virtuous men and women. Yet they also talked of the West as "Satan's seat." The primary campaign for Christianity, they maintained, should be fought beyond the mountains. The point, in any case, was that Protestants might as well let the cities go and work elsewhere. In defiance of such views, urban missionaries insisted that it was as important to do God's bidding in the slums as in the West or in foreign lands and that, moreover, Christians encountered special problems in urban areas, requiring special solutions and much exertion.

By the mid-1830s missionary and tract workers also challenged—albeit temporarily—the old sense that poverty could not be done away with and that it was the fault of the individual. The millennial faith of the evangelicals was sorely tried by reality and did not last long, but it was an admirable starting point. Until men and women felt social conditions could be improved, as evangelicals insisted, there was litle prospect anything would be done about poverty, other than to dispense alms and criticize the indigent. Almost without thinking about it, urban missionaries increasingly gave attention to the social factors that kept people from escaping the slums—unhealthy food and housing, bad family life, evil companionship, unemployment, and ignorance. The notorious first report of the New-York Magdalen Society, for instance, explained that much prostitution was "the result of sheer necessity, poverty rather than [preference]." That simple observation was accurate and an admission that degradation could be the product of economic and environmental forces.

Somewhat subdued, Protestant charitable endeavors continued past the Panic of 1837 and eventually blended into twentieth-century types of social welfare. The New York Association for Improving the Condition of the Poor proved to be the best example of how the transition was made. Formed in 1843 to relieve the New York City Tract Society of administering alms, it resembled earlier organizations by gathering data on health, education, and crime, and by using the old system of home visitors. But its volunteers functioned somewhat more like twentieth-century case workers, dispensing relief to particular clients and acting as intermediaries between them and the city's charitable and governmental services. As time went on, the association's approach became still more "scientific" and its staff less amateur. It tried to make charity rational and systematic, and it lobbied for governmental action in such fields as education and treatment of juvenile delinquents. The association also focused attention on tenement housing and saw the slums as a menace to "public health." (That argument became fashionable after the Civil War—it played to the self-interest of middle-class urbanites, who did not care greatly about the poor but who were concerned about epidemics and disease.)

Despite its "modern" approach, the association—which lasted into the twentieth century—took decades to rid itself of its antebellum and Protestant presuppositions about poverty. For years it counseled paupers to solve their own problems by righteous living and by going West. Its long-time agent Robert Hartley coupled detailed investigations of slum conditions with sour remarks about the less worthy indigents, whom he called the "debased poor" and whom others referred to as the "dangerous classes." If anyone mistook the Association for nothing more than a secular social-service agency, Hartley's words would have dispelled the illusion. His commitment and mentality were thoroughly evangelical. One can hardly imagine a twentieth-century social worker, no matter how desperate for funds, making the kind of religious and poetic appeal Hartley made in his eighth annual report (1851):

> Give alms: the needy sink with pain;
> The orphans mourn, the crushed complain.
> Give freely: hoarded gold is curst,
> A prey to robbers and to rust.
> Christ, through his poor, a claim doth make,
> Give gladly, for thy Saviour's sake.

(It is not entirely clear whether Hartley was more concerned about the recipient's soul or the donor's.)

By the late nineteenth century, the Protestant charitable apparatus grew to formidable proportions and it remains large today, even though the government has assumed many of its functions. Its beginnings, however, were in the late eighteenth and early nineteenth centuries and for a time it was the best provider of essential services for the destitute. Yet in the antebellum years it was difficult for evangelicals, or any middle-class people, to see poverty very broadly or very intensely. Although the cities might have looked awful to them, their own style of life was improving. Men and women of goodwill could honestly believe that free land, moral uplift, and divine intervention would cure whatever ills there might happen to be. Given that perspective, charity workers deserve respect for their ability to learn and to adapt. Some of their number, like Hartley, could go a half step—no further—toward the view that prevailed in the twentieth century: the belief that social conditions, not just personal morality, have to be changed and that the state has a responsibility to do the job.

In a general way, the majority of antebellum reformers probably would have endorsed the efforts of Hartley and the urban missionaries (the Tappan brothers even helped with money). But few of them really gave much thought to poverty, and when they did speak sympathetically of poor people, they had in mind (as charity workers did) the helpless and virtuous ones—widows, orphans, and men ill or injured through no fault of their own. The honest workingman, according to reformers, had little to worry about. If he was temperate, thrifty, and careful about having children, he could (they thought) live in simple comfort. When they spoke of the "problems" confronting wage earners, it was to promote their own causes (temperance was the key to success, abolition of slavery would elevate the condition of free workers everywhere, and phrenology could assist in finding a job). When reformers such as the abolitionists talked about conflict between capital and labor, they claimed it could be resolved quickly once both sides realized each had an interest in the other's well-being. That analysis was as superficial as it was cheery.

There were those, honest workingmen among them, who were not convinced that labor's difficulties were so easily solved. Beginning in the 1820s an assortment of artisans, visionaries, politicians, and opportunists put together a series of organizations to help workers. In many respects these stand at the opposite extreme from Protestant missionary activities. The two kinds of endeavor shared virtually no personnel, drew leadership from different classes, and disagreed over the effectiveness of religion as a means of social change.

Antebellum reform, as a creature of its time and culture, could produce only a limited range of reactions to the dislocations of industrial society. Toward one end of that range were the efforts of evangelicals; at the other were workingmen's associations. The only other conceivable alternatives seemed to reformers to be barren ground: uncritical acceptance of the new order or radical rejection of it.

By the mid-1820s there were hundreds of local labor societies. They appeared only among skilled workers and, in form, fell somewhere between medieval guilds and modern unions. They provided a variety of mutual benefits and social opportunities, and allowed masters and journeymen to set rules and regulations for their craft.

There was, then, nothing exceptional about a journeyman carpenters' association that went on strike in Philadelphia in 1827. Its demand was similarly common in the 1820s (and for the next two decades): it was seeking a ten-hour, rather than sunrise-to-sunset, workday. The response of some fellow artisans, however, was unprecedented. The walkout, which failed, illustrated to them the need for skilled workers in every craft to pool their funds and coordinate their activities—otherwise it was difficult to win against determined employers. The result was the Mechanics' Union of Trade Associations, the first citywide federation of workingmen's groups. The fifteen or so member trades, hoping to find strength in numbers, pledged to aid one another's organizations in future disputes.

The Mechanics' Union was an important move toward solidarity among artisans, but it was also an isolated venture for several years. Lawsuits, politics, and an economic downturn took most of labor's resources between 1828 and 1832. Rather than banding together, workingmen's groups either put up candidates for office or struggled for survival. By 1833, nonetheless, Trades' Associations began to appear in New York and in cities as far-flung as Boston, Baltimore, Washington, and Louisville. They sponsored newspapers, lobbied for legislation, and gave financial support to striking unions. Even though many labor groups remained independent of them, these Trades' Associations signaled a mobilization of a large portion of the work force. Along with their growth came sharp increases in the number of local unions and strikes. By the mid-1830s over a hundred thousand (perhaps up to three hundred thousand) men and women belonged to some sort of labor society.

Much of the organizing energy of the 1820s and 1830s came from artisans, or mechanics, as they were also known. Frequently used loosely, the terms most accurately describe people who were knowledgeable in a craft requiring special training and equipment (shoemaking, for instance). They were divided into masters (who were self-employed and hired assistants), journeymen (who were proficient in the craft and usually owned their tools, but who worked for wages), and apprentices (who were learning under a master's supervision). Mechanics differed greatly among themselves in wealth and education, but in general they were something of a labor elite. Their skills gave them a measure of independence in choosing when and how to practice their trade. They also had self-respect, a high rate of literacy, and a tradition of political involvement going back at least to the Revolution. These were characteristics making them the segment of the labor force quickest to detect and to oppose threats to their well-being.

After 1800 economic change upset their world of small shops. Master mechanics took advantage of cheaper transportation and increased production to cover wider markets. Still considered artisans, such people really were more capitalists than workingmen and their interests often clashed with those of the journeymen they hired. Masters sought to keep wages low and output high. When they could, they replaced skilled help with unskilled and human beings with machines. Journeymen faced the possibility of being forced into the ranks of common laborers, with none of the autonomy and hope for advancement they once enjoyed. They resisted and some of the fiercest antebellum labor conflict, including the Philadelphia carpenters' strike, was not across class lines (as people perceived them), but rather between masters and journeymen in the same trade.

There was, however, more behind antebellum labor reform than the plight of the artisans. That is not, of course, to deny the importance of low pay and bad working conditions in setting off antebellum labor unrest. Many occupations were doing poorly, even in generally good years; and still more found their style of life altered by the factory system. Yet industrialization hit no group harder than the unskilled men and women who became machine operatives; they, nonetheless, seldom formed unions, were looked down upon by the craftsmen who did, and—through no fault of their own—remained on the periphery of the antebellum labor movement. Workingmen's societies always did best in periods of prosperity, when skilled employees were in the strongest bargaining position, and among many people (such as carpenters) who were unlikely ever to become factory hands.

Workingmen's organizations were stimulated—not always for the better—by ideas and tactics from other antebellum crusades. Seeing all manner of causes being promoted stridently, labor would have found it difficult *not* to enter the public arena. In addition, workers were inspired by the Jacksonian political style. They divided over Jackson himself, but his call for common people to participate in politics spurred them on. His attack on "monopolies" likewise encouraged them to mount their own campaigns against the economic privileges their employers and all wealthy men enjoyed.

The situations that triggered particular strikes varied and, overall, the grievances of the mechanics were several and complex, as were their capabilities and hopes. They were squeezed by inflation and their employers; they knew how to build organizations and were politically conscious; they felt skilled labor was not receiving the respect it deserved and that long workdays and harsher conditions were further debasing it; they saw the emerging capitalism of their day as a menace to their traditional prerogatives and to American liberty. They also had the typical antebellum sense that the world could quickly be made a better place.

In the summer of 1828, the Philadelphia Mechanics' Union of Trade Associations, itself an innovation, took off in a new direction. It resolved "to form a ticket for Assembly and City Councils to be supported by Mechanics and Working Men in the next General Elections." This inaugurated the first and last period in which substantial numbers of American workers formed labor parties, distinct from, and in competition with, all other political organizations. The Union made nominations of its own (they lost) and endorsed friendly candidates put up by both major parties (some of whom won). It had become a full-fledged political organization and within two years others like it appeared throughout Pennsylvania, New Jersey, New York, and New England. Working Men's parties achieved impressive victories in Newark, New London, and Wilmington, and they made considerable splashes in New York City and in New England. A few of these were spurious creations, assembled by politicians courting the labor vote, but many originated with artisans and were directed toward the issues they took most seriously.

The New York City Working Men's Party grew out of a series of mass meetings held in the spring of 1829 to resist an alleged plot by masters to extend the workday. (Ten hours was customary among the city's artisans.) A Committee of Fifty was appointed to coordinate future protests. In October it issued a ringing report containing many of the egalitarian ideas of Thomas Skidmore, a Connecticut-born machinist who appalled conservatives with his belief in equality of property. The document began with the premise that "all human society . . . is constructed radically wrong" and ended with a call for nominations for upcoming state and municipal elections. The ticket, with less than a month to campaign, did remarkably well. A carpenter won a seat in the legislature and other candidates, including Skidmore, fell only a few votes short.

During its glory days in 1829 and 1830 the party was a forum for a variety of capable and articulate people, not all of them workers. The best known were Skidmore, George Henry Evans, editor of the largest labor journal of the time, the *Working Man's Advocate*, and Robert Dale Owen, fresh from the failure of his father's communitarian society at New Harmony and convinced that education was what common people most needed. Perhaps there was an excess of strong-minded individuals in the party: after its spectacular beginning, it broke apart into bitterly hostile factions. By 1831 each was insignificant.

Partisan activity in New England took a slightly different form and met much the same fate. The initial issue there, as in New York, was the ten-hour day. New York artisans, however, sought to preserve it while New England artisans had been trying for years to get it. As part of the drive, a convention in Boston in the spring of 1832 brought forth the New-England Association of Farmers, Mechanics, and other Working Men. Its most distinctive feature was its comprehensiveness. In part designed to be a central union for the whole region, it opened membership to groups usually excluded, notably factory hands and (as the name indicated) farmers. The association also dabbled in politics, building on the scattered efforts of earlier New England Working Men's parties. In addition to campaigning in local elections, the Association endorsed a candidate for governor of Massachusetts in 1833 and 1834 (he did poorly) and suggested that labor ought to build an independent national political organization.

That did not occur. Before 1834 was over the association was defunct and there were few legitimate Working Men's parties of any sort left. They were weakened by personal and ideological conflict (Skidmore was adept at generating both in New York). They were frustrated by their inability to wean the mass of workers away from traditional party loyalties. The major parties, in turn, damaged Working Men's parties by infiltrating them, taking over their issues, or slandering them, whichever was most effective. By the mid-1830s some workers turned to Jackson's Democrats, others to their rivals. Labor was back to its usual strategy of voting to reward its friends of whichever party and to punish its enemies (often finding it difficult to tell which was which).

While they lasted, Working Men's parties consistently made several demands; these likewise appeared among the resolutions of Trades' Associations and were at the heart of labor reform. The ten-hour workday, whether as an objective or a right to be defended, was always high on the artisans' list of priorities. Anything more lengthy, they argued, deprived them of good health, a proper family life, and opportunities for self-improvement and political participation. Artisans also urged abolition of imprisonment for debt and demanded that the legal and electoral systems and the militia be made fairer to common folk. They sought passage of mechanics' lien laws: these entitled workers to make claims against the estates of deceased or bankrupt employers in order to recover back wages. Like the Jacksonians, artisans waged war on monopolies, by which they meant any sort of legally sanctioned economic privilege, including corporation charters. They regarded these as conferring benefits on a handful of idle and wealthy individuals and they called for open competition, with the government granting no special favors—hardly a radical suggestion. On no issue were Working Men's parties more insistent than on the need for free public schools. Artisans believed that equal access to knowledge would erase invidious social distinctions, provide all with a fair chance to rise in the world, and sweep away the baneful effects of ignorance and prejudice. "In obtaining an equal system of education," the Philadelphia party declared in 1830, "we will rid ourselves of every existing evil." That faith was pervasive, powerful, and as millennial as it was misplaced.

In the twentieth century the mechanics' programs look mild to the point of innocuousness. A few items were demands for fair play; most bespoke a firm confidence in self-advancement and in individual initiative. The stands against monopolies and in favor of public education, for instance, reflect the traditional hope of journeymen that they might themselves become masters, employers, and petty capitalists. Among the formal resolutions of the Working Men's parties there were no calls for anything resembling the modern welfare state, nor was there much evidence of a desire to change society, root and branch. The artisans were not so disgruntled by the early stages of industrialization—or so lacking in self-confidence—that they were willing to go on record as wanting more than to avoid being reduced to common laborers. They feared betrayal of the egalitarian promises of the Revolution and thought America might well be becoming like Europe, with its extremes of wealth and poverty. They wanted assurance that, with talent and hard work, they could continue to become small-scale entrepreneurs. In common with the evangelicals, they recognized the misery around them, denounced it harshly, and yet were optimistic about the ability of individuals to surmount it.

Yet there was a radical streak in labor reform in the 1830s. Artisans took to electioneering in the first place because of utter disenchantment with "the two great political parties which have heretofore misruled and misguided the people" (a feeling many middle-class reformers shared). Spokesmen for workers declared that the partisan organizations of the day were in the clutches of "aristocrats" and rotten to the core. Cautious labor leaders as well as radicals painted grim pictures of a political structure corrupt almost beyond redemption and of a nation blighted by poverty, degradation, and exploitation. That may have been good rhetoric, nothing more. Still, to talk in those terms was to deny the optimism that also appeared in workingmen's pronouncements and to invite disaffection with the economic system.

Labor reform did indeed attract legions of men and women with ideas about restructuring the social order. Abolitionists, temperance workers, and most conventional reformers may have shunned workingmen's organizations, but utopians flocked to them—Robert Dale Owen was merely the most famous of the lot. They rubbed shoulders with genuine radicals like Skidmore, who questioned the right of individuals to accumulate great wealth and who talked of the exploitation of labor by capital. Even the *Working Man's Advocate*, edited by Skidmore's moderate rival, George Henry Evans, began with a masthead proclaiming: "All children are entitled to equal education; all adults to equal property; and all mankind to equal privileges." (The middle term disappeared after the second issue, however.) For artisans to give such views a hearing in the 1830s indicates second thoughts about capitalistic individualism. There was a radical edge to the millennial expectation that workingmen could triumph "over every species of injustice and oppression."

Working Men's parties occasionally used the language of class conflict, but they were remarkably broad in the social composition of their membership. Artisans accepted as a brother or sister anyone who supported their programs and, as a consequence, the parties included masters, journeymen, politicians, men who never worked with their hands, middle-class or wealthy utopians like Owen, extremists, conservatives, practical unionists, and crackpots. Despite that diversity, many of these people shared characteristics setting them apart from other antebellum reformers. They differed, for instance, in status and theology from the directors of the Protestant "benevolent empire." Although Working Men's parties sometimes put wealthy non-worker candidates up for office, few genuine labor leaders had the social prominence or financial resources of an Arthur Tappan. An impressively large proportion did not share Tappan's theology either. More than any other crusade, with the possible exception of spiritualism, labor reform provided a haven for atheists, deists, and opponents of formal religion like Owen and his colleague Frances Wright. That was testimony both to the secular nature of workingmen's groups and to an undercurrent of freethinking among the artisans themselves. Also virtually unique to the labor movement were slender but significant ties between it and English radical traditions, a bond going back to the eighteenth century and personified by Tom Paine. Owen, Evans, William Heighton (a founder of the Mechanics' Union), and Thomas Brothers (Philadelphia hatmaker and radical journalist) were British-born and versed in the literature of European socialisms and working-class protest. The same sort of books and pamphlets they cited were reprinted in labor newspapers and quoted by native workingmen. Artisans had their international connections, just as evangelicals, abolitionists, pacifists, and temperance reformers did—although at different levels of society and of political consciousness.

The ideological and sociological mix of the Working Men's parties has led historians to question whether they really represented labor. Certainly they did not reach down to the lowest levels of the work force (the American labor movement seldom has). Equally true, the political naïveté of artisans—and their need to spend their days earning a living—made it easy for ambitious men, with money and leisure, to capture mechanics' organizations and use them to promote some other party or cause. Yet in terms of issues, candidates for office, and access to positions of authority, Working Men's parties at their worst did better by artisans than the Whigs and Democrats. Never after 1834 would America come so close to having a legitimate, viable labor party.

Labor reform, of course, did not die with the Working Men's parties in the early 1830s. As before, local unions and trade associations agitated for social causes and provided a home for utopians, even while pressing hard on economic issues. On all fronts they had successes. Wages seem to have risen by 1837 (so had prices) and the ten-hour day became commonplace for artisans in the East—in 1840 President Van Buren would establish it on federal projects. State governments began to meet the demands of workingmen's groups by abolishing imprisonment for debt and by making changes in the militia and in educational systems. In spite of the failure of independent political action, labor appeared to be making gains by the mid-1830s.

There was every reason to believe that better organization could accomplish still more. For a brief period, beginning in 1834, there was a first attempt at a countrywide federation of workers' groups, the National Trades Union. Seeking to "unite and harmonize the efforts of all the productive classes of our country," the union was a step toward consolidating and giving central direction to the labor movement. Before it met an untimely end with the Panic of 1837, it had begun to tighten its authority and had suggested such strong measures as general strikes in support of member unions. (One such strike in Philadelphia in 1834 focused upon the ten-hour workday and involved skilled, unskilled, and female workers.) Perhaps inspired by the union, at least five trades attempted to form their own national organizations in the 1830s.

The bottom dropped out in 1837. The Panic and the subsequent half decade of depression threw a third of the labor force out of work. Pay fell by a third, or perhaps a half. Workingmen's organizations collapsed.

Hard times only partially explain the falling off of labor reform in the late 1830s. It also suffered from institutional and ideological liabilities. The legal status of unions, boycotts, and strikes was dubious and labor leaders lived under the shadow of possible prosecution for conspiracy. That threat eased somewhat in 1842, with a landmark pro-union Massachusetts Supreme Court decision in *Commonwealth* v. *Hunt*. Employers, nonetheless, continued to coerce workers who tried to engage in collective action. Even without any sort of persecution it would have been difficult to fashion an effective nationwide labor movement in the antebellum years. Industry itself tended to be local and small. Trade associations had trouble coordinating terms of employment in different areas—there were too many producers to deal with. Workers, meanwhile, made use of cheap transportation, as their masters did, and slipped from place to place, seeking (and finding) different conditions.

Labor organizations created further troubles for themselves. They admitted people with clashing economic interests (notably masters and journeymen) and with different ideologies, ensuring a high level of internecine warfare. They also accepted assumptions that undermined the class consciousness and commitment to collective action a labor movement has to have. Like Ben Franklin, patron saint of the artisans, they believed that education, hard work, and thrift brought success. Such a view assumed that social mobility was a real possibility and that achievement was an individual matter. Why, then, take the risks of joining the movement when initiative and better schooling could lift one, or one's children, into the ranks of lesser capitalists?

As the economy revived in the early 1840s, so did labor reform, although with alterations in goals and tactics. Some turned toward individualistic and self-help panaceas, including temperance, as cures for working-class ills. By contrast, several onetime labor reformers committed themselves to communitarianism, especially to the Fourierist variety, with its elaborate mechanisms for allocating work. Others thought the answer was to set up producers' cooperatives so craftsmen could reap the full profit of their labor. Land reform also had its promoters. George Henry Evans emerged from retirement to propagandize for it through his National Reform Association, begun in 1844. Evans argued that the solution to labor's difficulties was to give public lands to settlers. Free farms in the West, he reasoned, would draw excess population from the East and raise wages for those who remained. If anything, the idea of homesteading gained more popularity among farmers and middle-class folk than among workers (by 1860 Northern Republicans and Democrats both endorsed it and in 1862 it became law). In any event, land reform's message for labor, like that of cooperatives and communitarianism, was to tell it to find salvation by avoiding conflicts with capital and by withdrawing from the factory system.

That may have been appealing advice, but it was not practical for the mass of workers. The majority of labor reformers turned away from utopianism in the 1840s, lost or muted their millennial zeal, and directed their attention to achievable, short-range objectives (a change many other antebellum crusaders went through in the following decade). Trades' Associations, dormant since the Panic, did not reappear until 1847, when they again flourished for a few years. Individual unions, meanwhile, concentrated single-mindedly on wages and working conditions more often than they had in the 1830s.

Labor's great collective effort in the 1840s was scarcely new, let alone radical. It was to bring the ten-hour day to artisans and factory workers who had not gotten it in the 1830s. Lobbying organizations appeared locally in Massachusetts by 1842. Female mill operatives, then forming their own unions, were particularly dedicated campaigners for the reduced workday (as well as for regulations protecting child labor). The cause seemed to get its biggest boost with the creation, in 1844, of the New England Working Men's Association, designed to coordinate efforts throughout the region. Its effectiveness, however, was immediately compromised by conflict among Fourierists, land reformers, and those who favored leaving such extraneous crusades alone. Power passed back and forth between factions until the association fell apart in 1848. By that time the ten-hour movement was safely in the hands of other groups throughout New England and, slightly later, in the mid-Atlantic states. The campaign was intense and significant for speaking to the condition of factory hands more than previous organizational drives had been. A few legislatures responded, beginning with New Hampshire's in 1847, but these victories were as modest as the demand: the earliest laws left workers free to contract voluntarily for longer hours, an option employers strongly encouraged.

In the 1850s labor organizations once again followed the business cycle—up in 1850–51, down in 1854–55, up again, then down sharply in 1857. The most successful unions of the period were, as usual, in the skilled trades and they had many of the features of their twentieth-century counterparts. They collected dues, provided benefits for members, bargained with employers, used strikes (about 400 in 1853–54 alone), and sometimes won. In general, they were more tightly organized than earlier unions and less involved in politics or in wide-ranging social crusades.

Perhaps the most impressive development in the 1850s was the reemergence of national trade associations. Over a dozen of them were formed between 1850 and 1860. Many were short-lived and ineffective but they represented an awareness that it was necessary for workers to have standard agreements throughout the industrial regions, lest producers use goods from cheap-labor areas to drive down wages paid elsewhere. Three of the nationals, moreover, broke with the older mode of organizing. These—molders, machinists, and cotton mule spinners—consisted for the most part of men who worked in factories at a single stage in the manufacturing process, rather than making a finished product. For them to put together a national union was a tacit admission that the division of labor was here to stay and that many wage earners no longer had the independence or skills that had once been the pride of the artisans.

Time vindicated the labor leaders of the 1850s. Their type of unionism outlived their organizations, survived the Civil War, and eventually succeeded in raising pay, improving conditions, helping brethren through hard times, and holding on to a dues-paying membership. Their practicality, however, was at the expense of the old radical spirit of men like Thomas Skidmore, which was mostly gone by 1860. (Immigrants would bring it back later in the century.) Largely gone also was the view—which caused so much trouble for the Working Men's parties—that all who toiled with their hands were brothers and sisters. It was replaced by a more selfish sense that each segment of the work force had to look out primarily for its own welfare, while the devil took the hindmost (or the least skilled).

The world-view in much of antebellum labor reform is alien to twentieth-century Americans. People who believe in today's practical, "bread and butter" unionism fault workingmen's associations of the 1830s for their political involvement and their utopian binges (as if idealism and imagination were sins in labor organizations). Radicals, on the other hand, are critical of antebellum labor leaders for their failure to develop a consistent class consciousness, or sense of class conflict, and for their basic acceptance of private property.

By whatever modern standards one uses, labor reform and evangelical Protestant charity before 1850 seem imperfect and unrealistic responses to urbanization and industrialization. But both define the outer limits of most Americans' ability to treat directly the problems posed by economic change. One cause was secular, the other religious; one had roots among artisans, the other was middle and upper class. Both had a brief millennial fling—a temporary belief that the Kingdom was about to come and that poverty could be abolished along with the rest of the world's evils. Neither was adequate to the job and each, by the 1850s, had begun to settle in for trench warfare against the disruptive effects of cities and factories: organized to endure and to fight for tightly defined objectives, with lowered expectations.

With variations, the story was much the same for many other antebellum reformers. Few of them ever aimed at a total transformation of society (communitarians and nonresistants were the prime exceptions). In their most enthusiastic moments—which likewise had become less frequent by 1850—they did talk about the march of civilization and paint pictures of a millennium soon to come. What they had in mind, nonetheless, looked like what America would have if it just lived up to its own Protestant and democratic pieties. It may, in fact, be in the nature of reform for it to appear terribly extreme in its day (as labor reform certainly did to middle-class folk) and yet to play an essentially unifying and conservative role. Much like the law, reform asserts values—usually generally held ones—and tries to reconcile reality with them. Rather than transcending society, it is a mechanism through which society debates, modifies, and enforces rules.

That is fine for everyone except those whose values are different and against whom the rules are made.

9. Institutions and Uplift

One of the basic problems in combating sin is to figure out who the sinners are. Some reforms, such as the Graham diet and phrenology, answer that we all are and direct their efforts primarily to curing the reformer. Most causes, however, identify somebody else as the culprit and aim at him or her. This act of labeling groups or individuals as evil or misguided can become important in itself. For antebellum reformers it was a means of setting limits to pluralism in an increasingly pluralistic nation.

There have been many outsiders in American culture, ranging from alienated heroes to despised social groups. Perhaps the most ironic of these is the Indian, who has the best claim, by length of residence, to representing the true American way of life. Indians never were a major concern of pre-Civil War reform but they figure in here primarily because attitudes toward them illustrate a point about social crusades and the objects of their attention.

Beginning in the late eighteenth century, missionary societies sent agents to proselytize red, as well as white, heathen in the West. Their goal was to do more than gather in converts. As a Methodist preacher admitted in 1857, missionaries sought "to teach the Indians to live like white people." To many present-day Americans, those words have a distasteful air of paternalism and colonialism. Yet there are worse ways of dealing with people different from one's own kind: at least the missionary assumed that Indians had the capability of becoming brethren in Christ and of mastering the arts and refinements of whites. Others, as we know, were not so charitable (nor always were missionaries). But whether whites advocated conversion or extermination, they thought of the Indian as a "savage" and his "barbarity" was the antithesis—and the measure—of "civilization." Whites gauged their own "progress" by their divergence from the Indian's style of life.

Outsiders are always similarly useful to the majority and to social activists alike. "Normal" people project hopes and fears onto them and, in the bargain, turn them into reference points marking the difference between what is good and bad. That is a common enough psychological process, and in the antebellum years, blacks, foreigners, and subversives (including reformers) served some people as much the same kind of negative reference points as Indians often did. Hatred and prejudice lay behind those feelings, but their function was to help groups of whites clarify in their own minds what was American and right by contrasting it with what was un-American and wrong.

Much the same thing went on with reformers. They expressed their sense of righteousness by describing unrighteous people. In the twentieth century many of their judgments seem just: if one has to have an opposite it might as well be a slaveholder, a warmonger, an oppressor of women or workers, a drunkard, or a glutton. Yet the comparison with anti-Indian, anti-black, and anti-immigrant sentiment ought to be a warning. There are dangers in drawing sharp, highly moralistic social boundaries like the ones often made by pre-Civil War reformers. If too restrictive and rigidly enforced, they stifle diversity instead of promoting justice and virtue. In the early nineteenth century that usually was not the case. Harsh as reformers were in denouncing vice, they relied on moral suasion rather than compulsion and believed that sinners should be accepted into the circle of righteousness after repentance. Things took a more repressive and pessimistic turn in the late 1830s, when temperance workers used legislation to force conformity to their view of drinking. Slightly earlier, others were developing different means of coercing people to uplift them and society.

After the War of 1812 state and local officials started to examine poverty, dependency, and crime within their jurisdictions. Massachusetts' legislature led the way in 1820 with a comprehensive study of indigence and its treatment. New York followed in 1823. Cities also inspected their primitive welfare apparatus. These investigations were in part inspired by sudden urban growth and by a depression that began in 1819; but even when they were undertaken in a mood of urgency, they displayed some of the same millennial confidence that evangelical charity workers had begun to radiate. Pauperism, the New York report declared, "may, with proper care and attention, be almost wholly eradicated from our soil."

It is no wonder that there were similarities in tone between governmental investigations and the rhetoric of urban missionaries. Protestant charitable groups, quickest to react to crises, prodded lawmakers and worked with them once they responded. In many cases, there would continue to be close ties between private and public benevolence for decades. State and municipal administrations, however, did dispense aid in a somewhat different manner from private charities. The latter ran some asylums (orphanages, for instance); more commonly, they gave assistance directly to individuals living in their own homes. Antebellum public officials spent proportionally less money on such "outdoor relief," often preferring to put troublesome human beings in institutions.

At first, inmates were easier to come by than buildings. The increase in almshouses, orphanages, jails, or hospitals for the insane is striking after 1820 and was far greater than population growth alone warranted. Equally impressive, during the same years these institutions changed in function and, sometimes, in form. Eighteenth-century almshouses, for instance, were rare and usually were places of last resort for the most helpless of the poor. Otherwise, families cared for their own and able-bodied paupers were set to work or hurried out of the jurisdiction, to become somebody else's headache. In the nineteenth century, practices were less flexible and the almshouse became, in many instances, the predominant way in which governments dealt with indigents. (For a decade, the Philadelphia and Chicago city fathers refused to give any outdoor relief whatsoever.) The nineteenth-century almshouse handled, at low cost, individuals whom families and neighbors no longer would care for in a mobile, heterogeneous society. In addition, it could, according to its proponents, be structured so as to reform most of its inmates. Presumably all but the hopelessly ill or very aged did some work and learned skills and personal habits enabling them to lead useful, virtuous lives. Eighteenth-century almshouses had not been burdened either with such a large clientele or with such grand expectations.

Prisons also underwent a transformation in the antebellum years. Since the late eighteenth century American and European philanthropists had been trying to make jails more humane. They had some effect in the United States, particularly in Pennsylvania, where Quaker benevolence was a force, and in New York. But it was after 1800 that prisons became a major issue, agitated effectively by new organizations like the Boston Prison Discipline Society, founded in 1825 by an agent of the American Bible Society. Such groups helped shape the many jails and penitentiaries built after 1810.

Especially influential—and hotly debated—were the systems implemented by New York at Auburn and Ossining (Sing Sing) between 1819 and 1825 and by Pennsylvania at Pittsburgh and Philadelphia between 1826 and 1829. The plans differed in detail and zealous admirers quarreled over the merits of each; but the hallmark of both was almost total isolation of prisoners from one another and from the outside world. New York made provision for some interaction among inmates, although virtually no verbal communication. In Pennsylvania, prisoners were kept in solitary confinement so absolute that they were not even to know the identities of fellow convicts. One or the other system was imitated in nearly a dozen states before the Civil War.

These antebellum penitentiaries were more than a response to what people regarded as a high crime rate. Certainly there were cheaper ways of dealing with criminals than erecting expensive stone fortresses, with separate cells for each inmate. The object was not strictly economy, or to ameliorate the suffering of the prisoner, the goal of eighteenth-century humanitarianism: it was to make the convict into a model citizen. Antebellum prison reformers assumed that the environment, not flaws in a person's character, produced sin. (Their view was close to that of Robert Owen and many communitarians, who likewise thought of moral behavior as a product of the conditions under which human beings lived.) Reformers attempted —with much success—to persuade state legislatures that if criminals were taken out of the situation that created them, and totally cut off from previous associates, they would be amenable to good influences. Convicts would have time to ponder their errors and to gain the self-discipline they had not learned from their families and communities. (In practice, many reacted to isolation by going insane or committing suicide.) Two French observers, Alexis de Tocqueville and Gustave de Beaumont, claimed the American philanthropists they met in the early 1830s "consider man, however far advanced in crime, as still susceptible of being brought back to virtue." The penitentiary "seems the remedy for all the evils of society."

As reformers learned more about the dependent classes, they came to see differences and to realize that even the best of almshouses and prisons were not beneficial for every sort of inmate. The insane and children, in particular, had a rough time when thrown in with seasoned paupers and rogues. Concerned men and women began to consider what sort of treatment might be more appropriate for them. The answer was new, special asylums. Just as some reformers' interests clustered around antislavery, pacifism, and woman's rights, the commitments of others focused on almshouses and prisons, and then broadened to include more novel institutions.

The first facility for juvenile delinquents, the New York House of Refuge, opened its doors to wayward boys and girls on New Year's Day 1825. For over a decade the city's Common Council had been concerned about mayhem from youthful vagrants and with the difficulties of placing them in existing institutions. It took the Society for the Prevention of Pauperism—among whose members was the mayor—to come up with a solution. Drawing on one person's knowledge of European experiments with problem children, a committee appointed by the society compiled a report which led to the creation of a Society for the Reformation of Juvenile Delinquents. Its mandate was to raise money for "a prison" for minors. Endorsing the idea, the Common Council donated the land upon which an outmoded federal arsenal stood. The United States government then sold the building itself to the society for $2,000. For its part, the society provided management and much of the money, at least until 1829, when public funding became a dependable source of revenue.

Boston built its House of Refuge in 1826 and Philadelphia's came in 1828. By the late 1850s they appeared in cities as widely scattered as New Orleans, Chicago, and Providence. Massachusetts, in 1848, and New York, in 1849, opened the first state-supported reform schools. Although most of these were publicly financed, they continued—in the tradition of the New York House of Refuge—to have generous assistance from charitable groups and individuals. In 1860 three of the major facilities for delinquents were still private corporations with some state regulation.

Many features of these Houses and Reform Schools are open to condemnation, particularly their use of solitary confinement and corporal punishment. The earliest and best of them, however, were remarkable for their honest attempts to help delinquents. Officials believed young wrongdoers were best "subdued by kindness." Discipline was never lax and moralizing was often heavy-handed, but it was aimed at teaching self-control and clean living to children who had known little of either. The Boston House encouraged a sense of responsibility by involving inmates in judging their own and each other's conduct, and by rewarding improvements in behavior. Formal instruction in the Houses ranged from the most elementary homemaking skills to conventional schooling, both of which were alien to many of the children. When a youth gave signs of being able to function as an independent, law-abiding human being, he or she was bound out as an apprentice to learn a trade.

Through the 1840s reformers were confident that the majority of their wards were amenable to such therapy. A hymn written in honor of the Massachusetts State Reform School assumed that if this "sweet retreat"

> . . . may win from folly's wiles,
>   The little wanderer's feet;
> Then from this guardian home will rise
>   The good and great, refined and wise.

That did not always happen. The Houses suffered from underfunding, too many candidates for admission, too few outside jobs for them, and too much illicit advice being communicated from older to younger inmates. By the 1860s the rate of "cures" was so disappointing that reformers were wondering whether the failure might not actually lie with the clients, rather than the institutions. Perhaps delinquents were innately bad, the offspring of "poor stock" and therefore unsalvageable.

Although it eventually became respectable to blame the underage criminal (or his "race"), dissatisfaction with the Houses themselves had been mounting through the 1850s. Private benevolent societies were particularly eager to come up with alternatives and to get to children before they were caught up in public institutions. As early as 1832, with the founding of the Boston Asylum and Farm School for Boys, philanthropists began to reach out for idle and rowdy minors who, if not helped, were likely candidates for the Houses. Of most consequence were the New York City labors of Charles Loring Brace, a former divinity student and ex-assistant to an urban missionary. His Children's Aid Society (1853) was an inspiration to public and private charities across the land. Having as its purpose elimination of pauperism and criminality, it was a well-diversified enterprise providing everything from education to lodging for city children—all the while being run on "scientific principles" and teaching self-reliance, hard work, and thrift.

That was a difficult performance for cost-conscious public officials to match, and few had the taste to try. The states, nonetheless, did become aware of deficiencies in the Houses and they began to make innovations of their own in the 1850s. Several began "reform schools" to take lesser offenders and those from rural areas. Massachusetts, with its Reform School for Girls (1855), and Ohio, with its Reform Farm (1857), experimented with a different mode of organization, a "family system" in which delinquents were placed in a country atmosphere, in smaller groups more nearly approximating a normal household.

After initiation of the "family system" there would be few changes in the handling of young offenders until the end of the nineteenth century, when separate juvenile-court systems were begun. Since then, the most important reforms have repudiated what was done earlier in the name of reform—especially the nineteenth-century eagerness to put minors in institutions. That skepticism about antebellum solutions may well be justified by the record. As time went on, the Houses of Refuge bore less and less resemblance to the good intentions of the men and women who created them (a pattern they shared with penitentiaries). Overcrowding and understaffing made personal attention difficult to give to delinquents. The Houses became dumping grounds for people too young for regular jails and too tough to be on the loose. But even the most perceptive and innovative of pre-Civil War figures came up with counterproposals of limited effectiveness, at best. Charles Loring Brace, for instance, recognized the failures of custodial institutions to cure delinquency. Yet among his favorite alternatives was placement of New York vagabonds on western farms. The plan neither succeeded in "draining the City of vagrant Children," as he hoped, nor served as much of a solution to the problems of poverty and juvenile crime.

The development of mental hospitals followed a parallel course to that of penitentiaries and Houses of Refuge. All derived from the notion, relatively new and exciting in the antebellum period, that asylums could be a tool of social and individual advancement. All stemmed from a recognition that different categories of poor and dependent people required different treatment. Yet even better than the Houses of Refuge, mental hospitals demonstrate how reformist goals could be betrayed by asylums as well as embodied in them.

After some lobbying by the Boston Prison Discipline Society and a young legislator named Horace Mann, the Massachusetts General Court in 1830 authorized construction of a hospital for lunatics, to be located at Worcester. The facility, which opened its doors in 1833, was not the first public insane asylum but it was the most modern and influential in its day (the other four in existence in 1833 were obscure and in slave states, where social services were ill maintained). The superintendent, Samuel B. Woodward, was an able administrator and publicist. He and his supporters soon proclaimed that Worcester was a model for the rest of the nation to emulate.

It took time to convince legislatures—only two states followed Massachusetts' example in the 1830s. The pace quickened in the 1840s, and again in the 1850s. By the Civil War, twenty-eight states, four cities, and the federal government had public mental institutions. That was an impressive amount of asylum building in view of the obstacles, foremost of which was the reluctance of antebellum lawmakers to spend money on the needy and on non-voters. Indeed, their willingness to construct mental hospitals is far more puzzling than their willingness to invest in prisons, since the sense of urgency about insanity was much less than about crime. Both seemed to be dramatically on the rise (madness probably was not); but, as a practical matter, a walk through parts of any American city would convince a taxpayer that there was more to fear from thugs than from lunatics.

Proponents of asylums won many of their victories by skillful agitation. They differed from other antebellum reformers in ways that made them effective at lobbying. Unlike many of their fellow crusaders, they trusted politicians and the political system and were very good at working through it. They tended to be religiously inspired but their theology was more orthodox and less offensive to the public than, for instance, William Lloyd Garrison's. If not extraordinarily wealthy, they were nonetheless comfortable and secure in status (a modest inheritance financed Dorothea Dix's career). Their respectability and moderate demeanor drew, rather than alienated, influential people. So cautious was Dix that she even refused to take a stand against slavery, making her one of the few New England reformers welcome in the South.

Dix and her colleagues had a conservative side to their ideal as well as to their tactics. They often blamed the strains of "civilization" for causing increasing amounts of insanity. The idea was common in both Europe and the United States and it could lead in different directions. For romantic radicals it implied a need for humans to liberate themselves from institutions and dogmas and return to a free, natural existence. That, however, was not what asylum builders had in mind. To the contrary, their concern was with freedom itself, which seemed to them to be excessive in nineteenth-century America. Pursuit of economic advantage, political turmoil, and the hustle and bustle of cities were more than fragile minds could bear. Reformers wished to see mental institutions instill in patients the internal guidance necessary for survival in such a confusing world of choices and fluidity. That meant learning Protestant morality, cleanliness, thrift, discipline, continence, and temperance.

In teaching those habits, mental hospitals both fulfilled a need created by the failure of families and churches and reproved an egalitarian, capitalistic society for driving people mad. (At the same time, of course, the ideal asylum would be producing precisely the kind of orderly, disciplined individuals essential to the factories and cities of an egalitarian, capitalistic society.)

The metaphysics of asylums probably had less effect on penny-pinching legislators than did the claims of professionals like Woodward that madness was curable. Europeans had long insisted that it was and Americans were not inclined to be any less optimistic. Woodward believed "judicious treatment" of "recent cases of insanity" would result in "as large a proportion of recoveries . . . as from any other acute disease of equal severity." Worcester, according to him, was able to discharge between 80 and 90 percent of those whom it got in the early stages of lunacy. Not to be outdone, his fellow superintendents presented similar figures, and two, in the 1840s, claimed 100 percent success. The statistics clearly were exaggerated: patients were counted as "cured" more than once, and there were other lapses from accuracy.

Still, the first asylums may have done well by their inmates. The institutions were small (Worcester originally had room for 120 patients), life in them was highly structured, and treatment was personal and gentle—a therapy of kindness that is often very effective. A twentieth-century authority puts the real cure rate at slightly over 50 percent, a fine showing by present-day standards. Yet even that might have been unacceptably below the expectations of reformers. Although sober, respectable men and women, they (no less than the wildest perfectionists) wanted to believe that no human was beyond redemption. With the proper application of scientific principles, the asylum—like the penitentiary and the House of Refuge—could take society's outcasts and make them virtuous and productive.

That was asking too much. Once asylums were built, people became more conscious of "insanity" as a "problem": there was a growing willingness to identify strange behavior as lunacy and to expect a rapid cure. Yet families and governments also quickly learned the advantages of locking burdensome people up where they could be kept cheaply and out of sight, with no unpleasant reminders of their existence. Many of these inmates were harmless and in earlier years would have been kept in private homes or left to wander. Some were senile, imbeciles, or syphilitics for whom improvement was impossible. Soon the hospitals were crowded; cities constructed their own institutions rather than ship lunatics to state facilities, located in the countryside. Those institutions filled. Small hospitals gave way to large ones; the superintendent became a bureaucrat rather than a healer; and individual attention and kindness were replaced by restraints and force.

As conditions deteriorated, optimism about curability faded. A report undertaken in 1854 for the Massachusetts legislature and written by a medical authority spoke of "inherent elements of poverty and insanity." That position, which was to become orthodox, shifted responsibility from the environment to the brain and justified the failure of mental hospitals to change their inmates. Like penitentiaries and Houses of Refuge, they were losing their reformist mission in the 1850s and becoming storage bins for society's outcasts.

There is a long postscript to the story of antebellum asylum building. Trends toward professionalization and bureaucratization, first evident in the 1840s, were destined to continue. In 1844 managers of mental hospitals formed the Association of Medical Superintendents of American Institutions for the Insane. It promoted the superintendents' viewpoint through conferences and a periodical, the *American Journal of Insanity*. By 1870 there was a National Prison Congress and in 1872 there began a series of international ones. Asylum administrators of all sorts gathered into organizations, conscious of being a group with distinct interests to promote and defend.

At the same time, the superintendent's power was being jeopardized by his clients, state legislatures, and his superiors. In the 1850s and 1860s ex-inmates published sensational exposés of maltreatment and wrongful incarceration in mental institutions. The subsequent outcry resulted in proposals for personal liberty laws protecting the rights of men and women committed to asylums. Little legislation was ever passed, but the prospect of it was enough to make administrators cautious. More of a threat to them were the very processes of professionalization and bureaucratization of which they were a part. By the 1850s cities and states were moving to consolidate public welfare activities, then administered and financed haphazardly. In 1863 Massachusetts founded its Board of State Charities, the closest thing at the time to a state welfare department. By the early 1870s many states in the Northeast and Midwest had similar agencies. The people who staffed them usually were professionals, like the asylum managers, but their goals were to cut costs, improve efficiency, and bring all public services under their jurisdiction. That necessarily worked against the autonomy of superintendents of particular institutions.

The city and state boards, furthermore, were signs that the original reformist expectations were departing in favor of the view that social problems had to be managed rather than cured. Board members often were less interested in trying to eliminate poverty, crime, and insanity—the dreams of the 1820s, 1830s, and 1840s—than they were in eliminating welfare. Yet neither they, nor (predictably) the superintendents, saw fit to challenge the notion that incarceration was the best treatment for deviance. That would remain an article of faith until well into the twentieth century.

Grim as asylums were, it would be foolish to deny the good they did, especially at first. No one can read of conditions in nineteenth-century slums and of cruelty toward the insane without feeling that many delinquents and madmen were better off inside institutions than out, at least those whose families could not (or would not) care for them. Even prison reform may have been a pleasant reality for convicts like those in Connecticut who were moved in the 1820s from an abandoned copper mine to a new state penitentiary. There were, moreover, other, lesser known varieties of asylums in the antebellum period, some of them remarkable for their accomplishments and general decency. Particularly impressive were the endeavors of Thomas Gallaudet with deaf-mutes and of Samuel Gridley Howe with the blind in his Perkins Institute, founded in 1832. Their work, and that of the earliest mental hospitals and Houses of Refuge, gave ample evidence that human sympathy was very much a part of asylum building.

But there were harsher aspects to it, and features that were downright insidious. By nature, asylums are repressive and, if anything, reformers made them more so by insisting on completely cutting the inmate off from his or her old environment. Of course, there are forms of behavior no society can tolerate and many men and women put away in prisons and mental hospitals would have been dangerous if left loose. But in less extreme cases, the condition being "cured" was more benign and did not require incarceration. Concepts of what is criminal or deviant, in fact, are social constructs, varying over time and from group to group. What one person or generation considers wrong or crazy may be acceptable to the next. Without meaning to, a nineteenth-century German medical student provided a perfect illustration of the point. He discovered an epidemic of madness in Europe and America and presented his findings under the descriptive title "On the Democratic Disease, a New Form of Insanity." By his way of reckoning, in the United States the lunatics were indeed running the asylum.

Since criminality and madness can be defined in different ways, critics have charged asylums with being designed to accustom unruly Americans to the time discipline of the factory or as being weapons against conduct that offended middle-class sensibilities. Certainly the potential for abusing asylums existed. Admissions standards were loose enough to allow public officials and relatives much latitude in determining who belonged in an institution. In 1826, for instance, Massachusetts permitted the Boston House of Reformation to take "all children who live an idle or dissolute life, whose parents are dead, or if living, from drunkenness, or other vices, neglect to provide any suitable employment, or exercise any salutary control over said children." Needless to say, the statute left a fair amount of room for value judgments. Within the asylum, superintendents had an equivalent amount of discretion. They expected inmates to learn the conventional virtues (it would have been surprising had they permitted anything else). Release from a House of Refuge—where juveniles were held on indeterminate sentences—or from a mental hospital usually depended on the inmate's ability to convince the administration that he or she was now prepared to conform to the expectations of decent folk.

These were not despicable standards, but they could be applied unfairly and against the interests of particular classes and ethnic groups. Catholics objected strenuously to Protestant evangelizing in the institutions. (In 1863 New York Catholics organized a reformatory to keep their delinquents away from Charles Loring Brace and out of the clutches of the House of Refuge.) Some inequities also clearly existed in admissions to institutions. Very early on, immigrants and poor people were overrepresented—some of it due to genuine criminality and insanity, the result of poverty and life in a foreign land (it also reflected the ability of middle-class Protestants to afford private care and good lawyers). Still, it was much easier for an immigrant or a pauper to be labeled as a deviant than for a person of standing. A Randolph of Virginia could act in a bizarre fashion, keep his freedom, and have a political career. If an Irish laborer muttered to himself, and appeared "superstitious" or quarrelsome, he was a prime candidate for incarceration. Once in the asylum, he was in the custody of people who did not like his religion, did not understand or sympathize with him, and considered him "different" even when he was behaving himself.

Little of the old reformist desire to perfect human beings survived in prisons, Houses of Refuge, and mental institutions after the 1850s. What remained was the idea of regimenting people in order to cure them. The choice, both in the asylum and in society, was clear by midcentury: either immigrants and poor people could conduct themselves in a "proper" and "American" manner or—literally —be outsiders, segregated from society.

Of all the institution building that went on in the antebellum period the most far-reaching and valuable was the construction of free public schools. They were not so repressive or demeaning as asylums (contrary to childhood folklore). They were, moreover, supposed to bring people into the mainstream of American life rather than isolate them from it, as asylums did. Both institutions, however, achieved reformist goals through indoctrination and discipline. Each tried to create a new person, incapable of immorality, and both served to define values and norms in a disunited society.

Education was not an antebellum invention. The Puritans of New England held to the traditional Protestant idea that all believers ought to be able to read the Bible and they had begun common schools in the seventeenth century. In the eighteenth century such influential figures as Benjamin Franklin and Thomas Jefferson wrote of the need for education and assisted in efforts to improve it. Schools, nonetheless, were poorly conducted and attendance was spotty until the middle of the nineteenth century, even in New England. Although there were local variations, in many places children of the wealthy were taught in private institutions or at home by special tutors; others paid fees to go to public schools or were designated "charity" cases, a label which offended parents' pride.

Between the 1830s and the Civil War a great change occurred, with Massachusetts leading the way. In 1837 its legislature created a Board of Education, the first secretary of which was Horace Mann, then forty-one years old, experienced as a legislator, and long interested in asylums. For over a decade Mann used his post to promote a number of innovations. The cause of school reform in Massachusetts was also aided by the state government's willingness to formulate educational policy and to implement it against the wishes of reluctant communities. The list of the state's achievements in the antebellum period—before, during, and after Mann's secretaryship —is formidable. Among the items on it are the first Board of Education, the first public high school (1821), the first normal (or teacher training) school (1839), and the first compulsory school attendance law (1852).

Mann and Massachusetts, nonetheless, were not the sum total of educational reform. Visionaries experimented with pedagogical theories of their own or ones borrowed from Europeans. (The communitarian societies at New Harmony and Brook Farm were notable in that respect.) Other states besides Massachusetts formed common school systems of some merit. Almost everywhere, the training of teachers became more formal and the profession rose in status and salary. All these developments were complicated and uneven, both between states and within them. Yet, whatever the situation was in any particular place, one thing was apparent. By 1860, Americans were becoming committed to free public education, at least through the primary levels. They were willing to pay a large share of their taxes for costly school systems, staffed by professionals and, increasingly, administered by elaborate bureaucracies.

Later generations accepted public education as one of the glories of the United States, conveniently forgetting how stiff opposition to it was in the mid-nineteenth century. Resentment came from local interests mistrustful of the state government, from old-fashioned teachers, from Catholics and immigrants who regarded the schools as bastions of middle-class Protestantism, from working people dependent on their children's income, and from wealthy conservatives who saw no sense in trying to teach the rabble. The battles did not cease once school systems were begun, as parents, school boards, religious and ethnic groups, and professionals argued over curriculum and control.

Yet educational reformers had a number of advantages in any conflict. Among antebellum crusaders they were the closest thing to political insiders. Mann, for instance, and Henry Barnard, Commissioner of Education for Connecticut (later United States Commissioner of Education), were Whig politicians and ex-lawmakers. Schools, like asylums, benefited from having the support of people who knew their way around the state capitol.

Educational reformers, in addition, got backing from an odd and effective assortment of groups, including many communitarians and phrenologists (who had strange notions about learning but who thought it was the key to progress). Evangelical Protestants realized that public education would be, from their viewpoint, morally sound and an ally for their own Sunday schools and Bible and tract societies. The more prosperous and skilled segments of the working class likewise demanded free schools, so long as they did not need their children's wages and had hope for upward mobility. Artisans especially were drawn by the idea, emphasized by Mann, that education would save America from the class system so obvious in Europe. Public schools, he wrote, were "the great equalizer of the condition of men."

The crucial elements behind educational reform, nonetheless, were the solid, respectable urban professional and middle classes, the people who would flee city school systems over a century later. They were not in such financial need that they had to have free schooling for their children, but they, too, found attractive things in the rhetoric of Mann and his colleagues. It reassured them that social tensions could be resolved easily and without radical change.

Education, Mann told them, "does better than disarm the poor of their hostility toward the rich; it prevents being poor." That idea was both comforting and an expression of the familiar millennial optimism: anyone could be improved; the nation was wealthy enough for everybody.

School reform, however, played equally well to the darker moods of middle-class men and women. Since the eighteenth century Americans had fretted over what would become of the republic if its people declined in virtue. That appeared to be happening—politics fell into the hands of demagogues; foreigners and paupers made the cities unpleasant and threatening for respectable folk. Schools were the answer. In Mann's words, they were the means for decent Americans to "free ourselves from the low-minded and the vicious; not by their expatriation, but by their elevation." Education would teach good behavior and make the dangerous classes trustworthy.

Those goals were reflected in curriculum. "Our system," Horace Mann wrote, "inculcates all Christian morals." Although public schools had to steer clear of denominational issues, they often had readings from scriptures (required in Massachusetts in 1855). The Bible used, and the theology, were Protestant—a fact that angered Catholics. Schools did train the minds of students and tried to balance mental with physical activity. Yet everything had its moral purpose. Exercise and play were supposed to create sound bodies; and sound bodies, antebellum Americans assumed, were less likely to sin. Textbooks taught virtue as much as literacy. A popular reader of the 1840s, for instance, had a lesson entitled "Danger of Bad Habits." It warned that "vice is not a thing to be trifled with." (Another section praised the mother, then added that "next in rank and in efficacy to that pure and holy source of moral influence is that of the *schoolmaster*.") There was no room here for doubt or disobedience. The child learned self-control, punctuality, all the Protestant and patriotic verities, and intolerance for different styles of life.

The schoolmen were proud of their work. In the 1850s the Boston School Committee, with the Irish clearly in mind, described its noble task as "taking children at random from a great city, undisciplined, uninstructed, often with inveterate forwardness and obstinacy, and with the inherited stupidity of centuries of ignorant ancestors; forming them from animals into intellectual beings, and . . . from intellectual beings into Spiritual beings." Schools—just like asylums—were institutions to instill a standard, sharply defined set of values to every class and ethnic group. They failed, of course, to create cultural homogeneity. That was not for lack of effort, but rather because of the overwhelming regional and sociological complexity of the United States and because of the weakness of the classroom when it comes into conflict with the student's family life and peers.

Asylums and schools did help many people lead happy and productive lives. If the repressive side of such institutions has been emphasized recently (as it is here), the reasons are several. As time went along, Americans became more and more aware of the gap between what the nation's much-vaunted educational system was supposed to be and what it was. From being pictured in the nineteenth century as the cradle of democracy public schools came to be attacked in the mid-twentieth century as elitist and a hazard to mind and body. Prisons and asylums similarly degenerated or failed to match the expectations their proponents raised.

Some of the attack on school systems and custodial institutions, however, has had little to do with their actual performance. It comes from a growing appreciation of the manner in which bureaucratic structures can perpetuate themselves, even when they do not work properly, and a sense that they often impinge on personal freedom and cultural diversity (the latter being more valued by twentieth-century Americans than by their ancestors). People today have likewise become suspicious of professional managers—asylum directors, school administrators, and the like—feeling that they have a vested interest in finding people to fill their establishments and in containing, rather than solving, problems.

Antislavery was the most significant and temperance had the largest number of adherents of the antebellum crusades. Communitarianism, nonresistance, and branches of labor reform were the most radical. Yet school reform brought together the most strands and, in some respects, was the epitome. It was endorsed by nearly all reformist groups: evangelical Protestants, utopians, artisans, and even pseudo-scientists like the phrenologists. It combined optimism about human nature with a desire to shape it by means of a rational system. It had millennial and perfectionist touches—all could be taught, all uplifted—and it ended with lessened hope and an imposing bureaucratic structure.

Afterword:
A Matter of Time

Reformers may not be the best judges of their own place in the universe. True enough, antebellum crusaders assessed their social origins fairly well (they characterized themselves as hardworking Christians of modest means, neither very rich nor very poor). On non-sociological matters, however, they seem to have been less astute. Like most American reformers, they often envisioned themselves as part of some grand procession stretching across the centuries—soldiers in the long march of Protestantism, Reason, Progress, or Democracy. At other moments they (again like later reformers) regarded themselves as outsiders whose critical distance from their society enabled them to see its flaws. In both instances the basic assumption was that they were special people, either quite detached from their time and place or else having a peculiar position within it. There is truth to that notion and it is frequently echoed by historians. Certainly commitment to a cause does separate people from the apathetic or hostile majority. One of the attractions of antebellum reform clearly was the way its organizations and meetings provided moralistic men and women with little islands of righteousness amid what they thought was a vast churning ocean of depravity, acquisitiveness, and disorder.

Yet there are flaws to the idea that reformers and radicals are greatly different from their non-reformist peers. Whatever illusions crusaders may have about their uniqueness, they are products of a milieu. Antebellum reform could not have existed without contemporary developments in printing and transportation. It also reflected, sometimes indirectly, widespread concerns about family life, cultural diversity, economic opportunities, vice, and political turmoil. Above all, it provided men and women with one out of many possible means for comprehending, coping with, shaping, and occasionally ignoring the larger nineteenth-century processes of urbanization, industrialization, population growth, and immigration.

But it is not enough to root antebellum reform in economic, demographic, social, and technological changes. To leave it there is to miss the importance of style, by which I mean the way reformers perceived problems, strategies, tactics, and solutions. That is where culture enters the picture—it inevitably limits the number of responses people can make to a social situation and it determines the particular configuration of ideas, emotions, attitudes, insights, and blind spots characteristic of reformers and radicals in a given age. The style of antebellum reform, in its initial stages, was very much that of evangelical Protestantism, with a leavening of rhetoric from the American Revolution and a dash of economic and scientific thought, especially in communitarianism and labor reform. In the 1820s and 1830s reformers usually thought they were attacking sins, not social problems, and they urged individual repentance rather than legislation and coercion.

By the 1840s that had begun to change, understandably so because reform is never homogeneous or static (unless it has a rigid core of ideology, something American social movements generally lack). Moral commitments can lead in several directions and they tend to be modified by events, successes, failures, and even by boredom. In the case of antebellum reformers, dissatisfaction with religion and churches prompted exploration of such "sciences" as health reform, phrenology, and spiritualism (which often merely dressed Protestant pieties in non-theological language). The ineffectiveness of voluntarism and moral suasion pushed reformers into advocating diverse forms of governmental action, including temperance laws and construction of asylums to turn deviants into model citizens. A mode of reform which, in the 1830s, sought to transform the world, was itself greatly transformed by 1860.

Occasionally scholars argue about whether certain American

"movements" (antebellum crusades among them) were backward-looking or forward-looking. The answer for pre-Civil War reform is that it was both. It attempted to preserve and extend ancient virtues —orderliness, plain living, freedom from external restraints, and so on; but it also made some shifts in emphasis and added such newer goals as strict self-control. (The latter was advocated in nearly every cause from antislavery to the Graham diet, phrenology, and asylum-building.) If reformers could not entirely accept the behavior of their contemporaries, they nonetheless could not entirely reject the values and accomplishments of the social order then emerging in the United States. Like most of their contemporaries, they were simultaneously awed and made uneasy by the rising glory of the United States and by humankind's marvelous mechanical and electrical inventions. Only some less popular causes—communitarianism, feminism, nonresistance, and labor reform—came close to posing a threat to an urbanizing, commercial, and industrial society. The chief effect of other crusades—notably temperance, phrenology, and asylum- or school-building—was to encourage people to adjust to, rather than resist, the brave new world of the nineteenth century.

Most antebellum reformers were, at heart, trying to adapt old and respectable verities, plus a few new ones, to an age of cities, steam-power, rowdy politics, and get-rich-quick schemes. To their way of thinking, that did not require stopping progress in its tracks. Proper morality, they assumed, would ensure that God's (or nature's) plan would continue to unfold as it was supposed to. For them, reform explained what was wrong with individuals and the nation, what might go wrong in the future, and how to avoid it without sacrificing the historic mission of Americans to increase and be prosperous.

It is one of the minor tragedies of antebellum reform that no one noticed its death and few mourned its passing. The old millennialism and the ability to believe in several causes simultaneously began to slip quietly away in the 1850s. By the 1870s they were all but gone.

Perhaps the analogy is wrong. Eras do not die, like living creatures; they merge and blend into each other. Antebellum reforms did set the tone for much of what was to come afterward: the search for scientific (or at least secular) modes of social thought, the quest for equality for women and black people, the professionalization of reform, and much more. But the future belonged to new sorts of people: to those who accepted the human body as a positive good; to those who could tolerate diversity and believed that morality was not absolute; to those who had faith in improvement and adjustment rather than in the millennium; to those who saw economic and urban problems as economic and urban problems, not moral failures; to those who believed that human beings are not masters of their destiny and that social change does not depend on overcoming the sinfulness of the human heart. Above all, the future of reform belonged to institution users—to men and women who thought of bureaus, agencies, and the government generally as instruments of social policy.

I have in mind, of course, the strand of liberalism stretching from Progressivism through the New Deal to the "Great Society" of the 1960s: it was at once more practical than antebellum reform and less radical. It seldom sought to transform America; more often, it tried to make the system run better. Except in rare radical moments (there were some in the 1960s), hope for a new heaven on earth, commitment to reform as a style of life, and repudiation of sin and governmental coercion—characteristics of some of the greatest of antebellum reformers—were ground up by the machinery of modern times.

Bibliographical Essay

To do without footnotes goes against a historian's instincts and there is a temptation to add a massive bibliography by way of compensation. I have resisted that impulse. A broad and interpretive book such as this stands or falls on the strength of its narrative and argument, not on particular pieces of documentation or on displays of learning. Academics will know the basic references or how to find them; general readers, very likely, will not be interested in the titles of obscure books and articles. I have cited the most comprehensive works and those most useful to me. That meant excluding ones on peripheral subjects as well as excellent pieces which are too narrow in scope to warrant inclusion or which are overshadowed by another work on the same topic. My apologies go to authors whose significant contributions are ignored and my encouragement goes to readers who want to probe deeper and to move beyond this bibliography. A good beginning would be with the works of antebellum reformers themselves, readily available in print, on microfilm, and (especially in the case of temperance) in manuscripts in hundreds of local archives across the United States. The field is uneven, but rich.

General Works

The longest, most enduring narrative of antebellum reform is Alice Felt Tyler, *Freedom's Ferment: Phases of American Social History from the Colonial Period to the Outbreak of the Civil War* (Minneapolis: University of Minnesota Press, 1944). The faults in Tyler's work are easily detected: it rambles, largely ignores such "fads" as phrenology, and is both limited and dated in its interpretation. Yet it is a marvelous compendium which probably will never be supplanted for the information it presents. E. Douglas Branch, *The Sentimental Years, 1836–1860* (New York: D. Appleton-Century, 1934), is another older book of considerable charm and merit. It treats, with a light touch, many things Tyler left out. David Brion Davis, ed., *Ante-bellum Reform* (New York: Harper & Row, 1967), is a superior collection and some of the wisest words on the subject are to be found within it, particularly in John L. Thomas, "Romantic Reform in America, 1815–1865" (originally published in the *American Quarterly*, XVII [Winter 1965], 656–81). Although social history has changed much since Whitney Cross wrote *The Burned-over District: The Social and Intellectual History of Enthusiastic Religion in Western New York, 1800–1850* (Ithaca: Cornell University Press, 1950), the analysis of reform holds up well. As few, if any, other studies have done, *Burned-over District* depicts the social and cultural matrix of reform and demonstrates the interconnections between crusades. Another book in the same series as this one—Richard D. Brown, *Modernization: The Transformation of American Life, 1600–1865* (New York: Hill and Wang, 1976)—discusses, in a different context and with different emphases, the changes I see as touching off antebellum reform.

Chapter 1.   The Missionary Impulse

The interrelations between Protestant churches and reform can be traced in John R. Bodo, *The Protestant Clergy and Public Issues, 1812–1848* (Princeton: Princeton University Press, 1954); Charles C. Cole, Jr., *The Social Ideas of the Northern Evangelists, 1826–1860* (New York: Columbia University Press, 1954); and Clifford S. Griffin, *Their Brothers' Keepers: Moral Stewardship in the United States, 1800–1865* (New Brunswick, N.J.: Rutgers University Press, 1960). Timothy L. Smith, *Revivalism and Social Reform: American Protestantism on the Eve of the Civil War* (Nashville: Abingdon Press, 1957), has been an influential corrective to misconceptions about the evangelical sects. A good summary and analysis of the literature is Lois W. Banner, "Religious Benevolence as Social Control: A Critique of an Interpretation," *Journal of American History*, LX (June 1973), 23–41. Finney is well treated in William G. McLoughlin, *Modern Revivalism: Charles G. Finney to Billy Graham* (New York: Ronald Press, 1959), while Bertram Wyatt-Brown, *Lewis Tappan and the Evangelical War against Slavery* (Cleveland: Case-Western Reserve University Press, 1969), gives a clear sense of how the "benevolent empire" functioned. Edwin S. Gaustad, ed., *The Rise of Adventism: Religion and Society in Mid-Nineteenth Century*

America (New York: Harper & Row, 1974), contains useful essays on the ties between millennialism and various reforms.

Chapter 2.   Heaven on Earth

Of the general histories of communitarian ventures, I have found most interesting three by participants (including a modern one): John Humphrey Noyes, *History of American Socialisms* (Philadelphia: J. B. Lippincott, 1870); William A. Hinds, *American Communities and Co-operative Colonies*, 2nd ed. (Chicago: C. H. Kerr and Company, 1908); and Rosabeth Moss Kanter, *Commitment and Community: Communes and Utopias in Sociological Perspective* (Cambridge: Harvard University Press, 1972). Also informative are Mark Holloway, *Heavens on Earth: Utopian Communities in America* (New York: Dover Books, 1966), and Michael Fellman, *The Unbounded Frame: Freedom and Community in Nineteenth-Century American Utopianism* (Westport, Conn.: Greenwood Press, 1973), a perceptive examination of utopian thought. Karl J. R. Arndt, *George Rapp's Harmony Society, 1785–1847* (Philadelphia: University of Pennsylvania Press, 1965), is a thorough treatment of a major strand of German pietistic communitarianism. As might be expected, Oneida has attracted a great deal of attention. Maren Lockwood Carden, *Oneida: Utopian Community to Modern Corporation* (Baltimore: Johns Hopkins University Press, 1969), is especially noteworthy. Robert David Thomas, *The Man Who Would Be Perfect: John Humphrey Noyes and the Utopian Impulse* (Philadelphia: University of Pennsylvania Press, 1977), appeared after this book was written. Adin Ballou and Hopedale loom large in Lewis Perry, *Radical Abolitionism: Anarchy and the Government of God in Antislavery Thought* (Ithaca: Cornell University Press, 1973). Charles Crowe does well by his subject in *George Ripley: Transcendentalist and Utopian Socialist* (Athens, Ga.: University of Georgia Press, 1967). My favorite account of Ripley's creation, nonetheless, remains Lindsay Swift's charming *Brook Farm: Its Members, Scholars, and Visitors* (New York: Macmillan, 1900).

Chapter 3.   Earth as Heaven

Owenite communitarianism has been better analyzed than the Fourierist variety has. See, in particular, Arthur E. Bestor, Jr., *Backwoods Utopias: The Sectarian and Owenite Phases of Communitarian Socialism in America, 1663–1829* (Philadelphia: University of Pennsylvania Press, 1950); and J. F. C. Harrison, *Quest for the New Moral World: Robert*

Owen and the Owenites in Britain and America (New York: Scribner, 1969). Fourier's influence in America is more difficult to trace, but useful for understanding the French visionary himself are Jonathan Beecher and Richard Bienvenu, eds., *The Utopian Vision of Charles Fourier: Selected Texts on Work, Love, and Passionate Attraction* (Boston: Beacon Press, 1971); and Nicholas V. Riasanovsky, *The Teachings of Charles Fourier* (Berkeley and Los Angeles: University of California Press, 1969). There is a succinct, suggestive overview of secular communitarianism: Arthur E. Bestor, Jr., "Patent-Office Models of the Good Society," *American Historical Review*, LVIII (April 1953), 505–26.

Chapter 4.   Antislavery

The study of antislavery took a new turn with Gilbert H. Barnes, *The Anti-Slavery Impulse, 1830–1844* (New York: D. Appleton-Century, 1933), which stressed the connection between evangelical Protestantism and abolitionism. Of the several recent surveys, none is more up-to-date or better than James Brewer Stewart, *Holy Warriors: The Abolitionists and American Slavery* (New York: Hill and Wang, 1976). More specialized accounts of significance are the works of Lewis Perry and Bertram Wyatt-Brown (already cited) and Aileen S. Kraditor, *Means and Ends in American Abolitionism: Garrison and His Critics on Strategy and Tactics, 1834–1850* (New York: Pantheon Books, 1967); Donald G. Mathews, *Slavery and Methodism: A Chapter in American Morality, 1780–1845* (Princeton: Princeton University Press, 1965); and Benjamin Quarles, *Black Abolitionists* (New York: Oxford University Press, 1969). The early stages of antislavery have been traced in several places lately, most comprehensively in Winthrop D. Jordan, *White over Black: American Attitudes toward the Negro, 1550–1812* (Chapel Hill: University of North Carolina Press, 1968); P. J. Staudenraus, *The African Colonization Movement, 1816–1865* (New York: Columbia University Press, 1961); Arthur Zilversmit, *The First Emancipation: The Abolition of Negro Slavery in the North* (Chicago: University of Chicago Press, 1967); and in two books by David Brion Davis, *The Problem of Slavery in Western Culture* (Ithaca: Cornell University Press, 1966), and *The Problem of Slavery in the Age of Revolution* (Ithaca: Cornell University Press, 1975). The transition of abolitionism into politics is traced in Eric Foner, *Free Soil, Free Labor, Free Men: The Ideology of the Republican Party before the Civil War* (New York: Oxford University Press, 1970), and Richard H. Sewell, *Ballots for Freedom: Antislavery Politics in the United States, 1837–1860* (New York: Oxford University Press, 1976). James M. McPherson has treated the post-Civil War activities of abolitionists; most relevant here is his *The Struggle for Equality: Abolitionists and the Negro in the Civil War and Reconstruction* (Princeton: Princeton University Press, 1964). I have said most of what I have to say in Ronald G. Walters, *The Antislavery Appeal: American Abolitionism after 1830* (Baltimore: The Johns Hopkins University Press, 1976).

Chapter 5. Women and War

Peter Brock, *Pacifism in the United States from the Colonial Era to the First World War* (Princeton: Princeton University Press, 1968), is the most exhaustive treatment of the subject. Much briefer, and still of value, is Merle Curti, *Peace or War: The American Struggle, 1636–1936* (New York: W. W. Norton, 1936). Lewis Perry, *Radical Abolitionism: Anarchy and the Government of God in Antislavery Thought* (Ithaca: Cornell University Press, 1973), gives a sensitive account of nonresistance. Elihu Burritt's career can be followed in his own words and in those of Merle Curti in Curti, *The Learned Blacksmith: The Letters and Journals of Elihu Burritt* (New York: Wilson-Erickson, 1937). Works about nineteenth-century American women are appearing at such a rapid rate that any bibliography would be dated before it could be printed. Good as these books are, several older, quite accessible studies are fine starting points, especially Eleanor Flexner, *Century of Struggle: The Woman's Rights Movement in the United States* (Cambridge: Harvard University Press, 1959), and Barbara Welter's influential "Cult of True Womanhood, 1820–1860," *American Quarterly*, XVIII (Summer 1966), 151–74. William L. O'Neill, ed., *The Woman Movement: Feminism in the United States and England* (Chicago: Quadrangle Books, 1971), provides both an interpretation and source material, as does Aileen S. Kraditor, ed., *Up from the Pedestal: Selected Writings in the History of American Feminism* (Chicago: Quadrangle Books, 1968). The role of women in abolitionism can be followed in Alma Lutz, *Crusade for Freedom: Women of the Antislavery Movement* (Boston: Beacon Press, 1968); Gerda Lerner, *The Grimké Sisters from South Carolina: Rebels against Slavery* (Boston: Houghton Mifflin, 1967); and Katharine DuPre Lumpkin, *The Emancipation of Angelina Grimké* (Chapel Hill: University of North Carolina Press, 1974).

Chapter 6. Strong Drink

After a half century of scholarship the most reliable guide to the antebellum temperance movement remains John Allen Krout, *The Origins of Prohibition* (New York: Alfred A. Knopf, 1925). As an interpretation of the motives behind anti-alcohol campaigns, Joseph R. Gusfield, *Symbolic Crusade: Status Politics and the American Temperance Movement* (Urbana: University of Illinois Press, 1966), has attracted both followers and detractors. (My own interpretation differs from Gusfield's.) Ross Evans Paulson, *Women's Suffrage and Prohibition: A Comparative Study of Equality and Social Control* (Glenview, Ill.: Scott, Foresman, 1973), looks across both national and group lines.

Chapter 7.   The Body and Beyond

There is much data on the topics in this chapter in Edwin S. Gaustad, ed., *The Rise of Adventism: Religion and Society in Mid-Nineteenth Century America* (New York: Harper & Row, 1974). Although a great deal has been written on health reform in recent years, it appears in scattered places or in passing in books and essays on other subjects. One of the best studies has never been published—Stephen Willner Nissenbaum, "Careful Love: Sylvester Graham and the Emergence of Victorian Sexual Theory in America, 1830–1840" (Ph.D. diss., University of Wisconsin, 1968). See also Richard H. Shryock, "Sylvester Graham and the Popular Health Movement, 1830–1870," *Mississippi Valley Historical Review*, XVIII (September 1931), 172–83; Ronald L. Numbers, *Prophetess of Health: A Study of Ellen G. White* (New York: Harper & Row, 1976); and John R. Betts, "Mind and Body in Early American Thought," *Journal of American History*, LXIV (March 1968), 787–805. John D. Davies, *Phrenology, Fad and Science: A Nineteenth-Century American Crusade* (New Haven: Yale University Press, 1955), is a succinct treatment of its subject. The literature on spiritualism is extensive, although not outstanding. Some of the best of it has come from R. Laurence Moore in his "Spiritualism and Science: Reflections on the First Decade of Spirit Rappings," *American Quarterly*, XXIV (October 1972), 474–500, and *In Search of White Crows: Spiritualism, Parapsychology, and American Culture* (New York: Oxford University Press, 1977), which came too late to be of use in preparing this book. Robert W. Delp, "Andrew Jackson Davis: Prophet of American Spiritualism," *Journal of American History*, XLIV (June 1967), 43–56, is good, but there is room for some hardy soul to attempt a full-scale biography of Davis.

Chapter 8.   Dangerous Classes and Working Classes

Robert H. Bremner, *From the Depths: The Discovery of Poverty in the United States* (New York: New York University Press, 1956), is sketchy on the antebellum period. More useful, although less sweeping, are Carroll Smith Rosenberg, *Religion and the Rise of the American City: The New York City Mission Movement, 1812–1870* (Ithaca: Cornell University Press, 1971), and Raymond A. Mohl, *Poverty in New York, 1783–1825* (New York: Oxford University Press, 1971). Herbert G. Gutman, "Work, Culture, and Society in Industrializing America, 1815–1919," *American Historical Review*, LXXVIII (June 1973), 531–88, has challenged older ways of viewing the history of working people, as have other social historians in the past decade. Those older ways persist, however, as they do in this book. There are several standard surveys of American labor: for example, Joseph G. Rayback, *A History of American Labor*, revised ed. (New York: Free Press, 1966). Of enduring utility is John R. Commons, et al., eds., *A Documentary History of American Industrial Society*, 10 vols. (New York: Russell and Russell, 1958). Although disagreeing on some matters of interpretation, I have relied heavily on Edward Pessen, *Most Uncommon Jacksonians: The Radical Leaders of the Early Labor Movement* (Albany: State University of New York Press, 1967).

Chapter 9.   Institutions and Uplift

The historical literature on asylums and deviants has been strongly influenced by Michel Foucault and by American scholars in other fields, particularly sociologists and psychologists such as Erving Goffman, Howard Becker, and Thomas Szasz. So far as I know, there is no convenient introduction to this literature, although there is help to be found in Edwin Schur's now dated *Labeling Deviant Behavior: Its Sociological Implications* (New York: Harper & Row, 1971). Of works by historians relating to this chapter, the most stimulating have been David J. Rothman, *The Discovery of the Asylum: Social Order and Disorder in the New Republic* (Boston: Little, Brown, 1971), and Michael Katz, *The Irony of Early School Reform: Education and Innovation in Mid-Nineteenth Century Massachusetts* (Boston: Beacon Press, 1968). Gerald Grob, *Mental Institutions in America: Social Policy to 1875* (New York: Free Press, 1973), is more detailed, cautious, and balanced than Rothman's account. Joseph M. Hawes, *Children in Urban Society: Juvenile Delinquency in Nineteenth-Century America* (New York: Oxford University Press, 1971), has much to say about Houses of Refuge. The latest, extremely interesting work on nineteenth-century school systems can be followed through articles and reviews in the *History of Education Quarterly*. Carl F. Kaestle, "School Reform and the Urban School," *History of Education Quarterly*, 12 (Summer 1972), 211–28, is a wise review essay.

Index